M000105024

A COLUMNIST'S VIEW OF CAPITOL SQUARE

Series on Ohio Politics
John Green, Editor

Abe Zaidan, with John C. Green, *Portraits of Power: Ohio and National Politics, 1964–2004*

Lee Leonard, *A Columnist's View of Capitol Square: Ohio Politics and Government, 1969–2005*

A COLUMNIST'S VIEW OF CAPITOL SQUARE

OHIO POLITICS AND GOVERNMENT, 1969–2005

LEE LEONARD

UNIVERSITY OF AKRON PRESS AKRON, OHIO

Some material was originally published by *The Columbus Dispatch* and *United Press International* and is reproduced with permission.

14 13 12 11 10 5 4 3 2 1

LIBRARY OF CONGRESS CATALOGING-IN-PUBLICATION DATA

Leonard, Lee, 1939–

A columnist's view of Capitol Square : Ohio politics and government, 1969–2005 / Lee Leonard. -- 1st ed.

p. cm. -- (Series on Ohio politics)

Includes index.

ISBN 978-1-931968-69-0 (cloth : alk. paper)

1. Ohio--Politics and government—1951- I. Title.

JK5535.L46 2010

320.977109'045—DC22

2009041705

The paper used in this publication meets the minimum requirements of American National Standard for Information Sciences—Permanence of Paper for Printed Library Materials, ANSI Z39.48–1984. ∞

Cover design by Amanda Gilliland. Cover image: Library of Congress, Prints & Photographs Division, HABS OHIO, 25-COLB, 36. Photograph by Jack E. Boucher.

The interior was designed and typeset by Amy Freels, with help from Amanda Gilliland. The type was set in Stone Print, with Gill Sans display. The book was printed and bound by BookMasters of Ashland, Ohio.

For Ruth Lindlaw Leonard, my wonderful wife of 45 years, who kept dinner warm and the family together on many nights when the events described in these columns were taking place.

CONTENTS

PREFACE

For 36 years, Lee Leonard wrote a weekly column about the Ohio Statehouse, first for *United Press International* and then for the *Columbus Dispatch*. During that time, he became one of the most respected and admired journalists in Ohio.

I am honored that this collection of Lee's columns is the second book in the Bliss Institute's Series on Ohio Politics with the University of Akron Press. Lee approached me about this project shortly after the release of the first book in the series, a collection of columns and articles by Abe Zaidan, entitled *Portraits of Power: Ohio and National Politics, 1964–2004* (2007). Abe and Lee were friends and colleagues for most of their careers, and their books complement each other well. Together they provide an insightful picture of Ohio politics in the last third of the Twentieth Century.

I knew of Lee's work before I moved to Ohio in 1987, and I made his acquaintance shortly thereafter. Since then I have talked with him on numerous occasions, usually for one of his columns. Thus it has been a special treat to work with him assembling this book of columns, along with his commentary about them.

Perhaps the most fitting praise of Lee's work comes from the people he covered for nearly four decades. In 2004, Lee spoke at the Bliss Institute conference on term limits, and drew an unusually large crowd of respectful politicians, all eager to hear what he had to say. One of the attendees summed up the prevailing admiration this way: "Leonard is a special guy, humble and smart."

Lee was respected by politicians because he respected them. He had high regard for politicians as people—despite their flaws and foibles. But he also appreciated the difficulty of their jobs and valued the public institutions in which they worked. And sometimes he revered the goals of Ohio politics and government more than the practitioners did themselves—as he reminded them, firmly but fairly, when the occasion demanded. Such respectfulness arises from a humble heart.

Lee was admired by politicians because he knew what he was talking about. He never set himself apart from the people and events he covered at the Statehouse. His goal was to understand what was going on and then share his understanding with others. His primary audience was the reading public, of course, but many politicians were enlightened by his columns as well. Lee has the mind of a scholar and the temperament of a teacher.

All these qualities are abundantly evident in the columns in this book. But in addition, these columns are fun to read. It is indeed a special writer who inspires, instructs, and entertains—all at the same time.

John C. Green
Director, Ray C. Bliss Institute of Applied Politics

ACKNOWLEDGEMENTS

The author is indebted to Dr. John C. Green, Director of the Ray C. Bliss Institute of Applied Politics, for his advice and editing, and to Janet Lykes Bolois, Manager, Marketing and Events of the Bliss Institute, for her work on the manuscript.

The author also is grateful to *United Press International* and the *Columbus Dispatch* and its publisher, John F. Wolfe, for the opportunity to write the columns herein. Thanks to the staff of the Archives Library at the Ohio Historical Center for help in researching the project; to *Dispatch* Librarian Linda Deitch for retrieving selected columns and photographs from the newspaper's files; to Debbie Turpening for transcribing the many columns that were not electronically stored; and to Amy Freels of the University of Akron Press, who supervised the book's production.

Finally, the author acknowledges former state Rep. Madeline Cain of Lakewood, who was the first of several people to suggest that a collection of past columns would be a good vehicle for chronicling what went on at the Ohio Statehouse over 36 years.

ABOUT LEE LEONARD

Lee Leonard, a native of Summit, N.J., was raised in Ithaca, N.Y., attended Middlebury (Vt.) College and graduated from Cornell University. He began his career with *United Press International* in Boise, Idaho, in 1962 and covered the Pennsylvania Capitol in Harrisburg from 1963–69. He became Statehouse bureau manager in Columbus in 1969 and in the 1970s was voted one of the 20 most-respected *UPI* bylines in a nationwide survey of the wire service's subscribers.

Leonard joined the *Columbus Dispatch* as a Statehouse reporter in 1990. He covered 11 national political conventions and a wide variety of campaigns. Among those he interviewed were former President Dwight Eisenhower and presidential candidate Jimmy Carter.

Leonard lives in retirement in Reynoldsburg, Ohio, with his wife Ruth. They have two grown children—Douglas, of Columbus, and Valerie, of West Chester, Ohio.

INTRODUCTION

Through the 1960s and well into the 1970s, Ohio government was dominated by rural interests known especially in the legislature as the "Cornstalk Brigade." This was in the "dead ball" era of politics when government operated on the farmer's calendar and officials liked to "set a spell" before making any decisions. Building relationships and trust was key. Political correctness wasn't even a gleam in the eye of an idealist.

Now, it's all business. Officeholders are focused on advancing or extending their political careers. Election, swearing-in, budget, campaign . . . all fly by at warp speed and then the cycle repeats. There's a laptop on the desk of every legislator, and lobbyists keep pace moment-by-moment on cell phones and other electronic devices. Lots of the calls are about money.

A Columnist's View of Capitol Square: Ohio Politics and Government, 1969–2005 bridges the two eras. It's a collection of columns meant to convey a sense of what it was like at the Statehouse during that span ofAP time. The columns were written on a weekly basis for *United Press International* and the *Columbus Dispatch*.

The reader will be treated to colorful profiles of some of the most entertaining characters inhabiting the Statehouse, and to contemporaneous analysis of some of the most momentous events of those decades.

With some exceptions, the collection is organized under the two major headings that comprise state government—politics and governing. The two are very different, and many an aspiring officeholder, having conducted a masterful campaign has arrived in office only to flounder because of a lack of understanding of how to govern. A key column under the division headed *Campaign = Compete; Govern = Cooperate* describes the hazards of failing to recognize the difference between campaigning and governing.

Five sections of the book are about special phenomena characterizing Ohio politics and government over the 36-year period. One is the intensity with which Buckeye citizens guard their right to vote, and their propensity to vote "no" if at all in doubt about an issue. Another is their extreme sensitivity to taxation. The other sections deal with seemingly constant warfare between rural and urban constituencies, state and local governments, labor and business, and environmentalists and energy producers.

The absurd side of lawmaking is spotlighted and the author has reserved space for some opinions and four humor columns. With regret, not all events or characters are chronicled; space limitations prevented that. The columns were chosen according to how they fit the premise of the collection and how well-written they were. "Well-written" sometimes was a function of how much time was allowed to produce the column. Most were written under deadline, as explained here shortly. Readers will note that some of the columns of the 1960s and '70s seem quaint. Some contain terms now viewed as politically incorrect. That was the language of the day, and those were the issues of the day.

Many columns that you read opposite the editorial page are flat-out opinions, and many columnists have a predictable point of view. In a way, this is good; you have a stable measuring stick because the columnist is always coming from the same direction.

I preferred to use my column to educate—to expand on the stories of the week and tell readers some things that wouldn't fit into a daily news story. My measuring stick was not predictability. It was enlightenment. I wasn't consistent and sometimes I left readers wondering where I was coming from. I wanted to expose them to what went on behind the scenes, to different points of view, to what caused particular government decisions and political posturing.

I much preferred analysis and interpretation of the news to giving my opinion, although occasionally certain politicians or their actions were so blatant that they cried out for a written punch in the gut. That, I enjoyed delivering and felt it was justified. Because I usually spared the heavy hand, I established credibility with readers—a rare and valuable commodity.

As expressed earlier, most of these columns were written on deadline. Many of my acquaintances outside the business thought all I did was write the weekly column. In fact, I was responsible for daily news coverage at the Statehouse and would often have two, three or even four stories a day—more when I was with the "deadline-every-minute" wire service.

During the week, I would "gather string" for the column I knew would come due on Friday. One editor thought I was holding back material from the daily menu to use in my column. He was right; I was always thinking ahead. But it was never at the expense of the daily story. You could have a good daily story and still leave enough quotes and other information to produce your column.

You had to give yourself a head start because when Friday came, you might have to cover a breaking news story *and* write the column. The deadline was unforgiving. The column was due in the early afternoon. I could write a decent column in two hours, less than that if I was under the gun, especially if I had all my information on hand and didn't have to make a lot of phone calls.

I certainly didn't hold the record for speed. When I was a summer intern for *United Press International* in Boise, Idaho, in 1962, I learned at the feet of the bureau chief, R. Richard Charnock. To me, he was a crusty old veteran of the Capitol wars. I was a 22-year old greenhorn who typed with two fingers. Years later I calculated that he was only 31 or so at the time, but he seemed ancient. His fingers could fly and he could wrap his mind around the political events of the day. Here's how adept he was at writing columns:

In the Boise bureau, there were no Teletype operators. You had to "punch" your own copy. Most of the time, you typed up your story on the typewriter. Then, while looking at it, you re-typed it on the Teletype keyboard, cutting coded holes into a yellow paper tape that unwound from a roll. When you finished cutting the tape, you would start running it through the transmitter and send the story out on the wire to client newspapers and broadcast stations. That's what made the clattering noise that is now fondly recalled by old-timers in newsrooms.

Invariably, Dick Charnock would find the deadline approaching for his weekly column. He wouldn't bother with the typewriter. He'd sit down at the Teletype machine and start cutting his tape, composing his column right out of his head. He'd put the front end of the tape in the transmitter, and when the loop reached the floor, signifying three minutes worth of copy, he'd hit the "send" switch. "No time to get fancy now," he'd mutter as the tape started flying through the transmitter. Charnock would continue to pound away at 60 words a minute, and the loop would seldom come off the floor. Sometimes he'd even gain slack tape! And when he finished his column, he'd rip off the end of the tape and wait three minutes for the rest of it to go through. On paper would be a sparkling political column for Idaho readers.

Some editors (and readers) think reporters shouldn't be allowed to write columns; that there should be a firewall between the news page and the editorial page. I was fortunate to be allowed to have a column for 36 years, and I tried not to abuse it. Certainly it looks bad for a reporter to express his or her opinion in print. Reporters should report the news and allow editorial writers and paid columnists to comment, the thinking goes. But who better to columnize on an issue, event or politician than the person who lives and breathes the stuff every day? They know things, by intuition and instinct from virtually living with their subjects, that no editorial writer or columnist in a windowless upstairs room could ever detect. Now, there are "columnists" on the Internet who work on laptops from home, even from their beds, without ever interviewing their subjects, much less living with them for much of the day and night. The work of such writers should be viewed with extreme skepticism.

A true reporter with a column should write it carefully and with respect. I think I was allowed to write the column for so many years because editors and readers saw that I was using it to inform rather than to advance a personal agenda. Sometimes I even wrote the opposite of what I thought simply to bring that viewpoint out on the table. The columns included here were aimed at giving the reader not my opinion, but depth and background about Statehouse events and newsmakers of the times.

Sometimes it appears that I "picked on" certain politicians. I can assure you it was on an equal opportunity basis. Republicans who complained near the end of my career that we reporters unfairly bashed Gov. Bob Taft and GOP legislative leaders, were not around in the 1980s when we were savaging Democrats Dick Celeste and Vern Riffe week after week, month after month. Some examples follow. Any harsh treatment was not an attempt at personal vilification. Mainly it was to unmask the politicians who tried to fool the public with what came to be known in recent years as "spin." When you're writing news stories, you combat the spin by giving both sides. Unfortunately, no matter what they tell you, the politicians in power have the upper hand 90 percent of the time. At the White House, Statehouse or courthouse, they manage the news. News stories pit the entrenched officeholders against their political adversaries. Columns—whether they are analysis, interpretation or commentary—should attempt to put the reader behind the scenes as if he or she were there on a daily basis while all the machinations are going on. And the columns in this book are largely attempts to give fresh insight, to present a different viewpoint and to entertain while educating the reader about how and why the world of state government and politics works the way it does.

Lee Leonard

POLITICS

CHAPTER 1
POLITICAL PARTIES

The Republicans

I didn't know Ray Bliss very well. I was a high school and college student and a cub reporter when he was working his magic in Ohio and becoming a national political figure. But he must have trusted me as we munched hors d'oeuvres at a "who's who in Ohio politics" cocktail party one day. Obviously, he saw me writing down what he said about Gov. Rhodes and the Republican leaders that followed him. I knew he didn't want to see his quotes in the newspapers and I kept his confidence until after his death. His remarks reveal something of himself and of Ohio Republicans' leadership in the late 1960s and '70s.

Ray Bliss: Candid Thoughts on Jim Rhodes and the GOP

United Press International, Aug. 16, 1981

COLUMBUS (UPI)—In autumn of every even-numbered year, Ray C. Bliss, the lion-hearted former state and national Republican chairman, would stand before the Ohio Republican Convention and deliver a brief, punchy pre-election pep talk.

The GOP delegates, alternates and supporters would respond with thunderous applause. Then they would return home, pull up the covers, roll over and fall into a deep slumber.

Last September, Bliss took his customary spot on the rostrum and reminded his Republican friends that Gov. Thomas E. Dewey had been a prohibitive favorite in 1948, only to lose, and that John F. Kennedy was mystified "to his dying day" by a get-out-the-vote drive that defeated him in Ohio in 1960.

There is, Bliss said, no substitute for hard work.

"This is a Democratic state," he said. "They talk about all these new-fangled gadgets to win elections. I've never seen a computer take anybody to the polls yet. We need a new determination and a new will to win in this state."

"We need to support the whole ticket from the top to the bottom and forget about little petty differences," Bliss continued. "It's hard work that wins elections, not hot air."

For once, the Republicans paid attention. They shucked any Dewey complex, went out and brought Ronald Reagan home a winner, and handed the GOP control of the state Senate.

Bliss won't be around to give any pep talk in 1982, except in spirit. He passed away earlier this month. While he was encouraged by the GOP turnaround in 1980, he still harbored bitter feelings about the way the state party deteriorated after he left in 1965 to rebuild the national party.

When Bliss left Ohio, the Republicans controlled everything in government—testimony to his 16 years as party chairman. Now they have nothing, except the governor's office, the Senate and two out of seven Ohio Supreme Court seats.

Bliss unified the Goldwater and Rockefeller wings of the national party but there was one political animal in his own backyard he was never able to tame—James A. Rhodes.

Publicly, Bliss gritted his teeth and measured his statements carefully to put the state Republican Party's best foot forward. Privately, he spoke his mind.

On one such occasion, at a luncheon in December 1979, Bliss confided that it hurt him to see how the once-powerful Republican Party had withered under Rhodes and his handpicked chairmen, John S. Andrews and Earl T. Barnes.

Rhodes squashed any promising candidates who were a threat to his statewide domination; he raised money only for himself; there was no sacrifice; everybody wanted to be an instant star.

Sour grapes? Maybe, but listen to what Mr. Bliss thought but kept to himself for the sake of party harmony:

"We (Republicans) won (in the 1950s and '60s) because we built up a stable of candidates and put on aggressive campaigns. But nobody's willing to do that anymore. There's been no leadership in Ohio to get a stable of candidates or to find people to finance campaigns.

"To have a strong party organization, you have to have a strong chairman. He can't be the lackey of the governor. John Andrews and Earl Barnes had different ideas than I did. They thought the party ought to work closely with the governor. But Jim Rhodes never did anything unless it was to benefit Jim Rhodes.

"Sometimes, you have to sacrifice for the good of the party—run somebody who's not going to win. We had people who would do this. They'd help the party out—maybe run three or four times without success, but then they'd get their chance to win. Now these young fellows, they join the party one day and they want to be chairman the next."

Pretty tough talk from a pretty credible source. And unless the GOP breaks the Rhodes hammerlock and develops some new talent and leadership down the line, the 1980s may be a long dry decade in Ohio.

■ ■

Bliss proved prescient. The 1980s were a long dry decade for Republicans. They got hammered in the 1982 statewide election, losing everything but one lonely Ohio Supreme Court seat. It was 1990 before they began a comeback. And that comeback was started under a chairman eminently worthy of carrying Bliss's sandals; some said Robert T. Bennett surpassed Bliss's record of achievements. Bennett was especially adept at slotting candidates in races they could win and persuading others to back off for the sake of party unity. Republicans won back everything in the 1990s and early 2000s.

And they did it by following Bliss's directives—hard work and attention to details. In 2004, the Republicans handed President George W. Bush a second term by outworking and surprising the rabid Democrats in the field. But then the GOP went into decline because of scandal, infighting and failure to build a stable of candidates.

Here's what happened at the other end of Bennett's mighty reign:

Party Chief Bennett Has His Hands Full with Those Rumblin' Republicans

The Columbus Dispatch, May 3, 2004

Maybe Bob Bennett didn't get out soon enough. The Republican state chairman thought he had problems before in lining up his thoroughbreds for the statewide starting gate in 2006.

Now he's got to be scratching his head over how to keep the GOP aspirants from killing each other before 2006 even gets here.

Bennett, nearing retirement age, needs to be concentrating on getting out the vote for President Bush and Sen. George V. Voinovich, not settling food fights in the Republican dining hall.

The latest episode has House Speaker Larry Householder and Secretary of State J. Kenneth Blackwell at each other's throat, making the sparring between Auditor Betty D. Montgomery and Attorney General Jim Petro for governor in 2006 look like a marbles game in the schoolyard.

Not that Bennett isn't up to the task. In 1989, he skillfully persuaded Bob Taft to drop out of the next year's primary contest for governor with George Voinovich and to run for secretary of state, which the GOP badly needed to control the process for drawing state legislative districts.

In 1998, he induced Blackwell to back away from a clash with Taft for the good of the party, and there has been room at the table for all Republicans since then.

Until now. Knives, forks and other weapons of individual destruction are in play. Blackwell got under Householder's skin last year by declaring that he could produce a better budget than the Republican legislators did—and without raising the sales tax from a nickel to six cents on the dollar.

Householder fired back, saying it was easy to carp about the budget, but that Blackwell never had to deliver critical services to the people and come up with the votes to fund them.

Blackwell loudly announced a campaign to repeal the penny on the sales tax—which is worth $1.3 billion a year—six months early, earning Householder's contempt.

What we didn't know until last week was that the speaker's political cadre, known to themselves as Team Householder, had an $8.5 million plan to not only combat the repeal but to make Householder so popular that he'd be a natural player for statewide office in 2006.

The plan, written secretly in January, was kept under wraps until it leaked out a week ago, proving to be another embarrassment to Householder, who has been raked before on his heavy-handed fund-raising and campaigning style.

Press Secretary Dwight Crum took the rap for writing the plan, to which political operatives Brett Buerck and Kyle Sisk contributed. Crum said Blackwell's continued hostility toward his boss ate at him until he sat down at his personal computer and wrote in a fit of pique and frustration.

Crum's flying fingers produced 109 pages of a campaign plan down to the finest detail before the anger wore off. He ended with a disclaimer that the document was only a draft for internal consumption and had nobody's approval.

"I don't know how anything like this could be put in writing," Bennett said last week in promising to try to get Householder and Blackwell together to drink some sort of ego-reducing toast. He didn't get a chance to invite them before Blackwell vetoed the idea.

Only those who live and breathe political campaigns could have put this document together. It covered all the bases. It's not unusual for political strategists to map out plans for their bosses, but most never see the light of day until the proper time, if then.

Consultant Jerry Austin, a Democrat who just happens to be plaguing Householder with a spate of negative TV commercials, chortled at the Republicans' dilemma.

Austin used to do the dirty work for Gov. Richard F. Celeste, and Anthony J. Celebrezze Jr., who was secretary of state and attorney general in the Democrats' glory days. "I kept 'em all in my head," Austin answered when asked how come nobody ever leaked out his strategies.

The Householder leak was reminiscent of 1997, when Senate Democrats left in a committee room the draft of a plan on how to hang the Republicans on raising taxes for school-funding and then running against them on the issue.

Republicans shut the Democrats out of the process, the school-funding problem was only half-solved and the Republicans won all the elections after that.

Now, the shoe is on the other foot. Bennett will have to step lively to stem the tide of disarray. And Householder, who will be out of office in January, will have to get a new plan and hope the Republicans are in a forgiving mood.

The tide of disarray rolled. Republicans kept only one statewide administrative office in the 2006 election. True, they held onto majorities in the Ohio House and Senate, and won a 7-0 edge on the Ohio Supreme Court. But the infighting that Bliss and Bennett detested cost them the governor's office and more. Blackwell was trounced in the governor's race. Montgomery, the GOP's top vote-getter, dropped back to run for attorney general, an office she previously had held for eight years. She lost that race. Householder barely won for county auditor in his home of Perry County despite spending a half-million dollars he had raised on Capitol Square. His plans for statewide office seemed doomed, at least for the foreseeable future.

In case it doesn't come through in the column, none of the Statehouse reporters believed that Crum wrote the 109-page memo. They knew him too well, and he was not a convincing fibber. Brett Buerck was more likely the author. He had boasted to reporters that Householder would make everyone forget about Vern Riffe, the 20-year speaker who set the standard for raw power on Capitol Square. Buerck and Sisk got carried away, and took Householder down with them. Although the FBI, the IRS and Ohio inspector general never found after months of investigating that a crime (such as racketeering, bribery, tax evasion or misuse of campaign funds) was committed, Team Householder was stained and then dismantled. Bob Bennett glided toward retirement, several years too late, early in 2009.

■ ■

Rhodes Orchestrates Selection of a Female Justice

United Press International, September 4, 1981

COLUMBUS (UPI)—From the beginning, you knew it was going to be a political happening. A special Republican screening committee was meeting to recommend someone to Gov. James A. Rhodes for a vacancy on the Ohio Supreme Court.

Toward the end of the meeting, a telephone call came to Republican state headquarters, where it was answered by Lucas County Republican Chairman James Brennan, a member of the screening committee.

"He did what?!!" exclaimed Brennan when informed by a reporter that Rhodes had announced the appointment of Judge Blanche E. Krupansky to the Supreme Court.

The committee quickly took a vote, and the winner was Judge Blanche E. Krupansky.

Driving back to Cleveland from her interview with the screening committee, Judge Krupansky learned via the car radio of her prompt appointment.

When she returned to Columbus last week to be sworn in, she found the stage had been set by the governor.

This was not to be the typical oath-taking for a new Supreme Court justice in the decorous court chamber with jurists in their black robes and a formal tea-and-crumpets reception afterwards.

Instead, the cavernous Statehouse rotunda was the scene, to accommodate plenty of TV crews and political guests.

There would be a press conference afterwards in case anyone missed the point: James A. Rhodes had appointed the first woman to the Supreme Court in 47 years.

Rhodes opened the ceremonies with a statement proclaiming it an "historic day," as indeed it was. He said the fact that Judge Krupansky is a woman "was not the criterion" for her appointment, and he was partly right.

Judge Krupansky indeed is highly respected in the Cleveland legal community and has served as judge at the city, county and state levels.

Furthermore, she is politically strong in Cleveland, having defeated Edward Corrigan for County Court of Appeals judge in 1968 and former County Commissioner Hugh Corrigan for state appeals court judge in 1976.

Twice, the Democrats haven't bothered to oppose her on the ballot. That's the kind of popularity that sets well with Rhodes. The governor is expected to be running for the U.S. Senate next year with Cleveland a major battleground, and Judge Krupansky will be on the ballot.

In an unusual statement before she was sworn in, Judge Krupansky noted the historic occasion and delivered a commercial for Rhodes, saying he has "done more for the advancement of women than any governor I can remember."

"He is a man of great wisdom and foresight, and I hope he continues in office for a very long time," she added. Which office wasn't clear.

At her press conference, Judge Krupansky fielded some tough questions with grace and aplomb that brought a twinkle to the eyes of Rhodes, who was watching from the sidelines.

Questioned about the political motivation, she replied: "That doesn't bother me at all. Why should we look at the motives, if there are any?"

Sen. Howard M. Metzenbaum, D-Ohio, perhaps the target of all this, wasn't looking at motives, either, reserving any comments.

But Robert E. Hughes, chairman of the Cuyahoga County Republican party, said, "This was a good appointment whether Metzenbaum exists at all."

It should be. Hughes recommended it.

Krupansky was defeated when she tried to run for a full term on the bench. And reporters, the author included, made way too much of an anticipated Rhodes bid for the U.S. Senate in 1982. Rhodes left the governor's office and went into private business. But he seldom tired of fueling speculation about a possible bid for office. Neither did Hughes.

■ ■

Ohio Republicans Fight Among Themselves

United Press International, February 12, 1982

COLUMBUS (UPI)—Like a giant prehistoric tortoise on its back, the Ohio Republican organization last week made another heroic lunge to right itself. Instead, it rolled over on its shell again.

Not that Michael F. Colley, the new Republican state chairman, won't be in there pitching for the crucial elections this year, or even that he won't make a good party leader. He may.

But in a rerun of countless exercises of the past, the party was left in control of a veritable Mount Rushmore of Ohio Republicans, headed by 72-year old lame duck Gov. James A. Rhodes, plus big-city organizations.

With the resignation of Earl T. Barnes, the state party's chairman for the last five years, the contest for succession boiled down to Colley, the Franklin County Republican chairman, and state Rep. David W. Johnson, R-North Canton. The Toledo and Cincinnati delegations put up Lucas County GOP Chairman James Brennan as an alternative.

Rhodes pushed hard for Colley, whom he had earlier appointed to the Ohio Board of Regents, to keep the home-field advantage in party matters, even when he retires next year.

He was joined by former U.S. Sens. William B. Saxbe, Robert Taft Jr. and John W. Bricker, and by the Cleveland-area Republican organization, which furnished one-third of Colley's support.

Johnson, a conservative who was one of president Reagan's Ohio co-chairmen in the 1980 campaign, was the choice of the anti-Rhodes faction and the rural areas.

Although it took three ballots, Colley's election was nearly a carbon copy of the selection of Barnes as party chairman in 1977. Barnes, Rhodes' personal choice, received 24 votes—the exact number needed for election. So did Colley, after being stopped short on the first two ballots.

As he always does during and after one of these intraparty skirmishes, Committeeman Robert J. Huffman, an attorney from West Milton, Ohio, lambasted Rhodes for orchestrating the outcome.

"Everybody said this was the time for the changing of the guard," said Huffman, legal counsel to the 1976 Reagan campaign organization in Ohio. "But there has been no changing of the guard. We're still marching to the same tune that we always have.

"I'm tired of the state committee being viewed as beholden to him (Rhodes)," Huffman continued, blaming the governor for "the dearth of Republican candidates in the last 25 years. He ought to be a counselor and allow younger people to hold office and govern this state."

For his part, Johnson displayed no bitterness over the narrow defeat. He pledged his full cooperation to Colley and the party.

But Johnson is close to the Timken family of Canton and some other large contributors to the party. They have indicated they want some changes in the way the party does business before they are willing to make a sizeable financial commitment.

Johnson said he had help from "some people in Washington" but the President did not personally intervene. "I didn't want it that way," said Johnson, although he could have used some assistance from the man he helped elect.

"When people get in power, they don't always come out on the firing line for you," said Johnson, adding that as an elected representative he understands that political fact of life.

Colley is energetic and seems to have some good ideas for moving the party into the 1982 elections. He wants to refinance the party's debt and raise funds through personal contact, stepping up direct mail and having regional fundraisers to help the local GOP.

He is also planning to touch base quickly with national party leaders, Republican congressmen, state legislative leaders, the Republicans' top pollster and statewide candidates. One objective is to try to defuse the Republican primary for governor and forge a strong statewide ticket.

As Colley works, he can expect to see plenty of the same long arms and old faces that have dominated the party in the past—Rhodes and the big-city organization leaders.

> Colley didn't defuse the primary for governor. There were four candidates, and the winner, Congressman Clarence J. Brown Jr., got clobbered as Democrats took over the state government in a disastrous year for the GOP.

■ ■

Rhodes Blows the Dust Off Republicans

United Press International, September 21, 1984

COLUMBUS (UPI)—As Air Force II taxied toward the terminal at Port Columbus International Airport last week, the cream of the Ohio Republican Party milled around waiting to greet Vice President George Bush.

Among others, there was Republican State Chairman Michael F. Colley; Columbus Mayor Dana G. Rinehart; David W. Johnson, executive director of Reagan-Bush '84 and three of the four co-chairmen of the President's re-election committee; Woody Hayes; and former Gov. James A. Rhodes, who appeared to be whiling away a sunny late summer afternoon.

Any of them—the mayor, the party chairman, the director of the re-election campaign—could have been first to welcome Bush to Ohio.

But as the Vice President and his wife, Barbara stepped to the ground, it was Rhodes who had suddenly slithered to the head of the lineup to give the initial handshake and kiss to the nation's second couple.

The symbolism of the moment was not lost on observers, many of whom fully believe that when the starting gate opens for the race against Democratic Gov. Richard F. Celeste in 1986, the same James A. Rhodes, then 76, will have bolted to the head of the Republican line.

Helping to promote this belief was Rhodes' chief booster, Cuyahoga County Republican Chairman Robert E. Hughes, who delights in fueling the speculation. "He's got his dark suit on," Hughes grinned at reporters. "That means he's running."

When Rhodes got to the site of the Ohio Republican Convention, a group of college students dressed in exterminators' uniforms were prancing through a parody of "Ghostbusters."

"If you see a Democrat in your attic, or under your bed, who you gonna call?" "Fritzbusters'" roared the Republicans, who normally yell nothing louder than "Fore!"

Rhodes regarded the antics with detached amusement. It reminded him of his grandkids. But when the "Fritzbusters" finished, Rhodes was the first one on his feet applauding. He also knows the value of a good campaign gimmick.

Then it was time for Rhodes' introductory remarks. Some people started a chant of "Four More Years" for the man who's already been governor four times that amount. He did not try to quiet them.

Rhodes then proceeded to savage Walter Mondale. He accused him of joining with Jimmy Carter to "destroy the well-being of 50,000 steelworkers in this great state."

Rhodes said he was the only elected state or national official to go to Youngstown on "Black Monday" in September 1977 when Jones & Laughlin closed its factory because of excessive federal regulations. He said Carter and Mondale "turned their backs" on the people of Youngstown, and now Mondale has the nerve to "ruthlessly travel over Ohio and try to say that President Reagan is the culprit. He had nothing to do with it."

"Here we have a lifelong knee-jerk liberal who will tax, tax, tax, spend, spend, spend, and regulate, regulate and regulate the steel industry," said Rhodes, dredging up one old line after another and sticking in Mondale's name.

He drew horselaughs when he said Mondale promised to appoint a committee to study the steel situation, the same horselaughs as when he said in 1978 that Richard Celeste would appoint a committee to study the school situation.

He drew thunderous applause when he said Mondale "is not qualified to be president of these United States"—the same applause as when he said six years ago that Celeste was not qualified to be governor.

The audience loved it. "Rhodes is back," said one reporter.

To anyone who didn't understand, Rhodes explained: "Somebody's got to take after 'em."

So it was vintage Jim Rhodes, positioning himself for whatever looks good in '86, running if he thinks he can win, staying out if he can't.

There were some mutterings at the Republican event that he ought to give up and leave things to the younger folk.

But Rhodes doesn't hear those voices. He only knew that somebody needed to blow the dust off the Republicans and stir them to work against Walter Mondale and for Ronald Reagan.

Rhodes did it, and he made believers out of them.

The muttering continued that Rhodes ought to leave it to the younger folks; he didn't hear, and lost a bid to return as governor in 1986. But there's no doubt he always livened up the campaign trail.

■ ■

Brush Fires, Bush and Dole

United Press International, January 10, 1988

COLUMBUS (UPI)—There's a story circulating at the Statehouse that Cuyahoga County Republican Chairman Robert Hughes climbs up on a hill, rubs two sticks together, blows on the tinder and starts a fire.

On an adjacent hill is former Gov. James Rhodes, holding up a huge mirror. "Pretty soon," chortles one Republican, "people think there are 20,000 Aztecs out there."

What Hughes and Rhodes have done lately, to the chagrin of those who would like things quiet and peaceful in the Republican camp, is to press for a quick kill for Vice President George Bush in the GOP presidential sweepstakes.

What they are also doing is attempting to give Ohio a voice in the selection process at a time when the Buckeye State otherwise will have nothing to say about whether Bush or his chief rival, Sen. Robert Dole, R-Kansas, is the nominee.

Rhodes has called for an early endorsement of Bush by the Republican State Committee, and Hughes has scheduled a Jan. 23 meeting of all GOP county chairmen in Columbus, with the hope of getting a Bush endorsement. Dole supporters are not amused by the antics of Hughes and Rhodes. They believe the GOP leadership should keep hands off the nomination fight and allow rank-and-file Republicans to decide.

Keith McNamara, chairman of Bush's Ohio campaign, said such an endorsement would be discouraged. "We don't want to do anything that would be divisive," he said.

At the same time, McNamara did a pretty good job last week of creating the impression that there are 20,000 Indians out there for Bush.

He held a press conference with several respected party leaders, pointing out Bush's "unprecedented" organization in Ohio, and endorsements from a majority of elected Republican officials.

The Dole forces respond that this is a façade for weakness; that the Kansas senator is virtually even with the vice president when rank-and-file are polled.

Part of the sniping results from the loss of an early Ohio primary and the missed opportunity to have an effect on the GOP nomination.

The Ohio presidential primary was at one time set for March by an act of the Legislature. But it was returned to May, ostensibly because of the prohibitive $5 million cost of a second primary election.

However, neither the Republicans nor the Democrats at that time wanted an early primary. Gov. Richard Celeste was thinking about running for president. And with Bush fighting fallout from the Iran-Contra scandal, it looked like a wide-open Republican battle with a late decision date.

Now, the GOP contest looks like a two-man race, and Bush supporters are trying to close Dole out.

Dole found irony in this two weeks ago when he made an impromptu visit to Columbus. He was told most party leaders believe Bush has the nomination sewed up.

"That's not going to happen," said the senator. "Jim Rhodes said he was going to be the next governor in 1986, too. When he couldn't get anybody else to come, Bob Dole was out here working for Gov. Rhodes." Ouch.

Meanwhile, Hughes is promoting his Jan. 23 county chairmen's meeting in Columbus as the first big caucus in any state on the GOP candidates, bigger than Iowa. It will draw national TV and big-time political reporters, he says.

"If the interest continues, we may have to hold it in Ohio Stadium," said Hughes. If so, there'd be plenty of room for all the Aztecs, and more.

Of course Bush won the battle of Ohio and the election. But this was the tail end of influence, both for Hughes and Rhodes, in Ohio Republican politics as the era of George Voinovich and Bob Bennett approached. Dole was the party's presidential nominee in 1996 but could not overcome incumbent Democrat Bill Clinton. Ohio later went to the March primary in presidential years, trying to maximize its influence on the party nominees.

■ ■

The Democrats

The 1972 Democratic National Convention was the last great brawl at the major party conventions. This column was written leading up to it. Minnesota Sen. Hubert Humphrey, who nearly had won the presidency in 1968, was the favorite of organized labor and many party regulars. South Dakota Sen. George McGovern was preferred by the younger generation and left-leaning partisans. It was the mirror image of the Republicans' center/right intraparty battles in recent years.

Ohio Passes! Democrats in Deep Division

United Press International, May 13, 1972

COLUMBUS (UPI)—Frank W. King, former (Ohio) Senate Democratic leader and now Ohio's most powerful labor chieftain, is in a solid position to assume control of the Buckeye State's delegation to the Democratic National Convention in June.

It is an enviable situation for King—a complete turnabout from two or three months ago when it looked for all the world like Gov. John J. Gilligan would lead the influential 153-member Ohio delegation to Miami Beach.

The strange winds of politics blew Gilligan's horse—Sen. Edmund S. Muskie—out from under him and King is riding to the convention at the head of the parade astride Sen. Hubert H. Humphrey.

Humphrey wrote King last Friday advising his longtime ally to organize Humphrey's portion of the delegation "as soon as possible," along with Morton Neipp, Ohio campaign manager for Humphrey in 1968, and Frazier Reams Jr., former Democratic gubernatorial candidate and Neipp's business partner.

King will have plenty of material to work with. Included among the 38 at-large delegates pledged to Humphrey are veteran Democratic Party pros like Albert S. Porter, national committeeman; state Auditor Joseph T. Ferguson; former Democratic State Chairman William L. Coleman; former gubernatorial candidate Robert E. Sweeney, and Summit County Democratic Chairman Robert M. Blakemore.

Humphrey will have close to 80 delegates from Ohio, and 31 of them are organized labor disciples, six of them vice presidents of the Ohio AFL-CIO.

It all adds up to a powerful base for King, despite the fact that Sen. George S. McGovern has more than 60 of the delegates pledged to him.

King was prepared for a scrap for control of the delegation, which carries with it the power to name Ohio representatives on the convention's rules, credentials and platform committees.

He indicated that if McGovern's followers wanted to make it a test of strength, they would be given a strong dose of medicine to swallow.

It now appears there will be no such test. Leaders of the Humphrey-McGovern factions have conferred, and King has pledged to exercise firm but fair control so unity will eventually prevail.

"We've got to think about winning in November," King said. "All our decisions at the convention will be made in caucus. We will make collective judgments and work it as nice as we can."

McGovern's Ohio chairman, Robert McAlister, agreed his forces will "try to keep personal antagonisms in low profile" and avoid a repeat of 1968 when "we had a couple of different camps that regarded each other as blood enemies."

"Our attitude going in is really going to be one of participating in an overall delegation that can function," McAlister said. "We've got enough strength so we can't be ignored. We're going to try to be cohesive and work to pick up additional votes. We're not going to be McCarthyesque and go in there and say, 'If we don't get this we're going to storm out of the convention.'"

McAlister said there would be a truce on raiding delegates pledged to the two candidates.

"We're not going to try to get them to break their commitments to Humphrey, and we expect them not to do it to us," he said.

McAlister believes McGovern can become attractive to Humphrey delegates as the primary season wears on.

"Candidates can come and go," he said in referring to Muskie's demise last month.

There are those who would like to see Ferguson, the 80-year old auditor, head the Ohio delegation. There is also talk he may be named honorary chairman.

"Joe Ferguson is going to have a very big part in this," said King, who apparently is taking charge and shooting for unity.

The delegation was so evenly divided and the McGovern and Humphrey partisans so intense that the peaceful intentions evaporated. The Buckeye delegation made a national spectacle of itself in the cavernous Miami Beach convention center, unable to poll quickly on roll call votes. "Ohio passes!" King repeatedly had to shout, to the derision of other states.

The reference to "McCarthyesque" was to the 1968 delegates pledged to Sen. Eugene McCarthy of Minnesota, head of the anti-Vietnam War movement, who inflamed passions at the Chicago convention.

■ ■

Ted Kennedy Challenges President Carter

United Press International, June 27, 1980

COLUMBUS (UPI)—If President Carter gets into serious trouble during the next six weeks—the kind of trouble that could deny him renomination, he needn't bother to look to Ohio to bail him out.

Half of Ohio's delegation to the Democratic National Convention is firmly behind Carter's opponent, Sen. Edward M. Kennedy. And among the other half it is fair to say that only a minority would be willing to swim the ocean or jump off the mountaintop for the president.

Not that the ship is sinking. It seems highly unlikely that Carter will lose the nomination now. All he needs to do is control his delegates for the first ballot and it's over. But the cracks are there, and if a leak springs it could mean a fast trip to Davey Jones' locker, at least in the Ohio contingent.

The makeup of Ohio's convention delegation and the election a week ago of Cleveland labor leader Martin J. Hughes was a tipoff that Carter's support is a mile wide and about as thick as the paper you're reading this on.

First of all, Kennedy's delegates are the zealots. They will fight to the end for their man. They are like the Carter delegates of 1976—the outsiders, the downtrodden looking for somebody new.

The current Carter delegates are a curious combination—the true believers from four years ago, and the fair-weather friends; opportunists who just wanted to go to the convention.

Many in the latter category are the political pros who have infiltrated the Carter caucus by pulling rank. They were left off the ship last time because they were unwilling to ride with an untested candidate. This time, they have bought a passport to New York. It's easy to ride with the president. But it is the political pros who will be the first to desert Carter if he becomes an unmarketable commodity.

The first order of business for these public officials and lobbyists is to get with a winner. The lobbyists want somebody who can produce for them and the public officials are interested in preserving their own hides. If Ronald Reagan wins, they lose.

Except for Democratic State Chairman C. Paul Tipps, House Speaker Vernal G. Riffe Jr. and possibly state Treasurer Gertrude W. Donahey, none of the elected statewide public officials has been steadfastly behind Carter during his presidency.

So when Hughes, an international vice president of the Communication Workers of America, got himself appointed as a delegate and upended Tipps as Ohio delegation chairman it was a signal that all is not well for the president in Buckeyeland. Should things go sour for Carter, organized labor would be looking for an alternative. Hughes would be likely to join the search, along with the soft section of the Carter caucus. It's no secret where the 77 Kennedy delegates would be.

Carter hung onto the Ohio delegation and his re-nomination. But the Kennedy challenge softened him up for Republican Ronald Reagan, who won the 1980 election.

Marty Hughes was as fickle as they came. He wanted to be a player. At the Republican National Convention in 1996, Hughes was spotted at the San Diego convention center by a reporter before a daily session convened, sitting in the section reserved for the Ohio delegation. Apparently, he didn't get along with the Bill Clinton crowd.

■ ■

Hart Could Upset Mondale in Ohio

United Press International, March 23, 1984

COLUMBUS (UPI)—At first glance, it would appear that former Vice President Walter F. Mondale will sweep over Ohio like a prairie fire at the May 8 primary, particularly if he picks up momentum in New York and Pennsylvania.

Mondale has already sopped up some of the support that went for favorite-son John Glenn until Glenn dropped out of the Democratic presidential sweepstakes.

Organized labor is strong for Mondale, and the Ohio AFL-CIO, the United Auto Workers and the Ohio Education Association normally carry big sticks in Ohio Democratic politics.

"I think Mondale is going to win Ohio," said Martin J. Hughes, an international vice president of the Communication Workers of America and president of the 150,000-member Cleveland AFL-CIO.

"I think we need a candidate who can beat (President) Reagan," said Hughes, who happened to be the chairman of the Ohio delegation to the Democratic National Convention in 1980. "I think (Sen. Gary) Hart will be fading by the time we get to Ohio."

For Hughes, the transition from Glenn to Mondale was made easily. He was on President Carter's ball team in 1980. That was also Mondale's team. Furthermore, Hughes is bound by the national AFL-CIO's endorsement of Mondale.

Nevertheless, Hughes is not an outspoken cheerleader for Mondale . . . just in case. He wants to go to the Democratic National Convention in San Francisco. That means being flexible.

"I want to be in the back room (at the convention)," said Hughes.

Some of the Democratic heavy-hitters, including Gov. Richard F. Celeste, have it easy. They get one of the 21 automatic invitations to the convention as an unpledged delegate.

The governor, who can afford to wait and see which candidate looks like a winner, is trying to hold others back so the Ohio leadership will be unified in a choice. He may not be successful.

Celeste and other party leaders will be under tremendous pressure from organized labor to break toward Mondale and influence the Ohio voting.

With Carter's leftover support and organization, Mondale would seem to have things going his way in Ohio.

But Hart can't be discounted, especially in view of his demonstrated ability to make something out of nothing in other states.

"There's something out there that's anti-Mondale, anti-establishment, anti-institution," said one political pro who predicted that Hart will "reach around the edges of the party" and carry Ohio.

Hart could do it with the same types of Democrats who:

- Signed on with George McGovern in 1972 and battled to a virtual standoff with Hubert Humphrey, who had organized labor in his corner.
- Took a chance with Jimmy Carter in 1976 over the better-known Sens. Frank Church and Henry (Scoop) Jackson, and Rep. Morris K. Udall.
- Helped Sen. Edward Kennedy capture 46 percent of the vote in a primary contest with Carter, who was president of the United States.

This is why top Democrats without a vested interest in Mondale are nervous about endorsing him yet.

Almost a carbon copy of the Democratic leaders' mentality in 1980 as described in the preceding column, except this time Hart, the outsider, carried Ohio in the primary. He didn't win the nomination, though, and Mondale lost the election to President Reagan.

Here, Marty Hughes owns up to his description in the preceding column—he wants to be in the back room no matter the candidate.

■ ■

Geraldine Ferraro Produces a Buzz

United Press International, September 14, 1984

COLUMBUS (UPI)—Probably because she has a chance of becoming the first woman vice president, Geraldine Ferraro produces an electricity among certain women not seen since the days of John F. Kennedy.

Last week she visited Columbus and made four appearances carefully calculated to appeal to senior citizens, women, labor, party faithful and young women and men in the business community.

One event was to be an intimate gathering of about 25 leading women in Ohio, something that has worked well for Ferraro in other states. There is a two-way exchange of ideas and information, and the women get to know the candidate on a rather personal basis.

Soon, the word spread. Everyone wanted to be in that elite group of 25. It grew to 50, then to 100.

By this time, the idea of a roundtable discussion was out the window, so the state Democratic organization decided to make it a speech to politically active women.

The invitation list grew, and since the event was free, many of the women decided to bring their relatives and next-door neighbors.

When the door opened for the speech last Wednesday, the 300 seats were quickly snapped up. Next door in the partitioned hotel ballroom, breakfast was set up for a senior citizens' conference. The overflow began to invade that room.

Ferraro began to speak, and staffers began to get nervous, fearing an ugly scene. Those left out were disgruntled. "If Ferraro's next door, we want to see her," said one. Others began stamping their feet and banging on the partition.

Ferraro saved the day, saying she would make time in her schedule to visit them. And she did.

So charismatic is the Democratic nominee that when she posed for a few photos in the back of the ballroom, bystanders were nearly knocked down by some women rushing to get next to her.

"It's great to hear 'Ger-ry, Ger-ry' but it doesn't do any good unless we get people to go vote," said Ferraro, trying to harness some of that energy.

"Don't rest until the polls close," urged Dagmar Celeste, "It's only eight weeks. What's eight weeks compared with the rest of your life wondering if you did your part to advance the cause of peace and justice?"

> We saw the same excitement in 2008 with Hillary Clinton and, to a lesser extent, Sarah Palin. Ferraro was the great hope of Democratic women of the day.

■ ■

How About a John Glenn-Jesse Jackson Ticket?

United Press International, April 10, 1988

COLUMBUS (UPI)—Spring is the time for speculation on baseball and politics, and what better dream could the Democrats conjure up than a Jesse Jackson-John Glenn ticket for this fall?

Or a John Glenn-Jesse Jackson ticket?

Let's say Jackson finishes the primary season with more delegates to the Democratic National Convention than anyone else but not enough to get the nomination. You're into the smoke-filled room.

Jackson has to be on the ticket. To eliminate him would frustrate his legion of supporters, who are necessary to help defeat Vice President George Bush in the fall.

The Jackson-Glenn ticket is ideal. Jackson, the fiery, charismatic preacher, offsets Glenn's labored efforts to be exciting on the stump. Glenn, who has had 13 years in the Senate, offsets Jackson's lack of experience in Washington. His demonstrated stability offsets Jackson's radical image.

It is doubtful that Glenn could be induced to run for vice president under any other circumstances. His ill-fated 1984 campaign even brought home to him the negative realities involved in running for president.

But Glenn is deeply committed to the advancement of minorities, to the point that he might be persuaded to team up with Jackson in order to present to the nation a credible presidential-vice presidential ticket with a black man on it.

John Glenn was a pioneer in space 26 years ago. He went where no American had gone. Who's to say he wouldn't do it in the political arena, given the opportunity?

Jerry Austin, Jackson's campaign manager, believes the preacher will do better in Ohio this year than he did in 1984, when he captured 16 percent of the popular vote. "He'll do better almost every place in Ohio," predicted Austin, who managed Gov. Richard Celeste's campaigns earlier in this decade.

Austin said Jackson will carry the same message in Ohio to working class people, farmers and university students that's worked for him in other states because Ohio is a "microcosm" of the country.

"His message has universal appeal," said Austin.

Austin believes Jackson will be the Democratic nominee and, in typical Austin fashion, minimizes the chance of defeat.

"Anybody who thinks Jesse Jackson, if he were the nominee, couldn't beat George Bush is crazy," he declared.

Of course the "dream ticket" didn't materialize. John Glenn was on the short list of running mates for Massachusetts Gov. Michael Dukakis but Texas Sen. Lloyd Bentsen got the nod. Glenn was never again a serious contender for president or vice president.

Jackson did well in the Ohio primary and continued to be the point man for African-Americans in the 1990s. Then along came Barack Obama.

■ ■

The Conventions

This post-convention, four-item column was written in the press workroom in Madison Square Garden the morning after the convention adjourned.

Democratic Convention: Ohio Puts Carter Over the Top

United Press International, July 17, 1976

NEW YORK (UPI)—Ohio commanded a fair share of the national spotlight at the Democratic National Convention last week.

The "mother" of eight presidents may have produced another one by adoption when it threw Madison Square Garden into pandemonium Wednesday night by casting the votes which clinched the Democratic nomination for Jimmy Carter.

All eyes were on the Ohio delegation, which had helped to entangle the 1972 convention in partisan bickering.

And it was a proud moment when Christine Gitlin of Berea, the tiny blonde delegation chairman in a flaming red dress, proclaimed: "Madame Secretary, Ohio does not pass!" and then put Carter over the top.

Postscript: despite the heavy display of unity, some members of the Ohio delegation are not too sure about Carter, and some are suspicious of the mettle of Sen. Walter Mondale of Minnesota, the vice presidential nominee. But they are in the minority. The rest of Ohio's national attention went to Sen. John Glenn, who lost out in the finals of the vice presidential sweepstakes.

Ohio newsmen and politicians had joked long before the convention that once Glenn gave his keynote speech, he would be eliminated from consideration.

But even the most cynical Ohioans couldn't match the national media, which declared Glenn "dead" in print and on the airwaves after the speech.

That cut the Senator deeply, and he criticized the media for grasping at every straw and interpreting "the turning of a doorknob the wrong way" to mean something.

The speech may have been a factor in Glenn's rejection, but it probably was more the delegates' ho-hum reaction than the speech itself.

Carter may have sensed that Glenn would not be as dynamic a campaigner as he would like. But he said he felt personally more comfortable with Glenn than with the other prospects he interviewed.

Glenn showed a sense of humor throughout the suspenseful four days of waiting for Carter to make his choice, and he indicated he feels that being in the final six will propel him upward in the Senate pecking order, where he is near the bottom now.

Lt. Gov. Richard F. Celeste kept a high profile at the convention, and if his political timetable doesn't call for a shot at the presidency within a decade, a lot of Ohio convention watchers will miss their guess.

All Celeste did, while not even a delegate, was:

- Promote a "Welcome" rally for Glenn when he arrived at his hotel and lobby vigorously for him as the vice presidential choice.
- Send a dozen youthful supporters into various state Democratic caucuses to get to know how they operated and who were the movers and shakers.
- Deliver a speech on a proposed party rule on the floor of the convention, while most of the delegates were present.
- Host a cocktail party which attracted about 250 guests, many of them politicians from other states whom Celeste may call upon in the future.

A long shot, way down the road, maybe, but that's the way Celeste does business, far ahead of time.

The "proportional representation" move guaranteeing equality for everybody may have gone too far, even in the eyes of some liberal Ohio Democrats.

A "men's liberation" caucus was struck up within the delegation when older white males found themselves cut out by organized minorities.

The "equality" movement, long espoused by state Rep. Michael P. Stinziano, D-Columbus, came back to haunt him. Stinziano was indignant because the women in the Ohio delegation, whom he aided by sponsoring the Equal Rights Amendment to the U.S. Constitution, helped defeat him for a spot on the Democratic National Committee because they were afraid he would bump a woman and they would have only three of the eight posts instead of half.

"I'm going to see that some changes are made," said one top-level state official and prominent Democrat attending the convention.

This convention was especially fun for Ohio reporters because their man was one of three finalists for vice president. The reporters spent a number of hours camped in the corridor outside John Glenn's hotel room waiting for the phone call from Carter. When the call came, the news was not positive.

Celeste and his groupies truly made a marvelous effort, working and learning behind the scenes so they could have an impact at a future convention. Only Celeste's libido stopped this army from charging into action in 1988. He was ready and qualified to compete for the nation's highest office.

■ ■

This column, written the day after the end of the Republican National Convention in San Diego, is a lament over the lack of spontaneity and fireworks at modern conventions.

Politicians Everywhere Try to Duck Tough Issues

The Columbus Dispatch, September 2, 1996

When you stop and think about it, the national political conventions aren't too much different from what goes on at the Ohio Statehouse, in this way: Winning is everything and political philosophy means nothing.

Oh, sure, both the Republicans in San Diego and the Democrats in Chicago wrapped themselves in red, white and blue, cheered their leaders, reviled the opposition, batted balloons, waved American flags, and blew horns and whistles. But they were careful not to offend anyone within the ranks because to do so would destroy unity and endanger the prospects of winning the big prize in November.

And so it is at the Statehouse. Politicians calculate every move with the next election in mind, carefully preparing a portfolio of accomplishments to impress the voters and avoiding any embarrassing incidents that could be exploited by opponents in 30-second television commercials.

Think about it. In the General Assembly last year, the thorny issue of abortion was handled with back-room maneuvering, producing a bill that supporters could crow about, although opponents claimed it would have little effect. At the conventions, the issue was finessed with clever semantics and scheduling of speakers.

Maybe it's a sign of the times. Maybe it makes good sense to have everything managed, scripted. Maybe the public doesn't have the time or the stomach any more to sort through backbiting political debate. Maybe the politicians just want to cut to the chase, dispense with the preliminaries and get to the main event: the election.

Once Bob Dole became the obvious Republican presidential nominee by crushing his out-organized opponents in a series of major state primaries, the GOP buttoned itself up. Conservatives were pacified in several ways and issues were put to bed.

The San Diego convention was tame because Republicans knew that a split would blow any chance they have of recapturing the White House. Delegates might as well have mailed in their votes. They were party-line soldiers who exhibited no independence of thought.

The Democrats were no better, and for the same reason: They want to win. Except for some mild criticism of President Clinton for signing a welfare-reform bill and a few other mutterings, the Chicago convention was an orchestrated TV commercial for Clinton-Gore.

Many no doubt believe it's past time. They say good riddance to the hour-long "demonstration," the lengthy parliamentary maneuvering over the "seating" of renegade delegates and droning debate over minutiae in the platform. They are relieved that there's no more wrangling for the microphone by delegation leaders or the monotonous pounding of the gavel accompanied by the shout of, "Will the sergeant-at-arms please clear the aisles?"

And they're right. The disappearance of the circus atmosphere has made the conventions much more efficient, and less fun. The train runs on time, and maybe that's the way the public's business should be conducted.

The news is gone, too, a lament often repeated during the last three weeks.

Why is it gone? Because the political parties have rediscovered the old school-days bromide: cooperate and graduate, or in this case, cooperate and get elected.

How does this resemble the situation at the Statehouse? Many years ago, the legislators and the governor's administration used to fuss and fight over everything. Then they realized that if they cooled the public rhetoric, they could get more done. So they clammed up and did their fighting behind the doors. Any passionate speeches were reserved for people who would give them money for their campaigns.

Now, issues are less debated than cared for in a choreographed way and then catalogued for display during the next campaign. Weak members, usually freshmen, are given custody of important bills, whether they know anything about the subject matter or not. Then when the bills are passed, through the efforts of the leadership, they can trumpet the accomplishment to their constituents on the campaign trail.

Last week, Gov. George V. Voinovich assembled key administration officials and Republican legislative leaders in an ornate room known as the Stateroom, to heap praise on each other for managing the state's finances.

The occasion was a celebration of the upgrading of the state's bond rating and apparently to counter all the free publicity the Democrats were receiving in Chicago.

Voinovich even borrowed from Clinton's observation from the 21st Century Express that America is "on the right track."

"We have a great team here in this state," said the governor. "If we stay on track and move through to the next century, we're going to be ready."

By the time the next century gets here, legislators and convention delegates may be E-mailing their votes in, and speeches may be delivered by videotape.

This has been a recording.

Reporters salivated in early 2008, thinking that the Democratic National Convention would be a knock-down, drag-out affair between delegates pledged to Barack Obama and Hillary Clinton. Obama fixed that by holding his edge through the primaries and Clinton chose not to carry the fight further. She was rewarded with an appointment to be secretary of state.

But even term limits did not alter the backroom choreography in the Ohio legislature.

■ ■

The Great and the Near-Great

This column was written immediately following President Nixon's resignation, but had more to do with the new president, Gerald R. Ford, a regional friend of Ohio Republicans, and the fallout from Watergate, which was underestimated.

GOP Hopes Ford Makes Watergate Disappear

United Press International, August 10, 1974

COLUMBUS (UPI)—President Nixon's resignation and the elevation of Gerald Ford to the nation's highest office can do little but help Ohio Republicans as they prepare to battle for their very lives this fall.

This feeling is expressed by a number of GOP politicians and shared by some Democrats.

Naturally, the rub-off is not going to be great in state and local elections. It may only affect close races.

But it will be better than nothing for the Ohio Republicans, who have been shackled, whether they believe it or not, by the Watergate issue for more than a year.

Prior to the events of last week, they had to fall back on statements like the one President Ford offered Ohio Republicans at a fund-raiser in Columbus two months ago:

"There's no Republican candidate on the ballot in 1974 who had anything to do with Watergate in any way whatsoever, so Watergate should not be an issue in 1974 in Ohio or anywhere else."

This sounded hopeful, but hardly practical. Even if Watergate was not to be a direct issue in the Ohio campaign, it created a climate to discourage campaign contributions and participation at the polls.

Money and votes will be highly important this year for a political party trying to regain control of a state government.

Now, the Ohio GOP seems to have been given a new lease on life.

"It's over with," said one Republican. "It's behind us and there are no more lingering questions that seemed to come up day after day."

"Whatever the resolution of the problem," said another, "just getting it over with has to have some beneficial effects for Republicans."

The most visible effect likely will be in the congressional races, where Republicans have 13 incumbents running and Democrats have eight.

Each of those incumbents, by virtue of Nixon's resignation, has been spared a record vote on impeachment although each has made his views known.

Instead of alienating a fraction of their constituencies with a vote on impeachment, the incumbents will be able to emphasize other aspects of their record.

Republican congressional candidates, new and old, may also be able to take advantage of Ford's natural popularity in Ohio. He is a fellow midwesterner who put in five appearances in Ohio during his vice presidency and may make more.

Furthermore, the new president will still be on a honeymoon with Congress and almost everyone else during the election campaign. Attractive Republican candidates ought to be able to convince their voters to help give Ford a friendly Congress for two more years.

There is even a possibility that voters who feel Nixon was hounded out of office may come out to vote against his detractors. They would largely be voting in favor of Republican candidates.

Statewide and legislative races will be determined on the basis of state and local issues. But there is still room for the close ones to be swayed by the takeover of a new administration in Washington.

For example, Republican Party officials already foresee an upturn in campaign contributions as Watergate fades.

And they are hopeful their followers, discouraged until now, will turn out and vote Republican in Ohio races. More of the independent vote may be captured, officials say.

Perhaps the GOP candidate who needs it most will benefit least from events in Washington. Cleveland Mayor Ralph J. Perk, Republican nominee for the U.S. Senate, faces former astronaut John H. Glenn Jr., a non-incumbent Democrat with instant recognition, a clean background, high prior service to his country and an appeal for conservatives.

It is doubtful even President Ford can do much for Perk against that kind of an opponent.

Watergate did NOT fade. John Glenn walloped Ralph Perk for the Senate seat, Democrats won control of the Ohio Senate and Ford lost Ohio to Democrat Jimmy Carter in 1976. Going against the tide, James A. Rhodes was the only Republican in the nation to defeat a sitting Democratic governor in 1974.

■ ■

Nixon Tries to End His Exile in Columbus

United Press International, February 20, 1981

COLUMBUS (UPI)—It was like Richard Nixon opened the closet door, peered cautiously in both directions to make sure no bogeymen were lurking nearby, and then tiptoed quickly to the sanctuary of a cozy living room for a chat with friends.

The scene was the Sheraton-Columbus Hotel, where the former president last week addressed a $300-a-plate fund-raiser for Ohio Senate Republicans, mingled with guests at a cocktail party and signed so many autographs he must have had writer's cramp.

Some called it a "coming-out" party. Others described it as a "carnival." By any account, it was a curious event with something to offer for everyone involved. For the GOP, it was money—more than $100,000 to use as an excellent financial springboard for strengthening its grip on the state Senate in 1982. For diehard Nixon fanatics, it was an opportunity for an up close and personal look at their hero.

For wealthy curiosity seekers, it was a chance to view what one person called a "three-headed kangaroo"—a president elected by the second-highest majority in American history only to plummet to an ignominious resignation in less than two years.

And for Nixon, it was hopefully a way to end almost seven years of exile and begin a new career as an elder statesman whose transgressions are forgotten and whose advice is respected.

Nixon, no doubt, needs most of all to know that somebody still loves him; that his 5 ½ years in the White House counted for something; and that he can still improve his position in the polls by which historians rank presidents.

With the mood of the country turning conservative, with Ronald Reagan in the driver's seat in Washington, what better time for Nixon to re-establish his political presence? And what better place than Ohio, where he never lost a national election?

When Sen. Thomas A. Van Meter, R-Ashland, first came up with the idea of inviting Nixon to Ohio to raise money, the response was underwhelming, as if he was inviting a case of bubonic plague.

As the time approached, there were still unbelievers who chose not to get involved. Republican State Chairman Earl T. Barnes had a responsibility to the party, and Gov. James A. Rhodes perhaps was looking toward a future campaign. Both indicated they had to go home and sort their socks the night of Nixon's appearance.

But most important for Van Meter, the Statehouse lobbyists came, and brought their money, even though a lot of them would also be down the street at the Democrats' fund-raiser this coming week.

And Nixon obviously enjoyed his visit—reminiscing with Woody Hayes and former Sen. John W. Bricker, shaking hands with well-wishers, waving to the crowds and seeing the TV lights and flashbulbs aimed in his direction under pleasant circumstances.

He even made it a point to initiate conversation with the news media, who came to see if Dick Nixon was still kickable.

When it was over, everyone was satisfied, even the demonstrators who got a chance to put on their Nixon masks and resurrect some old slogans.

"This event cannot be duplicated by us or anybody else," said Senate President Paul E. Gillmor, R-Port Clinton, who helped organize it. "Even Richard Nixon could not duplicate this."

That's not to say he won't try again soon.

The reference to the news media seeing if Nixon was "kickable" refers to Nixon's bitter remark to the press after losing the California governor's race in 1962: "Well, you won't have Dick Nixon to kick around any more." There was plenty more kicking, however, after Nixon won the presidency in 1968.

Rhodes's exact quote for blowing off the Nixon soiree: "I have to stay home and pay the paper boy."

■ ■

Senator Woody Hayes? It's Your Guess

United Press International, May 5, 1979

COLUMBUS (UPI)—Is he or isn't he interested in a political career? Only Woody Hayes knows for sure.

And when you ask him if he'd like to run for the U.S. Senate all you get is two arms criss-crossing vigorously like they're signaling an incompleted pass.

"I'm not going to talk about that," he says. But he says it with a smile.

Conceding the remote possibility of a Hayes candidacy for the Republican nomination to run against Sen. John Glenn, D-Ohio, next year, it's easy to set down the pluses and minuses.

The Republicans have to find somebody to run against Glenn, if only to make him spend a lot of Democratic money. They might as well go with a wild card instead of a professional politician. Hayes has an enormous following. His philosophy would be attractive for conservatives and, to say the least, he would bring a fresh outlook to Washington.

But, as one Statehouse observer put it last week, "Woody Hayes is like birth control, he has as many enemies as he does friends."

The former coach's temperament and his loathing of nagging news reporters are ill-suited to a political career.

Putting all this aside, we tuned in last Friday as Hayes addressed a luncheon meeting of the American Bottled Water Association in Columbus, to see if we could detect the start of a campaign.

We could not, but the potential is there.

For example, Hayes' normal 45-minute speech was cut down to 30 and the usual bellowing, fist-pounding delivery was replaced with genuine good humor and that "honest-to-gosh" voice quality Hayes gets when he talks about America, little kids and people who work for a living.

He talked, naturally, about positive accomplishments:

- How the Ohio State athletic department netted $50 million during his tenure and spent it on developing other worthy sports.
- How "we run a clean program and make sure others do, too."
- How you have to "be there," as he was, if you want to stop rioting on campus or lend support to the Vietnam War effort.

All of the above could easily be turned into campaign material.

Hayes also demonstrated he's come to terms with what made him an ex-football coach—the sideline explosion at the Gator Bowl during which he tried to deck a Clemson linebacker.

He conceded "I got fired" and even joked about the incident in recalling that a former player "came rushing up to me as I was walking across campus and grabbed me by the shoulders. He grabbed me, I didn't grab him!"

He told good jokes, like the one about a former player who went on to become an Olympian, won a gold medal "and was so proud of it he brought it back and had it bronzed."

He scolded "politicians" for "making hay by jumping on the NCAA. There would be no great college athletic programs without the NCAA," he said, adding that Teddy Roosevelt established the NCAA.

"Teddy Roosevelt was a great man," said Hayes. "He's the kind of a guy we need today. Maybe he could sit down with the Russians and make 'em understand SALT."

He said Americans have forgotten in peacetime how to work together as they do in war. "We're setting ourselves up for any invader that wants to take us," he warned.

Hayes made special note of the fact that he is a Republican. He also observed that he's lived in Columbus for 28 years and will probably do so for another 28. "I don't ever plan to leave Columbus," he said.

Woody Hayes and politics? Make your own guess.

SALT was a reference to the Strategic Arms Limitation Talks with the Soviet Union.

Successful football coaches often are recruited to run for office. Hayes never ran, but he was an unabashed supporter of Republican candidates and sometimes appeared at Statehouse rallies for GOP candidates. He died in Columbus in 1987 and former President Richard Nixon spoke at his funeral.

■ ■

Chef Jim Rhodes' Campaign Recipe for Ronald Reagan

United Press International, August, 31, 1980

COLUMBUS (UPI)—Ronald Reagan apparently has decided to follow the recipe of the master chef, Gov. James A. Rhodes, to concoct a victory in Ohio this November.

Rhodes has a good formula with some useful ingredients, but as Reagan found out last week, sometimes the success of the dish depends on who's doing the stirring.

The former California governor breezed into Columbus for a meeting with the Ohio Conference of Teamsters and was promptly intercepted by Rhodes, who asked to see his speech.

Reagan's address apparently was too tame for Rhodes. It talked about Samuel Gompers founding the AFL-CIO in Columbus, and about human rights in Poland. So Rhodes picked up a couple of tins of spice and began shaking with both hands. He had a whole extra page written into the speech, blaming President Carter for a "severe depression" and saying he is "insensitive to the problems of working people."

Rhodes had the speech loaded up with references to Cleveland, Akron, and Youngstown so it would hit home. And it did. Except that Rhodes is prone to exaggerate with his blustery, one-sentence declarations.

Somehow, the Rhodes rhetoric just didn't seem appropriate coming from the man who used to visit America's firesides through television to present the G.E. Theater. When Reagan was finished serving up his peppery "ad lib stew," there was a slight case of indigestion over whether America was ready to be characterized as being in a full-scale depression.

Reagan aides ran quickly to the medicine chest and came up with some bicarbonate in the form of "clarifications." They'll need to keep a full supply of home remedies on the shelf if their candidate is to cook in the Rhodes kitchen this fall.

Speechmaking aside, Reagan could do worse than follow the governor's advice when it comes to where and how to campaign in Ohio.

Rhodes wants the Republican nominee in as often as possible, and he wants him in the economically troubled cities, talking about plans to create jobs, cut inflation and solve the energy problem.

The first target, within the next two weeks, is Youngstown. Look for Reagan to hold forth in an empty steel mill, blaming the vacancy on Carter.

Rhodes also wants to put the candidate in Cleveland, Akron, Toledo, Dayton, Lorain-Elyria, and into the southeastern Ohio coal fields.

And the Reagan staff seems eager to follow that advice, which was echoed by the GOP governors of four other Great Lakes states in a private meeting.

"He's got to do it," said Rhodes, meaning he's confident Reagan will see the light, shun the lawn parties, roll up his sleeves and hit the streets.

There are 133 electoral votes in seven Great Lakes states—half the number needed to win the election.

By the time Reagan left Ohio, he appeared to understand that to beat Carter, he must return time and again to the Midwest this fall, rub elbows with blue collar Democrats and independents, come up with workable plans for the economy and sell them. That's all the master chef is asking.

Indeed Reagan followed Rhodes' advice. He cut a TV commercial in front of an abandoned, rusted-out steel mill in Youngstown and he went after the blue collar Democrats and independents, who came to be known as "Reagan Democrats."

Rhodes knew how to win in Ohio. One time, George H. W. Bush was asking for advice. Rhodes pulled out his wallet, slammed it on the table and said, "This is what you gotta talk about. They want to know whether you're gonna put money in or take money out." It was that simple.

■ ■

Salty Senator William Saxbe Jabs Nixon

United Press International, December 30, 1972

COLUMBUS (UPI)—Top-level Ohio Republicans are buzzing, and Democrats are looking on with bemused interest, about the possible after effects of U.S. Sen. William B. Saxbe's harsh denunciation of President Nixon's strategy of renewed bombing in Vietnam.

Saxbe, the senior Republican senator from Ohio, set off a premature New Year's Eve explosion late last week by indicating the President might have "lost his senses" in ordering the latest turn of events in the war.

The senator, who has parted with the President before on Vietnam and other issues, said he would join in support of legislation to end the war in 1973, and he was especially critical of Nixon's silence on the U.S. tactics, both on the battlefield and in the negotiating arena.

Ironically, 1973 also is the year Saxbe will have to decide whether to run for re-election, for governor or for nothing at all. If he chooses to run, 1973 will be his year to prepare for a probable primary fight in 1974.

So there was plenty of speculation about whether Saxbe's outburst at the President made good political sense.

Ever since Saxbe and Nixon arrived in Washington in 1969, there has been some distance between them. The senator has supported the President in a number of areas, but has never been afraid to differ with him.

Saxbe would not likely attract a lot of help from Nixon anyway if he decides to run for re-election.

But the real question is whether he read the Ohio electorate accurately in making his sharp criticisms of the President.

Ohio gave Nixon a thumping 883,000-vote plurality less than two months ago despite mounting antiwar protests. Whether sentiments have changed that drastically because the war did not end after the election is something only Saxbe may be able to tell in reading the voting public.

"I wonder if it wasn't Saxbe and not Nixon who slipped a cog," exclaimed one observer.

Another veteran politico thought Saxbe might be "knuckling under to the pressure of the news media" in criticizing the President, although the senator has never knuckled under to much of anything. "Maybe he has stronger feelings against the war that he can't hold back any longer," speculated one inside Republican, "or maybe he's sensing a stronger feeling on the part of the average guy.

"If there's a quick settlement of the war, he wouldn't look too good. But if it drags on for four or five months, and he's on record in support of a cutoff, he might end up looking favorable.

"Bill's his own man and says pretty much what he thinks. This may rattle some people, but in large measure, people like a guy who says what's on his mind.

"When he first went to Congress, he made some votes on a couple of pieces of legislation that were questionable, and his ratings up in the northeastern part of the state were tremendous because he was his own man."

Saxbe hadn't served in the Senate for two years before he said he was fed up with the ways of Congress and might not run again.

So it may have been Saxbe's blunt manner rather than any political ploy that led to his statements.

One veteran politician summed it up with this recollection:

"One time the Ohio Senate was fidgeting around toward the end of a session, waiting for a message from the House so the two chambers could proceed according to protocol toward adjournment for the rest of the year.

"Tom Bateman, the Senate clerk, sent over a carefully worded message requesting the House's permission to adjourn *sine die*, and so forth. They got a message back from Saxbe, who was (House) Speaker, saying: 'Hell, we already have.'"

The exact quote out of Washington was that Nixon had "taken leave of his senses" in resuming the bombing. The following week Saxbe, in Columbus, encountered an acquaintance who asked if the quote was accurate. Laughing, Saxbe answered, "No, I said he was out of his fucking mind."

■ ■

Liberals

Kucinich's Credibility Sags after Quitting Governor's Race

United Press International, August 31, 1986

COLUMBUS (UPI)—When he was mayor of Cleveland, he was Dennis the Menace. Now he's just Dennis the dropout; he'll menace no one again.

For Dennis Kucinich, who played the public and the press for fools with the skill of a P. T. Barnum, has canceled any credibility he had left by quitting a battle for governor he said he would fight to the bitter end.

In February, Kucinich trumpeted himself as the unbossed alternative to the two major party candidates, whom he called Tweedledee and Tweedledum. Last week, the party bosses got him to endorse Tweedledum.

Dennis Kucinich said he was going to take the "for sale" sign off the Statehouse but it ended up over his own door.

It is not yet quite clear what Dennis received for abandoning the contest to unpopular Democratic Gov. Richard F. Celeste and once-popular Republican Gov. James A. Rhodes.

Kucinich said it was the satisfaction of knowing he can help the Democratic Party to mend its ways, and influence voters to support Democratic candidates. You believe that, and the tooth fairy will visit your bedroom tonight.

Some think Kucinich mortgaged his candidacy for national and state party support in a future bid for public office. Which one is unclear, because Kucinich probably would be lucky now to be elected mayor of his own neighborhood.

What does the Kucinich withdrawal do to the governor's race? It narrows the scope of the debate and eliminates an alternative for Ohioans.

There will be no discussion of nuclear power plants, the farm problem or hunger in Ohio. There will only be Jim Rhodes and Dick Celeste hammering each other over who attracted the most jobs to Ohio and who is the most corrupt.

Secondly, those who would have voted for Kucinich now have three choices. They can vote for Celeste, vote for Rhodes or stay home. Some will stay home. But many, particularly in the northeastern part of the state, will reluctantly switch their votes to Celeste.

So on balance, the Kucinich withdrawal probably hurts Rhodes' chances of overhauling Celeste the way he caught then-Gov. John J. Gilligan in 1974 when third party candidate Nancy Lazar Brown drew 95,625 votes away from the Democrat.

Rhodes needs confusion and disenchantment to win the race, and Kucinich's withdrawal helps clear the picture for voters.

In welcoming Kucinich back into the fold, Democratic leaders had to grit their teeth. Grit they did, because it was worth it to have Dennis out of the race.

What will they do with him now that he's on their side again? "I want his active involvement in the campaign," said Gerald Austin, the campaign manager for Celeste.

What he probably meant was, he'd like to put Kucinich on a slow boat to the Azores for the rest of the campaign so he won't be out telling people how great Celeste is.

After all, how can you believe somebody who says the day after quitting the campaign: "I've never backed out of a race in my life."

Detect a note of cynicism? Reporters were disappointed that he dropped out because Kucinich made good copy. He would have livened up the race. But they were also disappointed because instead of being the maverick tilting at the establishment, Kucinich exposed himself as just another politician.

Actually, Dennis Kucinich was not washed up, as the column erroneously predicted. He got elected to the Ohio Senate and was a pretty good senator in the minority caucus. He said it was the best office he ever held, but that might not have been the truth either, because he ran for Congress at the first opportunity and got elected several times. Then he made a national caricature of himself with his antics—running for president and trying to impeach Vice President Dick Cheney.

■ ■

Legislature's Liberal Icon Left Legacy of Many Smiles

The Columbus Dispatch, January 25, 1999

As a legislator for three terms in the 1980s, Bob Hagan was out of place in the Ohio House of Representatives under legendary Speaker Vern Riffe.

Hagan, who died last week at 77, was a card-carrying liberal Democrat who wore his philosophy on his sleeve and enjoyed trying to convert anyone who would listen.

He would have been more at home in the legislature of oh, say, the 1850s, when Lincoln-Douglas style debates were popular.

In fact, the lanky, craggy-faced Hagan looked so much like Lincoln that he would dress up as the Great Emancipator each Feb. 12 and address the House from the speaker's chair, where Lincoln once sat during a visit in 1861.

But Hagan's speeches were more Mark Twain or Will Rogers, carrying more of Hagan's political philosophy than Lincoln's. And he was far more humorous even than Honest Abe, having written comedy for Danny Thomas and Phyllis Diller, and laugh lines for former Gov. John J. Gilligan and Sargent Shriver, the Democratic nominee for vice president in 1972.

Hagan was an interesting character long before he entered politics. He ran a construction company and built bridges, a fire station, a hospital and a cathedral in Youngstown, where he honchoed the aerial installation of the cross from a helicopter. He patented easy-to-assemble construction scaffolding, then sold the patent for a song. He patented tubular steel picnic tables that folded up and stored easily.

Then the political bug bit Hagan and he became a Trumbull County commissioner and served two terms. "Politics ruined his business mind," said his son, Robert F., now a state senator from Youngstown.

When Hagan returned to the Statehouse in 1993 and dressed up to commemorate the anniversary of Lincoln's campaign speech, Sen. Richard H. Finan, R-Cincinnati, pointed out that the Atrium, an open-air portico in Lincoln's time, now was enclosed.

"Your plaque will not be subject to attacks by pigeons," said Finan.

"There may not be pigeons in here," replied Hagan-Lincoln, looking skyward, "but there are senators."

Hagan was only half kidding, as he had contempt for those who didn't see things his way. "When he thought you were wrong, he not only *thought* you were stupid, he *told you* you were stupid," said Hagan the son.

During the heyday of the Galleria Tavern, a watering hole across the street from the Statehouse, the elder Hagan would sip soft drinks all evening, soberly expounding on issues of the day and verbally taking on all boozing comers.

The younger Hagan, who roomed with his dad, thought he should lighten up. "At the end of the night, he'd still be debating. I'd tell him, 'You may be arguing and convinced about this, but they are drunk and asleep and couldn't care less.'"

Democratic State Chairman David J. Leland said Hagan viewed liberalism as a badge of honor. "I think he viewed it as a title of someone who cares about other people," said Leland.

Hagan and his wife, Ada, had 14 children. That led one anti-abortion lobbyist to think he was fair game for a sales pitch. Hagan asserted: "I'm pro-choice. My wife and I chose to have 14 children."

"I didn't know anybody who stood more strongly for what he believed in, even when his philosophy was not in vogue," said former Rep. Joe Secrest, a Senecaville Democrat.

This staunchness alienated Hagan from Riffe, who wanted all Democrats to toe the mark on certain bills. But Riffe could never punish Hagan, because Hagan never wanted any favors.

Hagan, in fact, served a useful function in the House Democratic caucus. Leland recalled that he and Hagan came into the 1983 session as freshmen and had to vote on collective bargaining for public employees and an income tax increase.

"It was kind of a rough session," said Leland. "We had some tough caucus meetings. All of a sudden, he'd come out with some wisecrack that would bring everybody back to Earth."

A sampling of Hagan humor: He hated utility lobbyists, and the first month he was in the legislature, he met with some. Afterwards, he put out a memo to other legislators, "Thought you'd like to know how my meeting went." Below, there was a picture of Reddy Kilowatt with a long Pinocchio nose.

Hagan also posted a sign on his office door: "No Prostitutes or Utility Lobbyists Allowed." Later, he crossed out the word Prostitutes.

But even as he battled cancer, Hagan battled the Republicans trying to throw President Clinton out of office, faxing U.S. House members acerbic denunciations.

"He hated the Republicans in Washington for their hypocrisy," said young Hagan. At the end, as the family sat by Hagan's bedside, son Bob tried to pry loose some words of wisdom about the legislature. Hagan said, "It's tough workin' with dummies."

■ ■

Better Late Than Never: Liberal Democrats Honored Post-Riffe

The Columbus Dispatch, January 1, 2001

Welcome to a new year, a new millennium (2000 was a rehearsal) and a new General Assembly.

Tuesday, the first group of legislators with eight-year term limits over their heads will be sworn in.

Forty-five new ones in the House, according to those who know them, are an independent lot. They are highly principled and eager to change the face of Ohio, either by doing what government can do or getting its nose out of people's business.

Among the 28 new Republicans, we hear, are some hard-boiled conservatives, nearly enough to dominate the House GOP caucus that has long been controlled by moderates.

This transition is coming on top of a fascinating deed quietly performed last week as the 123rd General Assembly ended. Some highly principled former legislators from the other end of the political spectrum—liberal Democrats—were belatedly honored for their service to the House. Real belatedly.

The final act of the House in the 1999–2000 session was to pass resolutions honoring 10 former representatives who served in the 1970s and early 1980s. The Wednesday "skeleton" session amounted to Speaker Jo Ann Davidson and two other lawmakers. Davidson said she was asked to pass the commendations by Rep. David Hartley, a Springfield Democrat who was term-limited out in December after 28 years and received his own resolution.

The honored 10 shared two things with Hartley: all were Democrats and all, at one time or another, had defied legendary House Speaker Vernal G. Riffe Jr., who loathed independent thinking when there was a job to be done.

Had Riffe denied them the laudatory exit resolutions?

"He didn't do it deliberately," Barney Quilter, Riffe's former assistant, said from his home in Toledo. "If he did, it was another side of Vern I didn't know about."

As it turned out, Hartley spoke with some of his liberal comrades-at-arms from the 1970s and determined that they hadn't received formal plaudits. "It was his last chance of honoring his old friends," said Dennis L. Wojtanowski, a successful Columbus lobbyist who received one of the commendations.

Wojtanowski and Hartley were part of a group called "the crazies" because they leaned to the left on social issues and dared to taunt Riffe in an era when he ruled.

Hartley may have been the craziest. He was the only three-time loser under Riffe's system of rewarding loyal soldiers with committee chairmanships and firing them when they disobeyed. Hartley would do his penance and be reinstated, only to stray again.

Some Democrats would offer Hartley money to go up on the speaker's dais and sit beside Riffe during session just to see how long he could stay there.

Hartley once dared to vote no in the Democrats' private caucus when Riffe was nominated for speaker. Eugene Branstool, another "crazy" who was in the room that day, reports that Harry Malott, a Riffe lieutenant at Hartley's table, "turned his chair around in a nanosecond" so he wouldn't be facing the black sheep of the caucus.

Once, when (Columbus) Bishop Hartley High School had a championship basketball team, Democrats cut a headline out of the newspaper, "Teamwork Key to Hartley Success." They added Hartley's photo and got it circulated to state offices with the daily news clippings. No explosion was heard from the speaker's office, but he may have fumed.

Hartley worked quietly to help people on welfare and rid the state of toxic waste. He didn't seek publicity. His officemate, Branstool, became inquisitive one day as he was assembling a press release.

"You ever get your name in the paper?" Branstool asked.

"Yeah," said Hartley, fetching an article from a Springfield paper headlined "Hartley Arrested" for going 38 mph in a 35 mph zone.

"David's the least compromising person I know," said Wojtanowski, who was known as "the legislator's legislator" when he worked many late nights on social-services bills. Wojtanowski said Hartley is such a purist he won't even allow mulligans during a friendly golf game.

When a Cleveland securities company invited legislators to put on a seminar and handed out personal checks in excess of the legal limit, Hartley was the only one to return his when he saw how much was in the envelope. The rest were caught up in what became the "pancaking scandal" of 1993.

"He saw things in black and white, and had the courage to back it up," said former Senate Minority Leader Robert Boggs, another "crazy" who is now an Ashtabula County commissioner.

So, as the new members usher in the era of term limits, the advice from here is to learn who came before; in fact, who just left the door swinging on the way out. You can hang onto your principles and make a difference. You can survive the doghouse. And you may get recognized, even if it's 20 years later.

■ ■

'Choo Choo' Wilkowski Left Colorful Legacy, Unfulfilled Dream

The Columbus Dispatch, December 6, 1999

He had a grand plan to bring Ohio into the 21st century, but refused to talk about the price tag. Republicans pegged the cost at $10 billion or more and dubbed the proposal fantasy, and a boondoggle.

School funding?

No, the 16-year-old dream of Art Wilkowski to have a network of tracks carrying "bullet" passenger trains between Cincinnati, Columbus, Cleveland, Youngstown and his hometown, Toledo.

Although the dream has been derailed several times, it is still faintly alive. Wilkowski, however, died last week at 70.

His credentials as a prophet are in question but as an evangelist for high-speed rail they are beyond doubt.

Wilkowski, who retired from the state legislature in 1983 after 14 years, earned the derisive nickname "Choo-Choo" by pestering lawmakers for his pet project. But allies and foes admired his debating skills. He was one of the few who could change the minds of seasoned politicians with his verbal pyrotechnics.

The son of a union organizer, he once told an unsuspecting young reporter, "Y'know, I'm a Communist," but the only revolution he ever engineered was to help Vernal G. Riffe pull a coup d'etat. Riffe went on to become a legendary House speaker and Wilkowski was a platoon sergeant in his army.

Wilkowski, a liberal Democrat, worked for reform of the probate law, abortion rights and gun control. He was responsible for the Civilian Conservation Corps—a work program for wayward youth that still operates in the Ohio Department of Natural Resources.

But his passion was high-speed rail.

Traveling to Germany and Japan to view sleek 200-mph passenger carriers, Wilkowski saw them as a response to the hold Middle East countries had on the world's oil supply in the 1970s. He saw such trains as Ohio's response to the Sunbelt that was sucking citizens away from the rusting northern tier.

"The Amtrak system does not work in Ohio," Wilkowski proclaimed. "We will build this system on the ashes of Amtrak."

Despite Wilkowski's efforts, Ohio voters in 1982 crushed his initiative for a penny sales tax to fund the start of a high-speed rail system. Even a test track proposed for the Youngstown-Warren area never got past Gov. James A. Rhodes.

"Too costly," Rhodes recalled last week from his North Side apartment. That was more or less what Franklin County voters said last month when planners wanted seed money for normal-speed transit trains.

Rhodes, a four-term governor, recalled a practical side to Wilkowski. "He wasn't on the left wing when he wanted something," Rhodes said. What he wanted, and helped get, was a state office building in Toledo.

Wilkowski once spent $20,000 of taxpayer money for a magazine advertisement to promote high-speed trains. Taking offense was a young Republican state representative named Bob Taft, now the governor.

Taft tried to amend Wilkowski's test-track bill to outlaw future advertising.

With characteristic humor, Wilkowski addressed Taft with a yarn about a little old lady arrested for shoplifting in December. The judge suspended sentence but warned her to stay out of the department store. "OK, judge," the lady responded, "I've already done all my Christmas shopping."

"And I say to you, Robert," Wilkowski said, turning to Taft, "I've already done my advertising. There isn't going to be any more." Republicans broke up in laughter. One waved a white flag, and Taft's amendment was defeated.

Wilkowski represented the shot-and-a-beer culture from which he came. "He cared about those people," said former Rep. Ben Rose, a Republican adversary. "He wasn't going to let any bluenoses stand in the way of what he thought were those people's rights."

When Wilkowski stood to speak on the House floor, conversations stopped, because the members knew they were in for a treat. He might quote anyone from Chaucer to Churchill. The day he left the House for good, he invoked the names of Benjamin Franklin and Charles Dickens.

Wilkowski would begin each speech in a conversational, sometimes self-deprecating tone. If he were carrying a bill for racetrack owners, for example, he would look straight at the moralists and say in a mock whisper: "Oh-oh, here comes a HORSE RACING bill."

Then, speaking slowly in a nasal voice through clenched teeth, Wilkowski would build his case, working himself into a righteous lather until he was bellowing at his adversaries.

Carrying a legislative pay raise that many timid lawmakers were afraid to vote for in 1973, Wilkowski used the words "duty, honor and country" to justify it. It passed.

"He was brassy as hell," said Harry Meshel, the Youngstown senator who worked with Wilkowski for high-speed rail. Meshel recalled when the Toledoan appeared in his outer office, puffing a cigarette.

"There's no smoking here," the secretary said. "There is now," replied Wilkowski.

Chapter 2
Elections

Elections play a big part in Ohio politics and government. Some say there's too much emphasis on elections and campaigning. The planning is precise and the fund-raising relentless. No sooner is one election over than the next campaign begins. The columns in this chapter of the book are devoted to the preparation for and the execution of Ohio elections.

Memorable Campaigns

This section of the book is about the best of the campaigns in Ohio during the period.

The two U.S. Senate primary contests in 1970 were the first I was responsible for and it was one of the most memorable election nights of my career. Neither race was decided before sunup. There were no electronic vote tallies. Adding machines were used. Howard Metzenbaum beat John Glenn in the Democratic primary by less than one vote per precinct, and Republican Robert Taft Jr. beat James A. Rhodes by less than one vote for every four precincts.

Post-Mortem: Rhodes Loses; Metzenbaum Beats Glenn

United Press International, May 7, 1970

COLUMBUS (UPI)—Ohio's 1970 primary election results will be analyzed for a long time to come because they offer such a wide variety of angles for study. Any analysis is bound to focus on the U.S. Senate races, which saw one man do what he was told he could not, and another do what he was told he should not.

Howard M. Metzenbaum made believers out of those who scoffed at the idea back in November that he could take on the famed John Glenn and beat him for the Democratic nomination.

And Robert Taft Jr. politely turned down his party leadership's offer of second place on a "dream ticket," rolled up his sleeves and went to work, and defeated James A. Rhodes, a man who had lost only once before since entering politics in the 1930s.

To put the races in perspective, it must be remembered that they were close—so amazingly close that if Glenn had attracted one more vote in every precinct in the state, he would have won. Rhodes needed only one additional vote in every fourth precinct of the state. This means that for all practical purposes, Glenn is as popular as Metzenbaum among Ohio Democratic voters, and Rhodes has as much favor as Taft among Republican electors. But somebody has to win and somebody has to lose.

The somebodies who lost were none too cheerful, as can well be imagined. Glenn, who had held a premature victory party Tuesday night, looked the next day like he was having a bad dream and was waiting to wake up.

Rhodes did not even issue a concession statement to the press. He made himself scarce, failing to appear at a Republican unity meeting, turning down a trip to the Republican governors' conference and refusing to talk with newsmen about the election.

"It will be a long time before he'll have anything to say about it," said a spokesman, still in semi-shock. "We had the momentum going, but I don't know what happened. It could have been any one of a dozen things."

The spokesman said the answer would not be known unless someone takes a "post-mortem" poll, and none is planned.

Naturally, some educated guesses can be made about what happened to the man who carried the state by a record 63 percent of the popular vote in 1966. There was the *Life Magazine* article; Taft's magic name; a growing concern over pollution and crime which Taft played upon during the campaign; and perhaps most crucial, the activities of the National Guard troops on college campuses and the fatal shootings at Kent the day before the election.

One source hinted that "circumstances" played a large part in the governor's defeat.

Then, too, Taft hit hard on radio and television during the final week, perhaps even harder than Metzenbaum, who can credit the tube as the major factor in his victory.

Just as Taft exploded the myth that Rhodes had untold numbers of Republicans wrapped around his fingers throughout Ohio and was practically invincible, so did Metzenbaum explode the myth that an American space hero cannot lose.

Metzenbaum did it with massive media advertising, a campaign organization that was underestimated and an ability to get down on a level with the workingman.

Glenn played the favorite's role to the hilt, apparently saving some of his money for the general election campaign. He has now learned that everyone who rushes out to shake hands with a former astronaut isn't necessarily going to vote for him.

Metzenbaum won with heavy votes in the urban areas, indicating that Democrats there are in tune with his solutions to "earth man" problems and would rather get out of the space race for awhile.

The reference to *Life Magazine* was about a May 1969 article entitled "The Governor and the Mobster" and Rhodes' alleged ties to jailed Thomas "Yonnie" Licavoli, a member of Toledo's Purple Gang.

The way Rhodes dealt with campus disruptions actually may have helped his cause among Republicans. Polls showed he closed the gap on Taft at the end of the race. Student protests took place on many campuses; Kent State received all the publicity because of the shootings. But the disturbances on the Ohio State campus were much worse and lasted longer.

■ ■

John Glenn Arrives as a Politician

United Press International, September 21, 1973

COLUMBUS (UPI)—The time for John Glenn to jump to the head of the line in state politics may have finally arrived.

Ironically, his best chance comes 11 long years and two abortive U.S. Senate bids after he achieved the fame that made him a natural to enter politics in the first place.

The colonel from New Concord was a popular man in 1964 when he challenged U.S. Sen. Stephen M. Young, D-Ohio. He had just made America's first orbital spaceflight and was somewhat of a folk hero. But a bathroom fall damaged his inner ear and put him out of that campaign.

In 1970, Glenn returned from a soft drink executive's post in New York to run for Young's seat again. This time his opposition came from an unknown Cleveland millionaire who once managed Young's campaign, and Glenn was considered a shoo-in.

But Howard M. Metzenbaum became a household word in Ohio faster than anyone dreamed, spent money by the carload and blitzed Glenn's poorly-financed and ill-advised campaign. Metzenbaum won the Democratic nomination by 13,000 votes.

Now the same contest is shaping up again. One would think that Metzenbaum could start where he left off, with a well-recognized name, and trounce Glenn, whose space heroics are rapidly becoming ancient history.

However, something happened last week that could make Glenn a political hero and the frontrunner with rank-and-file Ohio Democrats.

What happened was that Glenn stood up and spoke out against behind-the-back slate-making, deals, big-money campaigns, buying elections, and everything else good Democrats are supposed to be against.

This was no idle speech. Glenn was accusing party leaders, including Gov. John J. Gilligan and Democratic State Chairman William A. Lavelle, of participating in these tactics to deny him the Senate nod, force him to run for lieutenant governor and let Metzenbaum spend some of his own money on winning the Senate in November 1974.

To believe the existence of this cabal to "stomp me into the political mud," one must believe Glenn. Gilligan has claimed executive privilege to refrain from public comment until Glenn accuses him of blackmail face-to-face.

But as one observer chortled last week after Glenn flopped the whole plot out on the floor at a meeting of the Democratic State Executive Committee: "Everybody knows John Glenn is politically naïve, but everybody knows John Glenn doesn't lie."

Having cut the cord, so to speak, from the Democratic organization, Glenn is free of some millstones and may be a more attractive candidate next year.

He already has been shown in the polls to be running ahead of Metzenbaum, as always, in the smaller counties and rural areas.

Big county Democratic chairmen have promised active opposition if Glenn tries to buck the party, but Metzenbaum won those counties in 1970 anyway. In fact, Metzenbaum won only 13 counties, and one of them was by four votes.

Glenn can be expected to be even stronger in the outlying areas where there is considerable anti-Gilligan sentiment.

And his disassociation with Gilligan can't hurt, either, in urban areas if organized labor has a rift with the governor before next May.

Perhaps most telling, the Metzenbaum ploy should be especially distasteful to the legions of young Democrats who literally pushed him to the nomination in 1970.

How many of them must have smiled ruefully when they saw a handpicked Metzenbaum—whose family contributed $497,500 to his 1970 primary campaign—reading Ohio's totals on the Democratic Telethon which was promoting $10 and $20 donations from the average working man.

New campaign spending limitations and a disaffiliation from organized politics could spell victory for Glenn next spring.

It did. Not long after this column was written, Gilligan appointed Metzenbaum to a vacancy in the Senate giving him a head start. But Glenn outdueled Metzenbaum in the 1974 primary contest and was elected easily in the post-Watergate era. Metzenbaum came back two years later and won Ohio's other Senate seat. There was tension between the two for a time, but eventually they learned to work together for Ohio's benefit.

■ ■

Glenn Bucks Governor, Beats Metzenbaum

United Press International, May 10, 1974

COLUMBUS (UPI)—Results of the Ohio primary have not been scientifically analyzed yet, but it is safe to say the Democratic party organization's marching orders worked for all but one man—U.S. Sen. Howard M. Metzenbaum.

The party organization helped furnish Gov. John J. Gilligan with 709,000 votes—more than 70 percent—the biggest endorsement for a Democratic gubernatorial candidate in 20 years. The organization also helped state Rep. Richard F. Celeste and state Sen. Tony P. Hall to win nominations for lieutenant governor and secretary of state.

But it was unable to pull Metzenbaum through against John H. Glenn Jr. in the battle for the U.S. Senate nomination.

The reason? This contest involved two well-known and highly talented campaigners who talked about issues, made issues out of non-issues, fought each other and generally made people aware of the election.

Democratic voters entering their polling places did not have to look at any card bearing the party slate to decide how to vote. They probably already had their minds made up, and firmly. A strong majority of them favored Glenn.

Despite the fact that the space shot that made him famous was 12 years and two Senate campaigns behind made no difference to Glenn. In fact, it may have made him more attractive to the voters.

"We think John himself made the difference," said Richard Bragaw, a member of the Glenn campaign staff. "He put on a much better campaign this time. He did his homework on the issues and his political maturity showed through."

Glenn began to show himself as a maverick last September when he jousted indirectly with Gilligan over who would be on the 1974 Democratic ticket and where they would be.

He further endeared himself as an underdog when Gilligan named Metzenbaum to an interim term in the Senate, against a lot of well-placed advice.

Shortly thereafter, Glenn got to bill himself as "Mr. Clean" when Metzenbaum made a payment of $118,000 in back taxes to the federal government—a payment he termed a "deposit" which would be refunded later.

Taking advantage of the post-Watergate emphasis on ethics, Glenn bared his finances in a 183-page document. It took Metzenbaum almost two months to match this disclosure, and by then it looked like the senator was playing catch-up.

Finally, there was the series of debates, which an incumbent almost never enters without good reason. Metzenbaum's reason was that he was behind.

His campaign staff is convinced that the first debate, on April 25 in Cleveland, may have been a turning point.

"We didn't do as well as we should have all through the northeastern part of the state in the Cleveland media market where that debate was telecast," said James Schiller, campaign manager for Metzenbaum.

That debate, in which Metzenbaum counter-attacked Glenn on his wealth and taxes, made the senator look like the aggressor. Glenn, in turn, responded coolly under fire during the fast-paced exchange.

The last straw may have been Metzenbaum's ill-fated remark that Glenn had "never held a job, never met a payroll"—a statement the senator later said he meant in terms of the civilian business world, not the military.

"He only said that once," Schiller said. "He never repeated it, but I'm sorry he said it at all."

Glenn's forces picked up the quote and broadcast it with Glenn's scathing reply. It may have been the most effective campaign commercial.

In the end, the black vote which had favored Metzenbaum in 1970 failed to turn out the Cleveland East Side in sufficient numbers.

To the contrary, a heavier turnout across the state boosted Glenn's margin in almost every county, and he broke through in labor-oriented counties like Trumbull, Summit and Lorain.

■ ■

Only after the 1976 Ohio Republican primary did reporters realize the strength of Ronald Reagan, who tested an incumbent President Ford with a minimal effort and a disorganized campaign.

Reagan on the Way Up; Ford on the Way Out

United Press International, June 12, 1976

COLUMBUS (UPI)—President Ford's victory in last Tuesday's Ohio primary may have been a pyrrhic one as far as the state's Republican party is concerned.

Although Ford carried the state by a 92,000-vote margin and won in more than three-quarters of Ohio's counties, much of his plurality was built up in major urban centers, especially Cincinnati, Toledo, Akron, Columbus and Cleveland.

Challenger Ronald Reagan held the president to small margins in most rural counties and even managed to win about 20 of them despite an unbelievably late start, a hastily-organized campaign and only two days of personal appearances in the state.

While Ford has apparently won all but six, or perhaps nine, of the 97 Republican National Convention delegates from Ohio, Reagan came remarkably close in several of the 12 other districts in which he competed but lost.

There is evidence, though not proof, that Ford's motorcade the day before the election may have salvaged victories for him in the 4th and 8th Congressional Districts.

But there is also a message that a good portion of Ohio Republicans are of a conservative nature—even more conservative than Gerald Ford.

Party regulars, once they rest up from the rigors of capturing the state for Ford and securing his nomination at the convention, assuming they succeed, will no doubt find a lot to worry about this fall when they have to put it all together again in battling Democrat Jimmy Carter.

In fact, dark thoughts are already being expressed about the possibility that U.S. Sen. John H. Glenn Jr., D-Ohio, might be Carter's choice for the vice presidential nomination.

One Republican shivered and looked skyward late last week when contemplating the possibility. He said not only Ford, but Sen. Robert Taft Jr., R-Ohio, would be in deep trouble if that happened.

Taft can expect a rough time anyway from former Sen. Howard M. Metzenbaum of Cleveland, whom he defeated by 70,000 votes in 1970 when Metzenbaum had run statewide only once in a primary.

True, Metzenbaum now has some scars to go with his recognition. He's had a run-in with the Internal Revenue Service and some skirmishes within his own party.

But he also has some ammunition to use on Taft and a taste of the Senate which no doubt will make his juices flow as the campaign heats up next fall. And Metzenbaum is a relentless campaigner.

Back to the Republicans. Ford's Ohio confrontation with Reagan has reopened an old split which may widen this week and be hard to heal.

The Reagan effort has brought party conservatives, hibernating since Republicans began losing the legislature in 1973, out of the weeds.

They toppled Kent B. McGough out of his Republican State Committee seat in the 4th Congressional District and are ready to tear into the party leadership Monday when an attempt is made to retain McGough as state chairman despite his non-membership on the committee.

Robert J. Huffman, the Miami County prosecutor and legal counsel of Reagan's Ohio campaign who defeated McGough, was perched on Rhodes' doorstep Friday trying to put a stop to the "save McGough" movement.

Huffman was given the bum's rush by the governor's office and retaliated by blaming Rhodes for the Republicans' minority status.

Huffman said Rhodes "owns Kent McGough lock, stock and barrel," adding that the two of them have allowed Republican state officeholders and legislators to go down the drain.

He said McGough has failed to adhere to the party gospel according to Ray Bliss, the former state and national GOP chairman who ran things successfully for years by "being attuned to the ordinary Republicans and not one man."

Bitter conservatives say that if Rhodes had pushed through a new legislative apportionment plan last year, "We'd be ready to take back the legislature in the fall." Instead, they report, Rhodes told them he was too busy with his bond issues and had no time to work on it. "Look at all the good that did," they complain.

While the Reaganites have been quiet for a few years, they are showing the same signs of unrest they exhibited in the early 1970s when they split the party over the state income tax.

They are a most tenacious group. Their appetites have been whetted by Reagan's showing despite hostile treatment by the party leadership. Ohio Republicans could once more be in for an uncomfortable period of time.

The Ohio primary was a harbinger of weakness for Gerald Ford, who was dragged down by his pardon of ex-President Richard Nixon and lost the presidency in the fall to Democrat Jimmy Carter. The primary also was the start of the Reagan movement, which succeeded four years later.

As for state party politics, Huffman was correct. Rhodes and his hand-picked leaders, including McGough, orchestrated things for another 10 years, to the detriment of the GOP. The conservatives never became a factor until late in the 1990s.

■ ■

Outsider Hart Upsets Mondale in Ohio

United Press International, May 11, 1984

COLUMBUS (UPI)—Now that the confetti and balloons have been swept up, the campaign placards deposited in the trash and the crying towels hung out to dry, it's time for a few observations about last week's Ohio primary.

Gary Hart won the Democratic presidential sweepstakes by 25,000 votes, out of 1.4 million votes cast, over Walter Mondale to keep the Hart campaign breathing.

How come Hart surprised the favored Mondale?

First of all, Jesse Jackson received 237,000 votes, most of which would otherwise have gone to Mondale, "There's no doubt Walter Mondale would have won Ohio if Jesse Jackson had not been in the race," said Gov. Richard F. Celeste.

Thanks to Jackson, Hart came out of Cleveland only 15,000 votes down, and he more than made that up in Youngstown, Dayton, Columbus and Akron, again with Jackson's help.

Outside of the big cities, Mondale's only gains came in southern and southeastern Ohio, where coal workers abound, and where Carter-Mondale put the giant addition to a uranium enrichment plant on the Ohio River, providing thousands of jobs.

Secondly, Mondale was lulled by heavy support from organized labor and his familiarity with top Democrats in Ohio, including the governor.

"Mondale tried to sneak one through this state," was the assessment of consultant Gerald J. Austin.

The former vice president was described by Senate President Harry Meshel as "like a comfortable old shoe, nestled in the closet with the other pairs."

Trouble was, Mondale got so comfortable he fell asleep.

When Hart came to Ohio, he rolled up his sleeves and went to work, visiting a farm and mingling with common laborers. Mondale made airport stops, and the Beechcraft and Piper Cub vote is not a big constituency here.

Little things hurt Mondale, and they all added up. Previous supporters of John Glenn weren't about to vote for his tormentor, Mondale. They backed Hart.

One Hart staffer even said the Russian boycott of the Olympics on Election Day may have swayed some votes, because it reminded people that President Carter pulled the Americans out of the 1980 Olympics in Moscow.

What now?

Nothing much good for Gary Hart, or for the Democrats in Ohio.

Because of the delegate selection plan, Mondale seems likely to get a majority of the Ohio delegation with the "unpledged" state officials, even though Hart won.

And Jackson's delegates, once they get what they're after at the Democratic National Convention, are sure to favor Mondale over Hart.

John J. Kulewicz, Hart's Ohio coordinator, plans to make it his business to see that "the Ohio delegation fairly reflects the proportion of the vote we received."

That would mean the Hart folks should lead the Ohio delegation.

"I'm sure they (the Ohio Democratic leaders) will heed the results of the election," said Kulewicz.

Maybe, maybe not.

Celeste still has not conceded Ohio to Hart and will do anything he can to make Mondale the nominee.

The governor declined last week to use his influence to see that the Hart forces are in charge of the Ohio delegation. Instead, Celeste said he will "work toward a unified delegation."

Mondale may be the Democrats' nominee, but he'll be in trouble in Ohio. "I don't think he can carry Ohio in the fall," said Austin, the political consultant. "If he can't beat Gary Hart, how is he going to beat Ronald Reagan?"

Austin was right. Mondale couldn't beat Reagan. And the next column shows that Celeste and the party regulars got their way, muscling out the Hart folks.

■ ■

This was at the end of a column on the state budget, but it's included here to point out that the Gary Hart forces were overly optimistic about how they'd be treated as the winners of the Ohio primary. Mondale & Co. used the automatic delegates—the party bigwigs now known as "superdelegates"—to gain control.

Democratic Organization Pushes Hart Aside

United Press International, June 15, 1984

. . . A postscript on the battle within the Ohio delegation to the Democratic National Convention: everybody got what they wanted except the winner of the Ohio primary, Gary Hart, and he was simply outmaneuvered by the professional politicians.

Democratic State Chairman James M. Ruvolo got the chairmanship of the delegation and peace, at least temporarily.

Celeste is honorary chairman and will be Ohio's focal point on national television.

Walter Mondale's people got the nomination; they don't need anything else.

Jesse Jackson got two Ohio delegates on the convention's rules and platform committees, when he would have had none.

Hart won the Ohio primary and the right to make noise about it. He got a neutral delegation chairman but little more. When Ohio stands up at the convention, it won't have a Hart hat on.

The conspirator in the whole thing was state Rep. C. J. McLin, D-Dayton, a veteran black politician who is pledged to Jackson but in effect was a "double agent."

A member of the Democratic National Committee, McLin is a longtime member of the Ohio party's inner circle, and he was dealing with the pros behind Hart's back to accomplish the final arrangement.

C. J. McLin, a Dayton funeral home owner, was one of the most underrated politicians of his era. He did all of his operating behind the scenes, getting little publicity, and he liked it that way.

■ ■

Campaign Holds No Joy for Bob Dole

The Columbus Dispatch, September 30, 1996

Back in 1970, Roger Cloud was the Republican state auditor running for governor. A former Ohio House speaker, he had a lengthy public service career and knew more about state government than any other Ohio official.

Cloud had never lost an election, but his campaign style was colorless. Once, when reading a speech, he actually pronounced to his audience the notation, "Add emphasis here."

Cloud had as much enthusiasm for campaigning as a lobster has for the pot of boiling water. "Well," he sighed one day upon boarding the campaign bus, "another day."

The memory of all this was triggered the other day when *USA Today* reported the following exchange in one of those campaign-plane interviews: "Asked if he's looking forward to the Oct. 6 and Oct. 16 debates, (Republican presidential nominee Bob) Dole said, 'Yeah, so I can get them over with.'"

Can you imagine a presidential candidate, well behind in the polls, wanting to get the debates over with? Doesn't it seem reasonable that such a candidate would view the debates as a wonderful opportunity to turn the campaign around?

Shouldn't Dole be looking forward to the debates as a chance to sell his 15 percent tax cut and tattoo President Clinton about Whitewater, Travelgate and anything else that comes to mind?

You can be sure that when Jack Kemp was the quarterback for the Buffalo Bills and the championship game was coming up, he didn't want to get it over with so he could go jackrabbit hunting with his buddies. He wanted to win.

This presidential campaign brings to mind the gubernatorial campaigns the Republicans ran in the 1980s against Democrat Richard F. Celeste.

Typical of the 1982 campaign was the autumn day Republican Clarence J. "Bud" Brown wanted to talk about highway funding and showed up late, keeping Gov. James A. Rhodes waiting.

The site of the campaign event was an incomplete intersection in southern Franklin County known as "the road to nowhere." And it turned out to be just that.

Four years later, it was Rhodes' turn to be buried by Celeste, although he tried to make it interesting. But in the last month, one pol close to Rhodes confided: "Jim knows it's over. He's just out there havin' fun."

This year, Dole doesn't even appear to be having fun. Nor do his surrogates.

Last week, the Ohio Republican Party brought its "Truth Trailer" to the Statehouse. The 25-foot recreational vehicle serves as a mobile operations center as the GOP follows the Clinton-Gore campaign around the state to "set the record straight."

Republican State Chairman Robert T. Bennett said the trailer will be cruising through all 88 Ohio counties until Election Day, reciting Clinton's "four years of flip-flops, fibs and fables."

At one point, Bennett's mind wandered briefly from the task and he referred to his candidate as "Bill Dole."

Nor was the honored guest—former conservative hatchet man Lyn Nofziger—much better.

Nofziger, the communications director in the administration of President Ronald Reagan, recalled the "Just Say No" anti-drug campaign of that era, then referred to Dole's anti-drug theme but couldn't put a handle on it.

"What's that other one, the new one?" he asked. "Anyway, he will do it."

Nofziger said Dole has to talk about taxes, drugs and character—the three issues that can turn the campaign around. He noted how successful the Democrats have been at attacking House Speaker Newt Gingrich of Georgia.

"They demonized him," Nofziger said.

And sure enough, the Ohio Democrats had a "Boot Newt" rally supporting their local congressional candidates, and they sent the announcement attached to winter boots designated for each Statehouse reporter.

Most of the boots were left-footed, and there was no explanation why they weren't kept in pairs and distributed to the less fortunate.

But back to Nofziger. He rated Dole as just as good a campaigner as George Bush, Gerald R. Ford and Richard M. Nixon, though not as good as Reagan. "You don't have to be a sweet, loving person to be president," he said.

Nofziger expressed optimism that the Dole-Clinton race will get closer in the next few weeks.

And he actually smiled when contemplating his "Truth Squad" role. "I like being critical," he said.

For the record, Roger Cloud lost the 1970 election and dropped off the political map.

■ ■

Ohioans Cherish Their Right To Vote

Ohioans will vote no when confused, but they covet their right to vote on candidates and issues they know little about, as shown in the next three columns.

Issue 3 Defeat Has Ironies

United Press International, November 8, 1987

COLUMBUS (UPI)—"Ohio is more like Texas than I thought," said a disgruntled Leslie Jacobs, president of the Ohio State Bar Association, shortly after a plan to appoint judges was thrashed by the voters Tuesday.

It seems that Texas, as Jacobs put it, "clings to the partisan election of judges," and so did Ohioans in rejecting by almost 2-1 a plan to have appellate judges appointed by the governor from a list of three candidates recommended by special lawyer-citizen panels.

It was clear from the outcome that Ohioans value their right to vote on something, even if they don't know anything about what they're voting on.

Except for the most dedicated citizens, most Ohioans base their choices for judge on the recommendation of political parties and skillfully produced television ads that shade the truth. A candidate's name is of paramount importance.

Trusting politicians to name judges is ironic, given the public suspicion of politicians. Yet that's how the judges get there. Few candidates slated by the political party are ever opposed in the primary, and then it's just a contest of Democrat versus Republican in the general election.

The Bar Association and the League of Women Voters were never able to get across their point that appellate judges, interpreting the finer points of law, ought to be nominated according to their legal expertise and not the whim of a county chairman.

Jacobs said those who favored State Issue 3 had thought it out. "It's a complicated intellectual process that involves understanding the way government works and the judicial process," he said. A "no" vote, he said, was a "knee-jerk reaction."

Jacobs said "merit selection" will come to Ohio only if a major political leader crusades for it.

"The only way this issue can be passed is instead of making it a grassroots issue, someone in high offices takes a lead in educating the public," said Jacobs.

Interestingly, John Thomas of the Ohio AFL-CIO, which opposed Issue 3, said those who understood the issue best opposed it. He pointed out that the voters who turn out in off-year elections generally are the most committed and take time to study the issues.

Thomas said that for "merit selection" to become a reality in Ohio, it would take a multi-year campaign by proponents to educate and persuade people.

Ohio is still waiting for merit selection of judges to become a reality.

■ ■

When in Doubt, Ohioans Vote No

United Press International, November 6, 1981

COLUMBUS (UPI)—In 1975, Ohio's business and industry spent $1.1 million to promote a series of giant bond issues dreamed up by Gov. James A. Rhodes to get the state's economy moving.

All four issues were drubbed, three of them by margins of more than 4-1.

This year, insurance companies spent more than $4 million to change the state Constitution so they could write workers' compensation insurance. They lost by a 4-1 margin.

That's inflation. It's also a signal that you can't sell an issue on the Ohio ballot by merely throwing money into television advertising.

State Issues 1 and 2 seemed to have the right things going for them at the outset. They were "citizen initiatives" placed on the ballot by petition drives.

Issue 1 promised competition for workers' compensation insurance, free enterprise and all that, while Issue 2 offered to take the backroom politics out of drawing congressional and legislative districts.

What could be more American?

The promoters of Issues 1 and 2 paid volunteers to collect signatures to get the proposals on the ballot. That's free enterprise, too, but it's hardly a case of Ohioans collectively rising up against an oppressive and tyrannical government in Columbus.

In fact, only 571,000 people voted for Issue 1. Almost that many people signed the petitions to get the issue on the ballot in the first place. That doesn't say much for the use of the $4 million during the campaign.

Despite the attempt to make it private enterprise versus bureaucratic and bumbling government, the proponents of Issue 1 failed miserably, perhaps because of their overplayed flag-waving.

The opponents—the entrenched bureaucracy placed in the position of protecting an ugly child—cleverly hung together and sowed the seeds of doubt. Who would want to change the system and why would they spend so much money? The answers were "insurance companies" and "profit."

The entire issue was clouded by nasty disputes and legal challenges over statistics on job safety in Ohio and cost-benefit ratios under various workers' comp systems. When Ohioans are in doubt, they vote "no," and that's exactly what they did.

Issue 2 seemed to have a good chance of passing. Some of the proponents were the same ones that used $702,000 successfully four years ago to overturn a law providing for "instant" voter registration—viewed as an invitation to election fraud.

This time, the Issue 2 commercials showed cigar-smoking politicians carving up the state of Ohio over a felt-covered table, swapping districts and conversing furtively out of the sides of their mouths.

Again, it was $1 million ill spent because the ads were too heavy-handed and the issue was too complex.

Many people don't understand the process of redrawing congressional and legislative boundaries, and how politics can be used to shape the districts.

But they know they are relatively comfortable with the existing system. The alternative was to vote for an unknown, and again the opponents planted the seeds of doubt—that Issue 2 would allow big business and utilities to control the districts, resulting in higher price tags. People understand that.

The message of the 1981 election is not so much that money won't buy victory. It is that for approval of a ballot issue, people must plainly understand a need for change and have somewhat of a passion to make that change. Otherwise, they will vote every time for the status quo.

The issue of creating an independent, non-partisan commission to draw legislative boundaries came up again in 2005. Curiously, a similar ad showing politicians (smoking was no longer in vogue) conversing furtively out of the sides of their mouths was used to promote fair redistricting. The result was the same. A majority of the people voted no.

■ ■

Instant Voter Registration Stirs Hornets' Nest of Emotions

United Press International, October 28, 1977

COLUMBUS (UPI)—Lou Jacobi, star of "Don't Drink the Water," bounded out for his curtain call last week at a suburban playhouse packed with lawyers attending a fund-raiser for Democratic Attorney General William J. Brown.

The Broadway actor was attired in a T-shirt sporting a map of Ohio, a yellow "sad face" and the words "Vote No On 1." The audience went wild.

State Issue 1 is captivating Ohio politics like few issues of recent times.

Republican State Chairman Earl T. Barnes said he hasn't seen such emotion in an Ohio campaign since organized labor tried to unseat the late Sen. Robert A. Taft in 1950.

Whether this excitement is rubbing off on the voters is questionable. That will be known Nov. 8, when they choose whether to pass Issue 1 and repeal election reform law passed by the legislature last May.

Campaigning for and against Issue 1 is accelerating. Democratic legislative leaders are spending almost full-time on the road speaking out against the issue.

Ohioans for the Preservation of Honest Elections (OPHE) has already spent more than $166,000 for passage of the issue, much of it from big business, and is shooting for $300,000 to $400,000 before the polls open.

Citizens to Save the Right to Vote (CSRV), with heavy contributions from organized labor, has spent more than $180,000 and is aiming up to $500,000, according to its chairman, Charles R. Baker.

Its broadcast media advertisements include Will Geer—TV's Grandpa Walton—speaking out against Issue 1.

OPHE is using the 600,000 persons who signed petitions for repeal of "instant" voter registration to help drum up support for Issue 1. It also plans a door-to-door leaflet campaign using college students and volunteers at the county level.

CSRV is coordinating an imposing group of organizations, including labor, teachers, blacks and senior citizens, which each have separate literature distribution efforts.

It wants to make sure voters don't think they should vote "Yes" if they want Election Day registration. "We're trying to say 'No' as loud and as often as we can," said Baker.

The key to the opposition's campaign may be a get-out-the-vote headquarters sponsored by organized labor, which hopes to encourage some 250,000 unregistered voters to go to the polls, register and vote "No."

The concentration will be on areas where there are likely to be Democrats, blacks, labor families, truck drivers, mobile home inhabitants, renters and young, mobile people like college students.

While the Democrats have come out unabashedly against Issue 1, Baker and Gov. James A. Rhodes have kept hands off. They don't want to alienate any Democrats who might be disenchanted with Election Day registration.

But despite the jousting about whether "instant" registration will increase voter participation or result in fraud, be not misled that the issue is nonpartisan.

Many Republicans believe they need a "Yes" vote on Issue 1 to save their party. "If this is defeated," said Secretary of State Ted W. Brown, "any organization that wants to will go out and register and vote 'em in buses with a keg of beer and ham sandwiches." He meant organized labor.

"The bottom line," said J. Patrick Leahy, executive director of the Ohio Democratic Party, "is that the Republicans think more voters will work to their disadvantage and we think it will work to our advantage. Everything else is just dressing."

Little wonder the politicians are excited about Issue 1. It's their bread and butter for the next few years.

■ ■

Campaign Finance and Redistricting

Nothing poisons the process more on Capitol Square than the astronomical sums of money spent on elections and the way legislative and congressional districts are drawn to favor the majority. The next four columns illuminate.

Campaign finance rules have created problems since regulations were first spelled out in the early 1970s. That's when public officials wanted to hide how much they were raising. In the column after this one, you'll read how it's evolved to the point where it pays to boast of huge amounts.

Those who make the laws will always create loopholes and the lobbyists will find them. Campaign finance "reform" is a perennial issue. The following column was just a benchmark on the continuum; some people thought the legislature solved the problem but it didn't. The issue is not a big one with the public, and the government officials know it. So they can afford to play rope-a-dope. Newspapers are among the few that care.

State Lawmakers Dodge Bullet on Campaign Reform

The Columbus Dispatch, May 29, 1995

For at least 10 years, state legislators and other officials have struggled with the issue of limiting the influence of money in political campaigns. Candidates and officeholders have decried the obscene amounts of money spent on campaigns, and the way large donations may influence legislation or behavior by the administration. But for various reasons, nothing was ever done about it.

In the early 1980s, the Democrats controlled the General Assembly and the governor's office. They didn't want any restrictions on their power. Even when Republicans gained a split in the legislature with the Democrats, no one wanted to disturb the resulting coalition government.

In the early 1990s, both House Speaker Vernal G. Riffe Jr., D-Wheelersburg, and Senate President Stanley J. Aronoff, R-Cincinnati, felt the public pressure to limit the influence of money on campaigns. But they didn't know how to do it without endangering their majorities. And after all, survival is what elective politics is all about.

Last week, Senate Bill 8 was signed into law by Gov. George V. Voinovich. It will govern money-raising in the 1996 legislative campaigns and the 1998 statewide elections.

Why did it pass after all the years of failed attempts? And why did citizens' petitioners, who wanted a much stricter version, agree to it?

The turning point came when Republicans captured the entire Statehouse in the 1994 elections, driving Democrats into the minority in both chambers of the legislature. Now they could work their will, and they did.

The Republicans took away one of the Democrats' main fund-raising tools—the ability of organized labor to match large corporate donations by making automatic union-dues checkoffs for political funds.

It didn't hurt that a conservative/liberal citizens' coalition, using petitions, placed its own bill before the legislature in January. That gave the lawmakers until May to act on the bill, or a reasonable facsimile. Otherwise, the petitioners would be entitled to petition for a public vote on their version.

The game thus shifted from Republicans vs. Democrats to Republicans vs. the petitioners. The GOP's job was to write a bill that would keep the petitioners from taking their own stricter version to the November ballot.

The Republicans succeeded, and the bill-signing ceremony last week was a celebration of that fact. Republicans packed the room. Democrats made themselves scarce, because Senate Bill 8 is a Republican campaign-finance-reform bill.

There are a variety of good ideas, studied and rehashed for years, in Senate Bill 8. For the first time, there will be limits on how much individuals, political-action committees and parties can give to candidates.

There are mechanisms to trace the sources of money in campaigns, more frequent reporting requirements and a tax incentive for small political donations.

Senate Bill 8 came nowhere close to the petitioners' proposal of a $1,000 limit on all campaign contributions and prohibitions against the transfer of money from one campaign committee to another.

Yet David Zanotti, president of the Northeast Ohio Roundtable Freedom Forum, and Janet Lewis, executive director of Common Cause/Ohio, attended the bill-signing ceremony and said they are forgoing a November public vote.

"I don't think there are any winners here," Zanotti said. "This reform marks a beginning and not an end," said Lewis.

Both Zanotti and Lewis said their resources would be better spent in a court challenge than by gathering more signatures to get their proposal on the ballot. And the reason is simple: They were snookered. In the most cynical one-upmanship, the Republican legislators managed to give legislative caucuses the unlimited ability to raise money in a law that limits everyone else.

How? They renamed the caucus committees and put them over in political party headquarters. Although there are dollar limits on party donations to caucuses, there is no limit on the amount of services (polling, television time and TV ad production) that may be supplied. And that's where the real funding is in legislative campaigns.

"I have to take my hat off to them," Zanotti said late last week. "It took them three times to figure out how to get around us, but they did it."

By changing definitions and section numbers in the law, the legislators eliminated the possibility that the petitioners' ballot issue could touch them, because the ballot issue can't be changed.

Zanotti believes that a legal challenge can be mounted to the way the lawmakers excluded their own caucuses from limitations. He says the Constitution requires equal application and enforcement of the law, and that by sheltering their fund-raising activities from the limits, the legislators have violated that requirement. In addition, labor groups are expected to go to court over what they view as shortcomings in Senate Bill 8. There may be a long and rocky legal road ahead before we see how the new law works.

■ ■

Campaign-Finance Disclosure Is Far From an Open Book

The Columbus Dispatch, July 8, 2002

When the state enacted its first primitive campaign-finance laws, political parties and candidates were not used to having their finances in the public spotlight, so it was painful for them to disclose that information.

The media's interest was a harbinger of bad news. So the parties and candidates disclosed as little as possible. Money in a campaign warchest was a badge of shame.

Gradually, the political parties and candidates realized that there was a flip. Maybe the public didn't care whether Candidate A had bazillions of dollars compared with Candidate B. But the oddsmakers cared.

So fund raising became a badge of credibility. If a candidate could raise money, he or she was deemed a good bet. Money begat money because the political pros like to support a winner.

One of the first noticeable examples of this phenomenon occurred in 1981 when Democrats were plotting a takeover of the governor's office. Four-term Republican Gov. James A. Rhodes was departing, giving Democrats a good chance to capture the state's highest office. Three-term Attorney General William J. Brown, a popular conservative Democrat with a good ballot name, was making his move. Richard F. Celeste had lost to Rhodes in 1978 and had been out of the state headlines since then. But he wasn't finished yet.

Celeste needed to jumpstart his bid for the Democratic nomination for governor. He did it by borrowing $400,000 from a half-dozen supporters, including his father, and quietly putting it in his nearly empty campaign treasury several days before the deadline for filing annual campaign committee financial reports.

Celeste quickly paid the money back, but the mission was accomplished when the report was made public: Celeste was a credible candidate on an equal footing with Brown, and the real money started rolling in. Celeste narrowly won the primary and went on to win two terms as governor.

Now, a huge campaign war chest is a badge of honor in politics. Candidates trumpet their fund-raising prowess. It may scare a rival out of a race or give the opposition an inferiority complex. It also persuades the news media that the well-funded candidate has the firepower to win, so it can set the tone of the campaign.

For example, Gov. Bob Taft's campaign unabashedly boasted in June of having more than $7.7 million on hand going into the summer months and gloried in the 39-1 edge in money over Democratic opponent Tim Hagan.

Candidates with a knack for fund raising, notably winners, have learned that while the public holds its nose over the influence of money in politics, the prevailing attitude is, "So what else is new, there's not much we can do about it." It's generally not the issue on which elections are won or lost.

This emboldens the candidates, caucus leaders and party chieftains to try to raise even more money. Sometimes they approach or even cross the line of legality. But whenever questions are raised about the propriety, they reply that campaigns are expensive, especially the media advertising, and they simply must get their message out.

The politicians have decided that Ohioans will not stand for the public financing of elections. Courts have ruled that it's unconstitutional to limit spending, which is a form of free speech. Lawmakers have placed limits on the size of donations, but loopholes make the law look like Swiss cheese.

The latest wrinkle is what Republicans have been saying for years: Disclose everything so people will know where the money came from and can vote accordingly. But even some Republicans are slow to warm to disclosure, especially after Ohio Citizen Action began insisting that the donor's occupation or employer be clear for every source of money.

Senate President Richard H. Finan, R-Cincinnati, said givers are shy and would prefer to remain in the background so they won't get on everyone's mailing list.

One of the biggest abuses is the way legislative caucuses, principally the majority, turn their troops loose to raise money, not for their own campaigns but to help the caucus protect weak members and retain control.

Sen. Michael C. Shoemaker, D-Bourneville, has proposed legislation to minimize this practice, but with Finan in charge, his bill will be consigned to a dark closet.

The aim of caucus fund raising is to "preserve good government," but good government is in the eye of the beholder. Or, rather, it's in the eye of the beholden.

■ ■

Minority Republicans Want "FAIR" Districts

United Press International, August 8, 1980

COLUMBUS (UPI)—In the fascinating law of man, not nature, the weight of an entire government or political system can be supported by a slender thread.

And so it is with Ohio politics and government, which may hang for the next 10 years from a small paragraph in the state Constitution containing 41 words.

The paragraph is what was left out of some of the petitions circulated by a group trying to get rid of gerrymandering—the use of political power to create districts for elective office.

The paragraph is what will come under close scrutiny in the courts during the next few weeks to see if it means enough to keep the Committee for Fair and Impartial Redistricting (FAIR) from getting its petition validated and taking its proposal to the Nov. 4 ballot.

Here's why that little paragraph is so important:

State legislative and congressional districts are drawn, following the new Census every 10 years, by the political party in power. In Ohio right now, that's the Democrats.

The districts are supposed to contain relatively equal populations, giving everyone equal representation. But skillful draftsmen can also manage to put the puzzle together so their party has a better-than-average chance of winning.

Since the Democrats reapportioned the state in 1971 they have gained control of both chambers of the General Assembly, closed the gap in the congressional delegation and captured every statewide executive office except governor.

FAIR, comprising mainly of Republicans who are out of power, wants to change the system so the boundaries are drawn by an independent, bipartisan commission, minimizing political overtones.

In order to establish the commission, FAIR has to amend the state Constitution and that requires a vote of the people. So FAIR has spent $375,000 over the last two years collecting signatures on petitions to get its proposal on the ballot this November.

If the plan doesn't get on the ballot this year, new boundaries may be drawn in early 1981 based on 1980 Census figures. They will be drawn under the same old system, and they will work to the advantage of Democrats. Assuming court approval, they will be good until the next Census in 1990.

So long, Republicans.

The FAIR committee's drive was going along swimmingly until last week. Petitions bearing 321,000 signatures were turned in at the secretary of state's office. Only 285,000 were needed to get the issue on the ballot.

Then up popped the crucial paragraph.

Secretary of State Anthony J. Celebrezze Jr., who happens to be a Democrat, discovered that some of the petitions contained the paragraph and some didn't. Neither type of petition had the needed 285,000 signatures, so he ruled the issue off the ballot. Celebrezze said the Constitution requires that all petitions contain "a full and correct copy" of the proposed issue.

FAIR attorneys argue that the key paragraph, inadvertently left out of some petitions by a printer's neglect, is part of existing language in the Constitution and is not part of the proposed change.

"This is a thwarting of the rights of the people on purely technical grounds," said William H. Schneider, attorney for FAIR and a former Franklin County Republican chairman.

Democrats around the Statehouse last week were gleeful at the turn of events. There were some indications they might have even tipped off Celebrezze to watch for the error.

And part of the political sideshow is the intrigue as to whether the FAIR campaign was infiltrated and sabotaged, or whether it was an innocent bungle.

The rest of the drama will be played out in some courtroom not immune to politics, and the small paragraph may determine the course of Ohio government in the 1980s.

The issue did not get to the ballot, but a similar proposal made it to the ballot in 2005, this time sponsored by the Democrats who had derailed FAIR in 1980. This time the out-of-power Democrats made the same arguments the Republicans had made in 1980, and this time the Republicans saw no need to change the system. Neither did the public, which apparently prefers districts drawn in backroom politicking over districts drawn impartially. Earlier columns in this chapter deal with the mindset of Ohio voters.

■ ■

The decennial exercise of realigning congressional and legislative boundaries provides ample fodder for columnists. Fiction couldn't be stranger.

Part Feud and Part Carnival, Legislative Reapportionment Returns to Ohio

The Columbus Dispatch, August 12, 1991

Like Halley's Comet, it comes along once in awhile to create a great spectacle, causing grownup public officials to revert to their schoolboy days of playground fighting. It's called legislative reapportionment, it happens every 10 years and it's about to return. Gov. George V. Voinovich has summoned the five-member board to his office in 10 days to start the process.

In 1964, the U.S. Supreme Court ruled that congressional and state legislative districts must be equal in population, affording equal representation for all. Thus, after each federal census, the district boundary lines are rejiggered to form districts of equal population. Just coincidentally (wink, wink) those districts are shaped to the advantage of the political party in power.

In the case of state legislative districts, the job is done by the Apportionment Board, which includes the governor, the state auditor, the secretary of state, one state senator and one state representative. This year, the board is controlled 3-2 by Republicans, who have been chafing within Democrat-drawn lines for 20 years.

The Ohio Constitution spends five pages on how legislative districts must be drawn to equal size, respecting existing governmental boundaries. Districts are to be compact, that is, devoid of arms, legs and whirligigs.

In practice, much of this goes out the window. "We won, baby, and now we get to put the crayons to the Rand McNally," is the way one Democrat described it in 1971.

Although Republicans control the board, the Democrats can be expected to offer some constructive criticism and obstruction. In 1971, for example, the board quarreled over who was to provide the maps and who would transcribe the official record.

In 1981, one nit-picking board meeting lasted for so long—seven hours—that reporters were taking bets on whether Gov. James A. Rhodes would break his own record for sitting still. He didn't.

Twenty years ago, the Democrats under Gov. John J. Gilligan convened the board and recessed under the pretense of studying all reapportionment plans that had been submitted after hundreds of hours of careful drafting. In half an hour, the board reconvened, and the majority Democrats pronounced all the Republican schemes unfit.

"We guide ourselves by the principles set forth by the highest court in the land, and are firm in our intention that the outcome of our efforts here will see the voices of all the people, not muffled or distorted by arbitrary constraints, but freely and clearly expressed and heard," pronounced a sober-faced Gilligan. Whereupon the Democrats released and rammed through their own plan over the shrieks of Republicans.

The Democrats' plan:

- Combined the districts of three pairs of Republican senators and 10 pairs of GOP House members.
- Included one Senate district stretching from the West Virginia line to the eastern border of Reynoldsburg, and another straddling I-71 from Columbus to the Ohio Turnpike just south of Cleveland.
- Contained a House district shaped like a bent stovepipe, running from the Pennsylvania line in Ashtabula County to a few miles east of Cleveland and then in a tunnel down to North Canton.

One district line was drawn around the block in Toledo where Republican Sen. Howard Cook lived, putting him in another senator's district.

The tactics worked. At least two dozen Republicans ran against each other, moved or retired in 1972. Democrats took over the House in 1973 and the Senate in 1975.

Sen. Harry Meshel, D-Youngstown, scratched his head in wonder over one Republican-concocted map in 1981. "The lines of this map resemble the early roads across this state," said Meshel. "As we chased the cattle over the hills and through the valleys, that is where we built the roads, and that is how these districts were drawn."

That was the same year Rep. Edward J. Orlett, D-Dayton, accused a House Republican employee of stealing some reapportionment work sheets from his office.

Rep. W. Bennett Rose, R-Lima, the assistant GOP leader, hotly denied the accusation and called a press conference to demand an apology. There, Orlett told Rose, "You are as full of crap as a Christmas goose. There will be no apology."

And so it will go this fall, although computers may have spoiled much of the fun, making a science out of putting equal numbers of people into the 99 House districts and 33 Senate districts.

But even though the Apportionment Board members won't be using crayons on the Rand McNally, there are still ample opportunities for mischief, and Ohioans should be on the lookout for it this fall.

The Republicans took control of the Apportionment Board in 1991 for the first time since the 1960s and, as expected, drew the lines to favor GOP candidates. It took the GOP two election cycles to capture the Ohio House, which it held through 2008. The Senate remained Republican. Each Senate district consists of three House districts put together.

■ ■

Ohio's Maligned 2004 Election

This column was included to show that Secretary of State Ken Blackwell, criticized in 2004 for his handling of the election in Ohio, actually proposed a uniform optical-scan system with a paper audit trail for every county three years before the presidential election, but the legislature dragged its feet.

Legislature May Be Stuffing the Ballot Box on Voting Reforms

The Columbus Dispatch, October 15, 2001

A panel assigned to improve Ohio's elections system is paralyzed by lawsuit terrorism and is two weeks late in issuing a final report.

The General Assembly finds itself in the awkward position of trying to tell its own advisory panel what to recommend to the legislature.

It might as well send this note:

Memo to self: Give Ohio a uniform voting system, but for heaven's sake, don't do anything that would provoke a lawsuit. And by the way, don't do anything to make the county governments mad, either.

That, in essence, is what the legislature is trying to do with the special panel assigned to perfect Ohio's system of voting and vote counting, in view of Florida's debacle in the 2000 presidential election.

The legislature assigned an 11-member commission headed by Secretary of State J. Kenneth Blackwell to make recommendations in the areas of voter registration, voter education, accessibility for the disabled and voting.

The panel has agreed on a final report in most areas but is hung up on the question of whether to force counties to phase in a uniform system or let them choose their own types of voting machines. There's no sign of a break in the deadlock at the Election Systems Reform Committee.

Blackwell wants to require counties to purchase voting machines that permit tabulating at the precinct level and provide an audit trail to preserve an accurate count. The machines also would give voters a "second chance" to check their ballots and make sure they are accurate.

But another faction of the panel regards this as an indictment of the punch-card system used in 70 of Ohio's 88 counties, even though Blackwell says punch-card machines can fulfill his three requirements.

Last week, the Republican-controlled legislature clearly was trying to alter the committee's report. In essence, the lawmakers asked the committee to make recommendations and is trying to influence those recommendations through Sen. Jeff Jacobson, a suburban Dayton Republican who serves on the panel.

Blackwell proposed that all purchases of voting equipment meet his three criteria and that by January 2006, all counties be converted to such equipment. In an alternative report, Jacobson removed all deadlines and incentives. The panel must choose between the two. Blackwell said he, in his role as secretary of state, is going to recommend equipment with the three capabilities, no matter what the committee says.

Big deal.

The legislature can do what it wants anyway. It can throw the recommendations from both Blackwell and the panel into the wastebasket.

So why would the legislature try to influence the very group that it assigned to make recommendations? Apparently because there are some things it doesn't want to hear.

Blackwell, as chairman, distilled the committee's discussions into the draft of a final report. Most of it was OK, but Jacobson balked concerning the recommendations on voting machines. He is the chairman of the Montgomery County Republican Party, and his county uses punchcards.

The Senate Republican caucus staff became involved in writing alternative recommendations for Jacobson.

"They (senators) were concerned it (Blackwell's report) didn't properly reflect their views," said Liz Connolly, a Senate Republican staffer.

Tracy Intihar, who works for House Speaker Larry Householder, R-Glenford, said she was involved in discussions to keep the House Republican caucus up to speed. "It's primarily a sharing of information," she said.

What it gets down to, believe it or not, is fear of lawsuits. If the legislature ignored recommendations of the very panel it assigned to study Ohio's voting system, someone could make an issue of it in court.

"I can see the vultures circling now," said Rep. J. Tom Lendrum, a Huron Republican who serves on the panel.

"It's a new day," said Senate President Richard H. Finan. The suburban Cincinnati Republican said the legislature has every right to influence the report it commissioned, because legislators are on the panel.

"I think you have to reflect what you expect to do," he said.

Said Lendrum: "We no longer have a republican form of government, where we elect legislators to represent us. We have legislation by lawsuit."

This was a case of hypocritical lawmakers asking a study committee for recommendations and then trying to skew the outcome. It also was the result of a political spat between two strong-willed conservative politicians who disliked each other—Blackwell and Jacobson—and were each trying to be king of the hill.

■ ■

Although Ken Blackwell fought against punchcard voting machines and generally conducted a fair election in 2004, he deserved to be brought up short for playing in the Republican political arena while he was supposed to be a neutral referee.

On Electronic-Slots Question, Referee May Be Stepping Over the Line

The Columbus Dispatch, April 28, 2003

Back in the winter, state Sen. Jay Hottinger got himself thrown out of the arena at a high-school basketball playoff game because he thought the ref's partiality was hurting his alma mater, Newark High School.

Now we have a referee of a different sort, Secretary of State J. Kenneth Blackwell, injecting himself into what could be a dandy fight this fall over slot machines at racetracks. Is this good or bad? You be the judge.

Blackwell, who oversees Ohio elections, asked Senate President Doug White last week to change the way the question will be put to voters.

In the state budget, House Bill 95, is a provision that would place on the Nov. 4 ballot the question of whether the Ohio Lottery Commission should be prohibited from installing electronic slot machines at Ohio's seven thoroughbred and harness-racing tracks.

Proponents of the slot machines say that since these are strictly games of chance with no skill involved, they are nothing more than another type of lottery game and thus permissible under current law. In fact, the proponents say, the commission could operate slot machines on every street corner in Ohio if it wished. What a blessing that they will be limited to racetracks under the proposal.

But the way the question is stated in the House-passed budget, folks would have to vote "yes" to prohibit the slot machines when all natural instincts will be telling them that "no" means no slot machines.

By the time the massive burst of television advertising finishes, poor Bob and Betty Buckeye will be so confused they won't know which way to vote—and that's the way the proponents want it. Because history tells us that when the electorate is confused, it votes no.

One need only to recall the effort in 1972 to repeal the newly enacted state income tax. It failed, partly because a "yes" vote was to prohibit repeal.

Blackwell is asking the Senate to reverse the question before passing the budget so voters will at least know which end is up when the commercials start. A "yes" vote will mean yes, we should have slot machines. This makes sense.

In Blackwell's own words: "I am seriously concerned that the language is likely to cause voters to mistakenly vote opposite to the way they intend to vote. It is my obligation as secretary of state to bring this confusing language to the attention of the Senate and urge the members of that body to make the language accurately reflect what is being proposed."

But is this his job? The law is silent on that.

For constitutional amendments passed by the legislature, the law provides for a five-member Ballot Board, which includes the secretary of state, to determine how the issues appear on the ballot. But on other issues, the Ballot Board has no say.

Furthermore, Blackwell is an outspoken foe of gambling and of this particular issue. It suits his purposes to try to reverse the language and take the edge away from the gambling supporters.

Blackwell will be supervising the counting of votes on election night. Is it fair for him to try to influence the process? Of course, his answer, as stated above, is that he's merely trying to assure a fair portrayal of the issue.

But Blackwell went further in his letter to White. He said the Ballot Board, not legislative leaders, should appoint individuals to write the official arguments for and against the gambling issue.

"The board is comprised of members of the public as well as legislators, and has a reputation for its neutrality in drafting the language for statewide issues," he said.

The arguments for and against the issue, maximum 300 words each, are part of the official presentation of the question. They are posted at polling places for all to read, and distributed with official election material. Their influence pales in comparison with the TV ads.

Nevertheless, the arguments at least put forth each side's best shot. Who better to frame the debate than the people who debated the issue in the first place? They may not have a "reputation for neutrality," but both sides have an equal chance and the most ardent representatives are usually chosen.

This seems like a case of the referee not only trying to influence the game, but to stick his head in the teams' huddles as well.

■ ■

The Republicans' plan for a massive get-out-the-vote drive 72 hours before the 2004 presidential election, described in this column for the first time, was a key to President Bush's re-election.

Ohio GOP Using Computers in Effort to Assure Bush Big Margin In '04

The Columbus Dispatch, May 12, 2003

Republican politics have come a long way since Martha Moore, the retiring vice chairwoman of the Ohio Republican Party, joined the state GOP committee in 1950—so far, in fact, that they've come full circle, with a little high-tech added.

Ohio Republicans, jolted by President Bush's narrow victory in 2000, are firing up a program to ferret out every Republican-leaning voter for 2004 to make sure the president carries Ohio by more than his meager 4 percent margin over Al Gore.

Using a so-called 72-Hour Plan, Republicans will be trying to identify every possible Bush voter, get them to register and target them with mailings and telephone calls as Election Day approaches. But this grass-roots movement will be computer-assisted.

At the state committee meeting last week, members were advised that 1.4 million eligible voters in Ohio are not registered. Among them are about 29,000 Republicans and 58,000 independents who have moved in from other states. They are what the party pros describe as "low-hanging fruit," because they have voted in past elections.

How do the Republicans know these things? They've done their research, and they have become students of computer-generated lists.

The Republicans were told they could increase turnout by 3.5 percent in their favor by motivating voters with a hot-button issue.

Their first job is to identify potential Republican voters by culling lists that are likely to contain conservatives—lists of individuals with hunting licenses and snowmobile permits, and lists of families that home-school their kids.

Because Ohioans don't register by political party, the political pros use lists of people who voted in primary elections, where they had to declare their party preference. Beyond that, they have ways of finding out a lot about households. They use automated phone calls to entice respondents into completing brief surveys about issues. They also have real people manning phones and volunteers knocking on doors to do the same. Finally, they have loyal party workers collecting the aforementioned lists.

When these efforts are combined, researchers can identify 64 percent of a previously amorphous list of individuals as to whether they are potential Republican voters.

The information is put online in something called a voter vault where, with the proper security code, it can be retrieved and used at the local level.

The weekend before the election, the telephone banks are mobilized, and recorded and live phone calls are made to households that are likely to produce Republican votes.

Republican State Chairman Robert T. Bennett, one of the most successful party chairmen in Ohio history, urged the faithful to get busy this year with the program of identifying voters, registering them and getting them to the polls.

"It is one of our highest priorities for the Ohio Republican Party," Bennett said of the two-year plan. Although 17 counties will get special attention, the GOP has set goals for all 88.

Bennett knows what he's doing; he didn't get the party where it is—controlling all of state government—without a lot of planning over the last 14 years.

Jo Ann Davidson, the former House speaker who has helped run presidential campaigns in Ohio, says it's a "new era" in politics where "to get your message out you have to look people in the eye and interact with the voters . . . make personal phone calls and knock on doors.

"We kind of got away from that," said the Reynoldsburg resident who serves on the GOP committee and hopes to be involved in the Bush re-election campaign.

Moore, retiring at age 84, is the senior member of the Republican National Committee and marvels at the changes almost as much as the party faithful marvel at her lengthy career. But she says the work still boils down to a personal, if computer-aided, approach.

She is puzzled by the difficulty of getting folks interested and involved in politics. "We have all this communication today," she said, "but a lot of people are involved in church and school. They always say, 'I'm too busy.' You have to keep after them, give them something to do."

Bennett has now given them something to do. He's given them plenty of time to do it, and they can even play on the Internet while working for the party.

■ ■

Blackwell's Focus on Issue 1 Resulted in Ballot Attractive to Bush Voters

The Columbus Dispatch, November 8, 2004

A year ago, it appeared that Ohio's presidential ballot would be muddled with a variety of unrelated issues. As it turned out, there was only one—protecting the sanctity of marriage—and it's being cited as one of the keys to President Bush's re-election. Accident? You be the judge.

This time a year ago, slot-machine fever was sweeping the legislature as a way of raising money for horse race tracks and for the state of Ohio. The issue was never going to make the early-March primary ballot, and some folks wanted to put it on in November.

There were fears that the gambling issue would draw working-class Democrats to the polls, but alternative speculation had the anti-gambling faction coming out to fight the slots and vote for the president, too.

As it turned out, the racetrack owners didn't want to pay for an expensive campaign for a constitutional amendment to allow the slot machines at the seven tracks. So it wasn't on the ballot. The issue apparently will be debated again in 2005 within the context of the next budget, which is starved for revenue.

Then there was the tax-repeal issue. How quietly that went away!

Secretary of State J. Kenneth Blackwell headed a group attempting to get the sixth cent on the state sales tax repealed early. It will expire June 30, but Blackwell's group wanted it to end at least six months before that.

Citizens for Tax Repeal were supposed to put the issue before the legislature by petition, and if the legislature did not act in four months, they would have been eligible to collect more signatures and get it on the statewide ballot.

Opponents to repeal—call them the tax-spenders—tied up the issue in court and it never even got to the legislature to start the clock running. Otherwise, it might have been on the ballot. It's hard to imagine the tax-repeal issue drawing even more voters than actually went to the polls, but it's possible.

The tax-repeal group put down the gloves during the summer. Maybe the conservatives found a better way. In Ohio and 10 other states, they got on the ballot—and passed—state constitutional amendments locking in the definition of marriage and apparently keeping judges from requiring state and local governments to offer benefits to couples other than heterosexual married ones.

They also drew huge numbers of Christians to the polls to vote for the amendments and for Bush.

Blackwell, as the state's chief elections officer, helped steer the amendment onto the Ohio ballot, ruling against the opponents when they attempted to derail it by challenging the petitioning process.

He had ample legal backing to dismiss the opponents' complaint on that issue, but he abused his position during the campaign by appearing in a TV commercial for Ohio Supreme Court Justice Terrence O'Donnell, a fellow Republican. Blackwell also made campaign ads in favor of Issue 1.

Ohioans don't want or need the referee to be taking sides on issues or candidates on the ballot.

Blackwell had the 88 county boards of election well-prepared, for the most part, to deal with a restless and ardent electorate, but he needlessly created the perception of partiality by appearing in the commercial.

The secretary of state's defenders say you can't take away his right of free speech. But if he wants to speak freely about candidates on the ballot, he should get another job. The person who certifies the vote should do everything possible to create an atmosphere of neutrality, even though we all know the position is a partisan elective office.

The secretary of state should take a position only on ballot issues that affect the way elections are run. An example would be repeal of the Election-Day voter registration provision in 1977.

Blackwell did not establish the best public relations in the run-up to the election. He jousted with a federal judge. He baited the news media into a lawsuit over who could be inside the polling places. By enforcing the letter of the law, he appeared to be trying to suppress the vote. But all things considered, he made his bravado stick. It was a fair election, even though many polling places needed more machines and workers. Even the punchcard voting, which he tried to eliminate after the 2000 election, went relatively well.

Blackwell will not be content to rest. He will pick up on the tax issue, this time on the side of cutting Medicaid costs in the upcoming budget. There is still plenty of work to do on smoothing out the election process. And he certainly is a live contender for governor in 2006.

Blackwell also was co-chairman of President Bush's re-election committee in Ohio, a clear conflict-of-interests for the overseer of elections. He was a lightning rod for criticism after the 2004 election and lost the race for governor of Ohio in 2006, chiefly because he was too conservative and he was burdened with following the Republican Taft administration that had been brought low by scandal.

■ ■

Lingering Ohio Election Brought Out the Worst in State GOP Boss

The Columbus Dispatch, January 17, 2005

OK, the presidential election is over. It's been over for a long while, but now it's really over.

It wasn't over when Sen. John Kerry conceded the morning after because we still had to make sure that the tallies were accurate in a few key states.

It wasn't over even then, because we had to make sure the official vote in Ohio—the real key state—showed that President Bush actually carried the Buckeye State.

But it wasn't over yet, because we still had to endure the inevitable parade of sore losers and conspiracy theorists, led by the obligatory appearances of Jesse Jackson, saying that tricks were played with the returns.

That, in a way, was brought on by Secretary of State J. Kenneth Blackwell. He actually conducted a pretty fair election considering the circumstances but chose to inject himself into the election's issues while serving as the referee.

Then it wasn't over because the challengers made the ridiculous assertion that exit polls were more accurate than the vote totals. As anyone familiar with polling will tell you, exit polls are not meant to predict or determine the outcome of an election. They are meant to ascertain why individuals voted the way they did.

It wasn't even over when the challengers took their case to the Ohio Supreme Court in a contest of the election, which they have every right to do.

And it wasn't over when Democrats in Congress lamely tried to nix Ohio's electoral votes, properly cast in Columbus on Dec. 13.

But it was over Wednesday, when challengers dropped their election challenge before the Ohio Supreme Court.

Unfortunately, Republican State Chairman Robert T. Bennett wouldn't let go. Having spent time in Cleveland, Bennett should recall that when the old Browns' fullback Jim Brown scored a touchdown, he handed the ball to the ref and left the playing field.

Maybe it's just today's culture, but Bennett chose to act more like the Vikings' Randy Moss; just scoring wasn't enough. Bennett accused the president's opponents of trying to steal the election. Get real. Convicts have a better chance of stealing from guards than Democrats have of stealing an election in Ohio.

"The 2004 presidential election produced the most outrageous behavior I've seen in my 40 years in Ohio politics," Bennett complained. He accused the president's opponents of voter-registration fraud, "manipulating the campaign-finance laws" and obstructing the electoral process.

"And now, they've even tried and failed to steal the election through lies and litigation," he said.

Sure, it was a close election, though not as close as predicted. Sure, tempers flare in the heat of battle, and, sure, Bennett is entitled to defend the honor of his president and his party.

But wasn't this piling on? A referee should have thrown a flag. Tweeeeet! "Conduct unbecoming a legend. The penalty is loss of down and an apology."

After the court ruling, Bennett said the challengers were "eager to cut and run." He apparently forgot that at about 2 A.M. the day after the election, his forces were insisting on national TV that Kerry concede to seal Bush's victory before the vote count was finished. National interest and all that.

Conspiracy theories are not limited to one political party, and they are best laid to rest by letting the process play out.

Before sunup on the day after the election in 1978, Republican Secretary of State Ted W. Brown wanted to lock down all the ballots, convinced that Democrat Anthony J. Celebrezze Jr. had stolen the election from him and put an end to his 28-year reign. Celebrezze did win, but honestly.

Maybe you can't blame Bennett for wanting to shut up the challengers. After all, we can't have the perception that America's election is flawed when it's trying to oversee one in Iraq.

But Bennett's late hit just adds to the polarization that already grips Ohio politics. He's already secured his place as one of the great Republican chairmen, if not the greatest. He's proved he can defeat Democrats. Why treat them like roadkill?

Chapter 3
Events and Issues

This chapter deals with issues that have occupied Ohio officials in various eras. It contrasts the issues of the '60s and '70s, in which views seem outdated, with the modern hot-button issues.

Four Memorable Events

Six-Day War: Democrats Lose Power Play on a Technicality

United Press International, September 26, 1975

COLUMBUS (UPI)—Last week's Franklin County Court of Appeals decision upholding the invalidity of six partisan Democratic bills rushed through the legislature in January carried a timeworn message—those that live by the sword die by the sword.

The bills, it may be recalled, included a new congressional redistricting plan calculated to furnish an additional two to four seats in the U.S. House for Ohio Democrats in the 1976 election.

There also were proposals to save more than 100 Democratic jobs in the executive branch, limit the powers of a Republican secretary of state and liberalize voter registration provisions and unemployment compensation regulations—both traditional Democratic objectives.

Democrats assuming control of both legislative chambers for the first time in 14 years, carefully chose the priority bills to push through during the first six days of the new session, so they could get them signed into law before Democratic Gov. John J. Gilligan left office.

They limited the list so there would be no delay. A bill must be considered for three separate days in each chamber, so they had little room for error. Seven days from the start of the session, Republican James A. Rhodes was to take office with veto power.

The Democrats carefully rehearsed procedures so nothing would go wrong. Court testimony shows they even had the final versions of the bills printed up in advance to hasten the process. No changes were to be made in the versions passed by the chamber of origin.

Republicans countered with their primary weapon—Lt. Gov. John W. Brown, a "lame duck" who was to remain in office exactly as long as Gilligan.

As presiding officer of the Senate, it was Brown's constitutional job to certify that all legislative requirements were followed, and he announced before the session began that he aimed to carry out that duty to the end.

Indeed, Brown guarded his authority so zealously that he slept in the Statehouse for two nights so the Democrats couldn't legally make an end run around him.

At last, the Democrats saw time running out and made the end run anyway, sending the bills to Gilligan without Brown's signature less than 48 hours before the administration changed hands.

Secretary of State Ted W. Brown, the real GOP ace-in-the-hole, blocked final enactment and threw the matter into Franklin County Common Pleas Court, where the bills were declared invalid last June by a Republican judge.

That decision was affirmed last week, to no one's surprise, by a panel of three Republican judges, two of whom had served in the Ohio House. Judge John W. McCormac, author of the unanimous opinion, offered this summary:

"A valid constitutional provision was found permitting speedy action by the General Assembly and it was utilized. Another equally valid section of the Constitution required, as an essential element to the validity of this legislation, that the lieutenant governor certify its procedural correctness. This provision was ignored."

John Brown has said since the so-called "six-day war" that had the Democrats given him the original bills as he requested, he would have had no choice but to return them promptly for correction of any procedural errors.

The Democrats, unwilling to gamble on any delay, bypassed Brown and took their chances in court.

In their written opinion, the three Republican appellate judges used the opportunity to rub salt in the Democrats wounds on this point:

"Even if devious conduct (on Browns part) had been intended," McCormac wrote, "no opportunity was given for it to take place and it cannot be presumed."

The jurists determined that the lieutenant governor "has no veto power over the substantive aspects of the legislation and he may not use a procedural subterfuge in order to effect a substantive veto power."

"If wrongful activity by the presiding officer had actually taken place, the result in this case may well have differed."

The Democrats no doubt take a dim view of this interpretive hindsight. They can't believe the result would have differed any more than they believe it will differ when they make their final appeal to the Ohio Supreme Court, also dominated 5 to 2 by Republicans.

In politics, the last weapon in the arsenal counts, even a technical sword.

■ ■

Democratic Sen. Morris Jackson Returns to the Fold

United Press International, December 17, 1982

COLUMBUS (UPI)—The gust of wind that rushed past your ears last week may have been the breath of Ohio's Democrats, led by Gov.-elect Richard F. Celeste, sighing with relief that they will rightly control the state Senate next session. The sounds of muttering came from Republicans, who took a calculated risk and lost their bid to organize the Senate under the presidency of Democratic Sen. M. Morris Jackson.

Jackson, the black Clevelander, came back to the Democrats to give them the 17-16 edge they need to run the Senate in 1983-84.

Why did he buckle when he seemingly had the Senate presidency in his pocket and the government of Ohio by the tail? To answer that question, one must understand Jackson's motivations.

After being second-in-command in the Senate from 1975-80, Jackson came up on the short end of a Democratic leadership squabble and was made an outcast. He felt like Rodney Dangerfield for the last two years. The Democrats were in the minority and didn't need him. He asked to be on a certain committee and was refused by Senate Democratic leader Harry Meshel.

"In 20 years of politics," says Jackson, "I learned how to be patient and use whatever leverage I have at the proper time."

The proper time came in late November, when it was suggested that Jackson join the Republicans in return for becoming Ohio's first black Senate president. It sounded like a good idea.

"I was looking out for me," Jackson recalls.

Some people thought Jackson should have insisted on more than just the Senate presidency. Even the Republicans were surprised at how cheaply he came.

If it had been a real power play, Jackson would have grabbed for more. But it later became clear: the senator merely wanted respect, spelled R-E-S-P-E-C-T, and he left an opening to return to the Democrats.

The Democrats handled the situation perfectly. They didn't try to bully or threaten Jackson. Instead, they calmly reasoned it out with him: if he joined the Republicans in organizing the senate on Jan. 3, they would control the committees and be able to block the programs of the administration of Gov.-elect Richard F. Celeste.

"I didn't think about some of these kinds of things," said Jackson, adding that he trusted the Republicans but his black friends in Cleveland did not.

"These people are looking for a ray of hope," he said. "That's why they voted 92 percent for Celeste."

It was pointed out to Jackson that if Celeste's programs failed, he might have to take the blame from his own community.

So Jackson came back, apparently for just as low a price as he had gone away. He will probably get a committee chairmanship.

Jackson may have gotten a couple of less visible concessions: that the Democrats will not embarrass him by retaliating against the Republicans next session, and that Meshel will tone down his blustery rhetoric of the past.

Jackson said last week it would be a "fatal mistake" if Meshel tries any kind of a vendetta against the Senate Republicans by hammering them in public or holding their bills hostage.

And he said he would be "surprised if Harry Meshel continues his arrogant ways, maligning people and stepping on anybody who gets in his way."

Jackson has made his point, the Democrats apparently have gotten the message, and the next Senate session probably will be run with the kind of caution exhibited by someone who lights a cigarette while walking past a fireworks factory.

With a 17-16 majority, Meshel did a masterful job of holding his caucus together. But the Democrats had to enact a large tax increase early in 1983 to fund the faltering budget, and they lost the Senate in the 1984 elections.

■ ■

Prison Riot Brings Same Reaction As '73 Uprising Did

The Columbus Dispatch, May 3, 1993

Consider the following quotations:

"These problems are not unique to Ohio; on the contrary, the situation at Lucasville is part of a nationwide phenomenon."

"While perfect security will never be possible, risks should be cut to the minimum. No one can foresee what crises may lie ahead. They should be limited to the single situation at hand, and met without panic or hostility."

"The situation at Lucasville remains dangerous. Many signs point to troubles: . . . the nature of the institution and its inmates; dissension among prisoners; hostility and fear in the wake of recent disturbances."

Last week's news? Nope, those quotes are 20 years old. They were issued after an uprising at the Southern Ohio Correctional Facility in 1973, not after the recent 11-day hostage standoff.

Nothing changes.

In 1973, two corrections officers were killed and the personal property of inmates was trashed by guards in retaliation. There were no hostages.

The circumstances leading up to that disturbance were also different than they were this year. Lucasville, opened just months earlier, was not overcrowded at the time. The inmates had their own labor union. Some weapons and drugs were being smuggled into the prison. There were no large religious factions.

But there were similarities, including many of the prisoners' demands and many of the recommendations made by a citizens' group sent in to determine the cause of the problems.

In 1973, Gov. John J. Gilligan named Simon Dinitz, the Bexley professor of criminology at Ohio State University, to his advisory panel on the prison system. This year, Gov. George V. Voinovich named Dinitz to head his investigating panel on Lucasville.

Nothing changes.

The recommendations during Gilligan's tenure were eerily similar to what is being discussed informally today: better training of prison staff, recruiting more minority guards, more education and job training opportunities for inmates, strict rules of conduct for inmates and prison employees, a better system for inmates to air grievances, changes in the commissary and an end to mail censorship. Officials also proposed more community-based correctional programs of the type now being pursued by the Voinovich administration.

"I don't think it (the prison) ever should have been built there (away from urban areas in southern Ohio)," said state Auditor Joseph T. Ferguson, whose son, Thomas, is now auditor.

Gilligan's task force described the prison as "an expensive monument to the ignorance of 19th-century penology, of which it is an excellent example."

Nothing changes.

William Weisenberg of the Ohio State Bar Association was a staff member of the Gilligan prison-reform task force and later was administrative assistant to the director of the Department of Rehabilitation and Correction.

"It's like Yogi Berra said, 'It's deja vu all over again,'" Weisenberg said last week. "Every time there's a disturbance, studies are made and reports are written. The problem is that very few of the recommendations that are made ever come to fruition. There is very little follow-up. What do we do? We build more prisons and put more people in them."

Weisenberg recalled that the administration in the early 1970s wanted to increase psychiatric services at Lucasville to correct the most deranged troublemakers. Last week, Lt. Gov. Mike DeWine said a major thrust by the administration will be to deal with mental problems at prisons.

Nothing changes.

Weisenberg said another blowup at Lucasville had been likely long before now. He said the department has its hands full "just fitting 39,000 prisoners in (the system) and doing it without letting them kill each other."

"Look at the odds against them," he said. "They are bulging at the seams. They get caught up bumping from one crisis to another.

"I'm not sure you can do more than maintain calm there (Lucasville)," said Weisenberg. "These people aren't there because they didn't give to the Red Cross. They are very violent and dangerous people."

"You've had prison riots since biblical times," said Senate President Stanley J. Aronoff, R-Cincinnati. "I'm not sure you're ever fail-safe. But you might have a better early warning system."

Senate Minority Leader Robert J. Boggs, D-Jefferson, said tensions between guards and inmates still have not been resolved. "Maybe they never will be," he said.

"It takes a tragedy to focus attention," said Attorney General Lee Fisher. "There will be more done about prisons this year than in the last 50 years because of Lucasville."

"I think it is probably accurate to say that more advances have been made in the last two years in Ohio (in prison reform) than in the previous 50 years."—Gov. Gilligan, Sept. 4, 1973.

■ ■

This column was written less than a week after man's first lunar landing. The descriptions early in the column were taken directly from the network television broadcasts that held a nation entranced at seeing a human being walking on the moon. The excitement hadn't worn off, but already plans were being made for a museum honoring Ohio's native son. Indeed, the museum was quickly built and it is still a tourist attraction in Wapakoneta, Ohio.

Spacewalking Armstrong Spawns Far-Out Museum

United Press International, July 25, 1969

COLUMBUS (UPI)—Imagine yourself strapped into a padded reclining seat, your head encased in a helmet equipped with earphones. You are floating suspended, almost weightless through blackness broken only by a thousand stars twinkling in the distance.

Suddenly you are hovering above a gleaming body of grayish-tan land full of craters and boulders. Rugged white hills spring from the horizon, and a bluish-green globe hangs in the darkness a quarter of a million miles away. The silence is deafening.

A shining metal structure on four spindly legs looms before you. It bears an insignia of the American flag. The hatch opens, and a white-clad spaceman backs out and slowly starts down the ladder, moving like a ghost.

The scene unfolds before you in gorgeous Technicolor. There is no distortion, no wavy lines, no picture roll. As the astronaut reaches the foot of the ladder, he extends his leg to the ground, pulls it back to the last rung, steps onto the pad of the landing craft and then plants his left foot firmly on the ground. Only then is the silence broken.

"That's one small step for man; one giant leap for Mankind," says the voice.

Fortunately, you can catch your breath, for you are not in the vacuum of the moon. You are inside the Neil Armstrong Aerospace Museum near Wapakoneta in western Ohio. This is just one of the mind-bending ideas envisioned by planners of the museum, which is to be started late this year and may be complete in 1970.

The actual re-enactment of the first step on the moon may be the center attraction at the museum if it isn't too costly. "We're thinking of a very dramatic effect as a central theme," said Daniel R. Porter, director of the Ohio Historical Society, which is moving quickly to enshrine the epic moon voyage at Armstrong's birthplace.

Porter went on to explain that the "first step" could be replayed by life-like mechanical figures such as those used in the Walt Disney exhibits at the 1964 World's Fair in New York. "The only limitations will be our budget and the space in which we are allowed to work," Porter said.

The $1 million museum is to be constructed on a 10-to-15 acre tract near Wapakoneta. Already, money and suggestions are filtering in.

The mind of the Historical Society is far from made up on the museum's features and design. One idea is to make it a replica of the moon. Gov. James A. Rhodes has suggested building it like the "Eagle"—the lunar module which made the historic landing.

"This is not going to be a traditional museum," Porter said. "We want it to be a building symbolic of the space age."

And he made it clear that the facility will be nothing like the musty corridors crammed with glass-encased relics that constitute the normal museum.

One of the ideas is a "mini-theater" for showing a film of the entire history and conduct of the moon journey. Porter pointed out that hundreds of feet of film taken by the astronauts may be made available. He also noted that the historical narration could include the deeds of other Ohio sons who made it possible to reach the moon—John Glenn and Donn Eisele.

Porter said the theater would not have to be conventional, with rows of seats. It could be a "stand-up, walk-around" theater with a 360-degree screen, using motion pictures in combination with slides, filmstrips and unique lighting effects. He said Armstrong's life might be portrayed in a vast mural, using his personal effects for illustration. And another part of the museum might be devoted to Ohio's contributions to the air and space age, beginning back in 1818 when the first balloon ascended west of the Allegheny Mountains in Cincinnati.

Porter hasn't given up, either, on the one exhibit that would put the frosting on the cake.

"We have high hopes of getting a piece of the moon, after the scientists are finished with it," he said.

■ ■

Kent State and Student Disorders

All you have to do is read the following to understand how Gov. James A. Rhodes reacted when students burned the ROTC building at Kent State University less than five months after this column was written. You could see it coming.

Rhodes Foreshadows "Kent State" With His Hard Line at Akron

United Press International, Dec. 12, 1969

COLUMBUS (UPI)—Sometimes, business and politics mix, which can be a big help if you're the governor and are running for the U.S. Senate.

Gov. James A. Rhodes ran into just such a situation last week when a small group of black students commandeered the administration building at the University of Akron to emphasize their demands for more recognition and participation in university affairs.

Rhodes' reaction was predictable and swift. It was predictable because he had promised last spring, while militants were practically dictating policy at colleges in other states, that misbehavior would not be tolerated on Ohio campuses.

The governor was so quick on the draw that his office had prepared and distributed a news release condemning the takeover before Statehouse newsmen had even heard about the incident.

Some newsmen, unaware of events at Akron, theorized in jest that the governor's reply could have been printed up in advance and released by mistake. They quickly found out the takeover was real.

Rhodes, still a step ahead of everyone, was true to his pledge. He had implemented his plan to deal surely and swiftly with campus rebels, beefing up Highway Patrol manpower at the campus and alerting 700 National Guardsmen in case the situation got rough.

As it turned out, a stroke of ink on some legal paper, and not a show of force, was mainly responsible for clearing the student rebels from the administration building.

But Rhodes wanted to be on the safe side. He had promised order on the campuses and nothing short of that would do, especially for a man who is running for the U.S. Senate on his record as governor.

Right or wrong, Rhodes is a man of action. He does not stand still. As he has said before: "I know that many people disagree with me. I've been more controversial probably than any other governor in this state. But you only get that way when you are doing things."

With that in mind, the governor hopped in his state airplane, summoned Columbus newsmen and whisked them to Akron. While the plane was in flight, word came that the students had heeded an injunction ordering them out of the building.

The situation was calm, but Rhodes pressed on for a first hand look. He met with university, military and police officials, shook a few hands and then sat down with the news media to deliver to the people of Ohio his philosophy on campus disruptions.

"The taxpayers of Ohio pay for these buildings and they help subsidize the students themselves," the governor said. "The public has a right to expect protection of their tax dollars and be free of organized civil disorders.

"We hear much about student demands at our universities. I think it's time the students hear about the taxpayers' demands. I believe the taxpayers of Ohio demand:

- "That the students conduct themselves in an orderly manner.
- "That they refrain from damaging public and private property in their dissent.
- "That they refrain from threatening or actually attempting bodily harm against those who disagree with them.
- "That they recognize that the people of Akron or anywhere else have a right to live in peace and security."

One could almost hear Joe Taxpayer cheering wildly as Rhodes spoke.

The governor then left, having nailed another plank into his platform for next year's Senate campaign. He denied he was taking a "hard" line in dealing with campus agitators. The voters could make up their own minds. It was a clever way to mix business and politics.

Although Rhodes narrowly lost the Republican Senate primary to Robert Taft Jr. the day after the Kent State shootings, it's believed his reaction, similar to the above, actually resonated with Republican voters and helped him.

■ ■

Kent State: Who Ordered the Guardsmen to Fire?

United Press International, Aug. 28, 1970

COLUMBUS (UPI)—Since the Kent State University tragedy last May 4, perhaps the major unanswered question is: Exactly what possessed the National Guard troops retreating up Blanket Hill to whirl and fire into a crowd of pursuing students?

Other questions, some of them more important, have been answered at least partially. There have been explanations of why the National Guard weapons were locked and loaded with .30-calibre ammunition and why students behaved in an unruly manner.

But discussions of the events around what the investigators are calling "Zero Hour"—the moment of the actual shootings—have produced a lot of vague information.

The public probably will continue to be in the dark on the matter until at least after a grand jury investigation is completed early in October. Crucial details about "Zero Hour" are lodged in the minds of National Guard officials and soldiers and will be shrouded in secrecy throughout the grand jury proceedings.

However, one theory about the fateful moment, advanced by a newsman who spent five days at Kent and sat through hours of legislative and federal hearings on the matter, has been acknowledged as a distinct possibility by sources close to the investigation.

This theory holds that the killings were an accident—a quirk of fate which occurred when a group of troops misunderstood a squad leader's order.

In theory, it works out this way:

Guardsmen had successfully broken up a noon rally on the Commons, splitting up the crowd and pushing down onto a practice football field at the foot of Blanket Hill. There, they regrouped for a retreat. "We felt we had accomplished our mission, and the troops were ordered to form a wedge and return to the bottom of the Commons," Brig. Gen. Robert Canterbury, assistant adjutant general and senior National Guard officer at the scene, testified before the President's Commission on Campus Unrest.

From time to time, groups of soldiers knelt and pointed their weapons as if to fire, hoping to intimidate the advancing, rock-throwing students. Canterbury said he did not know who ordered this maneuver.

Nor did Canterbury know, he testified before the Scranton Commission, if anyone ordered the guardsmen to turn and fire when they reached the top of the hill in retreat. The commission has testimony, however, that an officer in a soft fatigue cap raised and lowered his arm, turned toward his troops, then turned back toward the students, crouched and began firing a .45-calibre pistol into the ground.

It is conceivable that Canterbury was unaware of this maneuver. It is also conceivable that this officer commanded only a portion of the troops on the crest of the hill, for only a portion of them reacted.

Moreover, it is possible that their gas masks and the noise of the crowd obscured part of the order, if there was any.

Sources close to the investigation concede the officer could have said: "Fire over their heads!" and it could have come out: "Fire!" Even more startling, the officer could have cried: "Fire into the ground!" as he began to do a second later, and the guardsmen could have heard: "Fire into the crowd!"

In any case, the guardsmen, tired, taunted and no doubt confused, soon began to shoot in several directions, and there were four needless deaths. Most of those involved, including the students, would no doubt act out the senseless script differently if given a chance for a replay.

The author was the "newsman" in the column who speculated, based on sources close to the investigation, that the squad leader's commands had been misunderstood or perhaps only partially heard. There was a lot of noise and confusion on Blanket Hill that fateful day. Guardsmen were not well-trained to deal with campus protesting, and many of them had spent the previous week working long hours policing wildcat truckers' violence on interstate highways in northern Ohio.

The author was well-acquainted with William W. Scranton, chairman of the President's Commission on Campus Unrest, having covered him for *United Press International* when Scranton was governor of Pennsylvania from 1963-67.

The testimony about the officer in a soft fatigue cap was never given much publicity, and as far as the author knows, the speculation about the possible commands was never published elsewhere.

Having served in the Army reserves for 5½ years and having been a college student between 1957 and 1963, the author felt, based on the investigation, that the guardsmen received an unfair share of the blame for the shootings.

■ ■

The campus rioting and subsequent shootings by Ohio National Guard troops at the Kent State campus prompted a number of investigations. State legislators traveled to several campuses and in five months had assembled an interim report. Lawmakers tried to strike a balance, although there was clearly a sentiment among majority Republicans that the state should come down hard on "radical" students and faculty members. House Bill 1219, the bill that passed, became a byword for quelling campus disorder. Its supporters were known as the 1219ers and were basically the same lawmakers referred to elsewhere in this book as the "Caveman Caucus."

Legislators Want the Law Laid Down on Campuses

United Press International, October 9, 1970

COLUMBUS (UPI)—While the work of the Joint Legislative Committee on Campus Disorders is not yet finished, its interim report issued last week reveals some basic ideas of the committee members.

It is interesting to note that 12 of the 34 pages of the report are devoted to findings and recommendations on student and faculty conduct at state-operated universities. In fact, those two subjects are the first to be treated in the six sections of the report.

The committee recommends a code of minimum standards of conduct and discipline for students, either drawn by the universities and approved by the Board of Regents, drafted by the Board of Regents or by the legislature.

The message is clear—the colleges will get a shot at it. If they drop the ball, the General Assembly is prepared to act next year. According to the report, the universities should be responsible for enforcing the code (and) hiring the personnel needed to do the job.

At the very least, the report says, students should be required to abide by the law and the rules of the school, and to refrain from disrupting lawful activities at the institution, interfering with the rights of others and bringing discredit to the academic community.

Model punishments, according to the report, should range from warning to expulsion, with suspension or expulsion mandatory for these offenses: felonious misconduct, misconduct involving moral turpitude, drug abuse, cheating, plagiarism, threatening disruption or injury and "persistent misconduct."

Guidelines for the code suggest that university officials immediately suspend a student if they witness a destructive act on his part.

The committee also recommends financial assistance be withheld from "any student guilty of serious misconduct, regardless of his academic standing."

It also recommends a law requiring the reporting of serious criminal conduct to law enforcement authorities—an apparent attempt to force universities to police their ranks.

The report recommends a similar code of conduct for faculty members, established under the same terms.

This code would spell out faculty instructional obligations and make faculty members responsible for maintaining order and guiding students in proper standards of conduct.

It would set forth sanctions for professional and personal misconduct, to apply whether or not the offending faculty member has tenure. A one-year probationary period would be required before a faculty member achieves tenure.

The code, according to the report, should define "academic freedom." This term, the committee found, has furnished a convenient sanctuary for those in the university community who wish to dodge enforcement of high standards of personal and professional discipline.

The sobering aftermath of Kent State combined with summer vacation to put out the fires at college campuses. House Bill 1219 was enacted, universities became more attuned to student needs, authorities took steps to train enforcement officers and standards of conduct were developed. Once the politicians made their political hay out of the result, almost everyone forgot about the strict state stance and let the colleges handle any disturbances. Demonstrations were few, as college students generally became more concerned with making money than with correcting the ills of society.

■ ■

Ohio's effort to lower the minimum voting age from 21 was puzzling from the start. Why would a group of mainly old white males—Republicans—controlling the state legislature be interested in giving the franchise to college students protesting the Vietnam War?

The following column captures the frantic attempt by certain lawmakers to make Ohio the 38th and deciding state to ratify the 26th Amendment to the U.S. Constitution. It was a textbook lesson in how not to govern—excessive parliamentary maneuvering, blatant egotism and timing geared more to politics than careful consideration of legislation.

Extreme irony: You can see by the column that it was assumed Ohio had been the 38th state; later research showed the Buckeye State was a few hours too early. Ohio was the 37th state to ratify the Amendment. The next day, either Oklahoma or North Carolina won the honor.

The Strange Odyssey of Lowering the Voting Age to 18

United Press International, July 2, 1971

COLUMBUS (UPI)—When historians write about the 26th amendment to the U.S. Constitution, Ohio will rate a footnote as the state (that) gave 18-to-20 year olds the right to vote in all elections.

Little known and less remembered will be the machinations that went into making Ohio the 38th and final state to ratify the Vote 18 amendment. Let us chronicle them, before they are lost for all time.

The 109th General Assembly had barely been convened when Sen. Oakley C. Collins, R-Ironton, offered a resolution proposing that Ohio voters be allowed to amend their own Constitution in November to permit a reduction in the voting age to 18.

On March 25th, Sen. Stanley J. Aronoff, R-Cincinnati, chairman of the Senate Elections Committee, introduced a resolution to ratify the federal amendment. Aronoff said Ohio should wait until other states acted before proceeding on either of the resolutions.

On April 1, all 45 House Democrats offered the federal amendment on their own. Four weeks later, the Senate passed Collins' amendment and Aronoff said Ohio voters should be allowed to change their own Constitution; that the federal amendment was a "long way" from being ratified.

On May 19, the House passed the resolution proposing to amend the Ohio Constitution. It would have gone on the ballot, had not Rep. Harry J. Lehman, D-Shaker Heights, amended it to require a delay until Aug. 31 to see if the federal amendment was ratified.

The Collins resolution was sent to a House-Senate conference committee. It has never emerged and probably never will.

On June 3, Aronoff's committee released his resolution to the Senate Rules Committee, which sat on it until June 24. Aronoff said Ohio might try to be among the last few states to ratify.

On June 29, the Senate approved the resolution, 30-2, and Aronoff said the time to act was ripe. Thirty-five states had ratified the resolution.

House Speaker Charles F. Kurfess, R-Bowling Green, said he was "in no mood to play games" with the resolution, but if somebody else "wants to play the numbers games and make Ohio the 38th state, that's A-OK with me."

Within 24 hours, the resolution had been sent to the House State Government Committee where it received a three-minute hearing. One member missed the committee meeting because he had to make a telephone call.

Shortly before 8 P.M., Kurfess convened the House to consider the 26th amendment to the U.S. Constitution. What followed was more like a back-alley brawl than a chapter in history:

- Aronoff, whispering with leaders and giving the old infantry "go-go" sign from the back of the chamber, convinced the lawmakers that Oklahoma was in session at that very hour prepared to become the 38th state.
- Kurfess was persuaded to cut off debate after only 15 minutes, leaving Reps. James Thorpe, R-Alliance, and Richard G. Reichel, R-Massillon, screaming for (recognition from) the floor and alienating further a hard-core of Republican conservatives at odds with him over taxes.
- Democrats supplied 44 votes for the resolution, Republicans only 37.

Aronoff's information about Oklahoma being in session was proven wrong. He said his two-pronged plan to make Ohio flexible on the amendments had worked perfectly.

Years later, Kurfess acknowledged he should have telephoned Oklahoma Gov. David Hall, a friend of his, to see whether or not the Sooner State indeed was poised to pass the resolution that night.

Obviously, Aronoff was mistaken that his plan had worked perfectly; Ohio was premature. Informed in 2007 that Ohio was not the 38th state after all, he said: "You mean we went through all that for nothing?" and laughed heartily. Easy come, easy go.

■ ■

This column shows the continued strain on town-and-gown relations a year-and-a-half after the Kent State shootings. Although campus disruptions had abated, the Vietnam War was still on, and suspicions about college students still ran high in the community at-large.

Nerves Fray over Student Voting on Campus

United Press International, October 15, 1971

COLUMBUS (UPI)—Last week's court ruling permitting college students to register and vote in their college communities could, if it stands, have far-reaching effects on the government of certain university towns in Ohio.

The decision of a panel of federal judges in Cincinnati would permit college students to vote in their university communities starting next year if they wish to establish permanent residency where they attend school.

The ruling may be appealed, but if it is upheld it could have profound effects on communities whose populations are approached or outnumbered by the university enrollment.

The population of Athens, Ohio, is 16,000 and Ohio University has 18,585 students. "If students did register and vote, it could mean a tremendous difference in election results," said Mayor Raymond Shepard.

Oxford, Ohio, contains only 4,254 residents but the enrollment of Miami University is 13,133.

"The students could conceivably control elections," said Mayor Calvin Conrad.

Enrollments at the state universities in Bowling Green and Kent slightly outnumber the inhabitants of those cities, and it is easy to envision the students electing council members, as they have done in Berkeley, California, and Madison, Wisconsin.

One complaint already has been voiced—students pay no taxes but would be able to vote for projects requiring money—even long-term bond issues which they most likely would not be around to see paid off.

"They (students) are people who pay no taxes," Conrad said. "It is easy to spend if one isn't going to be there to bear the consequences." Of course, they wouldn't be there to reap the benefits, either.

But it is easy to see how things might get out of hand in a community dominated by a university.

Students could conceivably exert their voting powers to change local ordinances and upset the entire structure of the community. This thought already has prompted the suggestion that educational authorities clamp a lid on student enrollments at once and spread "student power" across the state.

It also has been suggested that student control of communities might drive the older generations out, leaving autonomous university cities run by the codes that now govern academia.

Large universities already can be described as cities within cities. They have their own police forces and governmental agencies. Why couldn't they extend themselves still further?

Some communities are dominated by large industry. Couldn't the parallel be drawn with institutions of higher learning?

A healthy sign or not, Secretary of State Ted W. Brown is not ready to panic. "All the hullabaloo is for nothing," Brown said.

He believes only the activists, "those who want to do it to torment people," will go to the trouble to change their legal address to vote in their college community.

The rest, Brown said, are the majority of students who will continue to register in their hometowns. And to encourage this, he has legislation now under study in the House to permit registration by mail for absentee voters.

Whatever the outcome, it should be an indication of how many students are willing to go to the trouble of participating to change the society in which they live at least nine months of each year.

Students may register to vote in a campus community if they can demonstrate that they are permanent residents. The paranoia in 1971 was justifiable for the times, however. The Sixties had just ended, the Vietnam War was in high gear and campus revolts had upset society in the prior year.

The matter of voter registration reared its head many times in subsequent years, the latest in 2008. Ohio's first early voting in a presidential election allowed a window when eligible Ohioans could register and vote the same day, leading to concerns about potential fraud. But the campus voting issue was long settled by then, and data banks made it easy to check if a college student was registered in his or her hometown or on the campus.

■ ■

Home State, Banking and Marvin Warner

Marvin Warner: Portrait of a Heavy Hitter

United Press International, July 15, 1983

COLUMBUS (UPI)—Marvin L. Warner eased himself in as chairman of the Ohio Building Authority last week about the way a warm knife eases its way into a tub of butter.

He was smooth. Oh, so smooth. But then you don't become a multi-million dollar construction company owner, or ambassador to Switzerland, or the owner of a United States Football League franchise (Birmingham) without a certain amount of finesse.

Warner, who helped bankroll Gov. Richard F. Celeste's campaign last year, was called upon by the governor to take over the OBA when the Democrats became convinced the Republicans were fouling it up with improper procedures on state building construction projects.

"I didn't want this job," said Warner, "But the governor asked me, and I'm going to do the best job I possibly can."

Warner was the designated hatchet man, leading two other Democrats into 3-2 domination of the board, but he acted more like a pussycat.

He began by asking, in his best Alabama drawl, for some "background" on the status of the second State Office Tower in Columbus—how much property had been purchased, how the architect and project manager had been chosen.

Of course, Warner was working from a crib sheet provided by Celeste's office, so he asked all the right questions, got the expected answers and made the logical recommendations.

Then he calmly directed the adoption of motions electing the other Democrats as officers of the OBA, firing the Republican lawyer and executive director, hiring Celeste's choice of counsel for the OBA and rescinding everything the Republicans did at the prior meeting.

During discussions, Warner took particular exception to the way the Republicans had chosen Turner Construction Co. to do the State Office Tower, and then planned to negotiate a price. "I don't see how you buy something at the department store without knowing the price," said Warner.

"You don't buy," responded Republican board member George Mutter, "But you take it up to the register and see if it fits your needs. If you're going to have brain surgery, do you ask the doctor how much it's going to cost and see if you can get it done for less?"

"Sure do," answered Warner. "We're not going to do anything without competitive bidding."

But Warner refused to make that official policy and refused to competitively bid the board's special counsel job, drawing scorn from the Republicans.

Less than two years later, Warner was at the center of one of Ohio's major scandals, largely because his flagship Ohio-chartered savings and loan company engaged in unsound investment practices. The following column deals with the fallout from the 1985 savings and loan debacle.

■ ■

The state savings and loan scandal was one of the biggest I reported on during my 36 years at the Statehouse. We worked on it night and day from March through June of 1985. Reporters from the *New York Times* and *Wall Street Journal* made themselves at home in our cracker-box Press Room. It had been two weeks since the scandal broke, but this was the first column I could write about it with any perspective.

Celeste Gambles in Closing Thrifts

United Press International, March 24, 1985

COLUMBUS (UPI)—There is plenty of second-guessing, and only time will tell whether Gov. Richard F. Celeste made the right move in shutting down the 70 state-chartered savings and loan associations, most of them for more than a week.

Initially, Republicans licked their chops over the prospect of the 1986 gubernatorial campaign. You could almost see them out there taking pictures of the signs in the S&L windows. "This office closed by order of Gov. Celeste."

Many remembered when former Gov. John J. Gilligan closed the state parks in September 1971 to put pressure on the legislature to enact a state income tax. The resulting public wrath contributed to Gilligan's defeat three years later.

Now the campaign rhetoric was beginning to come together: "Governor Celeste—he raised your taxes and closed your banks." But Celeste may have made the right decision after all, depending on how the affair turns out.

"I don't know what else the boy could have done," said veteran Republican Sen. Oakley C. Collins of Ironton.

When the Home State Savings Bank of Cincinnati first experienced runs, spreading to other S&L's, Celeste had a choice: Hope the panic would let up during the weekend, or close all the state-chartered institutions and regroup.

Tearing a page from the book of former Republican Gov. James A. Rhodes, Celeste chose a decisive course of action. Instead of sitting back and riding it out, he decided to exert leadership, much as Rhodes used to take command during floods, blizzards and fuel crises in the 1970s.

Celeste brought in the best Democratic political minds in Ohio to give advice. They included his father, Frank, a veteran Democratic politician; Democratic State Chairman James M. Ruvolo; and Celeste's former campaign chairman, political consultant Gerald Austin.

To make certain Ohio knew who was in charge, Celeste recruited an army of public relations people, the size of which was unmatched in the annals of the governor's office.

Most of them were less concerned with dispensing information than with putting out fires and getting the most mileage out of Celeste's efforts.

Celeste visited Cincinnati five straight days, and made statewide television and radio broadcasts. He sought, and received, federal help in Cleveland and Washington. He went on national TV to shine Ohio's tarnished image.

To capture the essence of the governor's leadership in time of crisis, a filming crew was brought in to record for posterity and the '86 campaign.

Celeste took another leaf from Rhodes' book at the outset: he brought in the legislative leaders from both parties and made them part of the solution to this non-partisan problem. It worked, although Senate President Paul E. Gillmor, R-Port Clinton, a potential rival for Celeste in 1986, looked like he would rather be somewhere else.

Still another page from the Rhodes book of survival: Celeste invited a special prosecutor to investigate any and all wrongdoing.

Another case of taking the initiative. A prosecutor can't do him any harm. He has already been tarred by his proximity to Marvin L. Warner, the owner of Home State who apparently sensed the impending disaster with ESM Government Securities of Fort Lauderdale, Fla.

Rhodes, who stood on the sidelines through it all, finally struck with criticism, saying Celeste should never have closed the S&L's; that he should have taken liquor and lottery money and backed them up.

Trouble was, the legislature had already done that, putting up $50 million in non-tax revenues the week before Rhodes, with his unparalleled timing, apparently saw that Celeste had stopped the "runs" on the savings and loans, and that he'd better get his licks in.

Whether the Home State affair is a genuine scandal reaching into the Celeste administration, and whether Marvin Warner's activities will rub off on the governor and other Democrats, those questions will be answered by subsequent investigations. The Republicans have got some good campaign fodder for next year, but Celeste seems initially to have held the wolves at bay.

It turned out that Celeste made the right call. His handling of this banking scandal was one of the highlights of his eight-year tenure. Depositors and the state received all their money back.

Celeste's director of commerce, charged with overseeing Ohio savings and loans, was relatively new at the time. But testimony at the state investigative hearings showed late in 1985 that Rhodes' superintendent of savings and loans had been warned by internal examiners in the early 1980s that all was not well with Home State, the flagship of the state-chartered thrifts. The warnings were ignored.

■ ■

Large commercial banks based in big cities in other states had long coveted the privilege of doing business in Ohio, but the Buckeye State's community banks always held sway in the legislature, and kept the big boys out. Just as a plan to phase in branch banking was about to pass, the Home State Savings Bank scandal broke and the New York banks cashed in.

Scandal Allows New York Banks to Invade Ohio Early

United Press International, April 14, 1985

COLUMBUS (UPI)—Exactly one month ago, two days before Gov. Richard F. Celeste closed the savings and loan associations, the Ohio House of Representatives passed a bill phasing in interstate banking over four years.

That bill would allow banks in neighboring states to do business in Ohio, and Ohio banks to go into those states. Two years later, the reciprocity would expand outward to the next ring of states. In four years, New York banks would be allowed into Ohio. The careful timing of that plan has since been upset by the Home State Savings Bank debacle, and the bill is now dormant in the Senate.

The New York banks don't want to wait four years, and they won't have to under the new scheme which is to be offered to the General Assembly this week. The New York banks will take over some of the state-chartered savings and loans now unable to operate, including Home State. In return, they will be given a head start on their invasion of the Ohio banking market.

The pressure building toward this week's showdown is well-nigh unbearable. It is best summed up by Sen. Richard H. Finan, R-Cincinnati, chief sponsor of the bill to permit the Home State sale to Chemical Corp. of New York. "You've got the depositors (of Home State) saying 'We want 100 percent of our money,'" said Finan. "You've got the taxpayers saying 'Don't use our money to bail out

Home State.' You've got the Ohio banks saying, 'Don't let (the New York banks) in,' and you've got the out-of-state saying, 'We'll bail out your chestnuts.'"

The Celeste administration and the lawmakers want in the worst way to unload Home State and get 100 percent of the customers' money back.

They are clearly annoyed that Ohio banks have not moved to acquire some of the closed S&L's without forcing the state to put up a sizeable guarantee. Lack of an Ohio bid also puts the administration at the mercy of the New York banks: There is no competition.

Ohio banks are just as annoyed that their New York counterparts are seizing the opportunity to take a four-year shortcut to interstate banking, with no agreement that Ohio banks can do business in New York.

A worse problem may be selling the idea of using tax revenues (there are not enough available lottery or liquor profits) to supplement the Chemical Bank deal. That would annoy taxpayers.

When Chase Manhattan jumped into the fray last week and promised to buy S&Ls in Mentor and Cincinnati, the Celeste administration made clear that Chase will have to buy some of the weaker ones, too, and not just the plums, if it wants Ohio banking privileges.

Behind all the tension is the spectre, down the road, of a New York monopoly of Ohio's banking system, controlling all the rates and services. "Do you think they care about you?" warned one observer last week.

> Not only did the big-city banks invade, but the huge banking conglomerates and their unsound investment and loan practices helped create the credit crunch of 2008. And notice, in the middle part of the column, how similar the reactions were in 1985 and late 2008 to a government bailout of the financial institutions!

■ ■

Hot-Button Issues

Meditation, Not Mandated Prayer, In Schools

United Press International, August 10, 1969

COLUMBUS (UPI)—During the last few years, public schools have shied away from devotional exercises, including anything resembling prayers and

Bible reading. Teachers and school boards have been unsure of just how far they could go under U.S. Supreme Court guidance. Rather than inviting a lawsuit, they have backed off.

Sen. Charles J. Carney of Youngstown, the minority floor leader in the Ohio Senate, thinks it is a shame that any school pupils might be deprived of the chance to participate in activities teaching them non-sectarian values such as brotherly love, the Golden Rule, charity and economic justice.

So Carney pushed a bill through the legislature encouraging teachers to conduct voluntary "meditation" programs in their classrooms. The measure, on its way to the desk of Gov. James A. Rhodes, provides for meditation for "reasonable periods of time" on a moral, philosophical or patriotic theme.

Carney's bill does not mandate meditation. It lets teachers know such programs are permissible under current law and it forbids boards of education to ban the programs if classroom teachers institute them. The meditation must be voluntary, and pupils do not require written excuses to be exempted from participation.

"I'm not trying to cram any religious belief down anybody's throat," Carney said. "I have received innumerable letters over the last few years saying that moral teachings are lacking in our time. This would encourage teachers to talk to their pupils about the fundamentals of morality and get them thinking about it."

Still, there are those who are not ready to accept Carney's proposal. In debate on the bill on the House floor, Rep. George E. Mastics, R-Fairview Park, said the proposal was "loosely worded," offered no guidelines and would be apt to make the teacher a "dictator."

"This precedent would be most dangerous," Mastics said. "What is a 'reasonable time'? Is it five minutes? Is it one hour? Is it all day long? How often could they do this? Could they do it in place of study?"

Mastics didn't answer the questions. He asked some more.

"What is a 'program?'" he inquired. "It's what the teacher decides to feed your kid. What is a 'moral program?' It could be a discussion of free love. What about philosophy? Karl Marx was a philosopher. Today's philosophy is 'do your thing.' Anything goes. And if we pass this bill, anything goes."

The bill was passed, and Carney is not afraid that anything will go. He believes that boards of education will be able to see to it that the meditation programs do not get out of line.

In the meantime, the meditation programs may remove some of the hostility toward the Supreme Court by those who want to "get the Bible back in the schools."

Not much changed in 40 years. Those who want to get the Bible back in the schools still regard the Supreme Court as a mortal enemy. And Mastics' questions still reverberate. In 2008, the Mount Vernon Board of Education attempted to dismiss a high school biology teacher for keeping a Bible on his desk and allegedly trying to teach creationism.

■ ■

One Person's Civil Right is Another's Civil Wrong

United Press International, July 17, 1969

COLUMBUS (UPI)—The civil rights movement is full of paradoxes. One group works for pure integration while another breaks its neck to get separate but equal facilities. One group advocates peaceful means of achieving its goals and another wants to make war, not love.

An interesting contradiction came to the surface in the Ohio General Assembly last week when the House passed, 70-14, a bill allowing the Ohio Civil Rights Commission to require employers and other persons to keep records of race, color, religion, national origin and ancestry of employees and applicants. In recent years, civil rights boosters have fought to get rid of such records. Questions on race, religion and ancestry were not to be asked in matters of employment or anything else in the public domain.

Now the General Assembly seemingly wishes to retrench and make a special exception for the commission.

The reason, according to the sponsor of the bill, Rep. Robert A. Manning, Akron Republican, is that the commission needs such records to find out if violations are taking place. Without the records, the commission has no way of proving that an employer, for example, is discriminating against Negroes in hiring.

"Ten years ago was the time when we were trying to get away from asking questions and keeping records on race, religion and national origin," Manning said. "We've passed through that phase now. Without the records, neither the employer nor the commission has tangible proof to show that there is or is not discrimination. The Civil Rights Commission can't even protect its own findings in investigations. If there is no concrete proof, everybody just cries 'whitewash' on a decision and says the administration is trying to protect somebody."

Another sponsor, Rep. Keith McNamara, Columbus Republican, claims the legislation is designed to protect both the commission and the employer.

McNamara recalled that Ohio State University was once accused of discriminating against Negroes and was asked to produce records for an inquiry.

The university said it was told not to keep such records, and thus was unable to defend itself.

On the other side of the coin, Rep. John A. Bechtold, Cincinnati Republican, one of the 14 opponents, protested that the bill would be unconstitutional.

"It forces the possibility that an employer may have to testify against himself," Bechtold said. "Furthermore, it is directly in opposition to the intent of the Civil Rights Act."

Another foe of the proposal, Rep. Walter L. White, Lima Republican, complained that the "one-sided commission" should have to prove the guilt of an employer without benefit of his records.

"It's up to the commission to show that there is a violation," White said. "It's not up to the individual to prove himself innocent. I was a prosecutor for eight years, and I didn't have criminals helping me prove my charges. The law tells us we should not keep records of these things, and then we turn right around and say, 'You must keep these to show your innocence.'"

Unfortunately, even this new weapon, should the legislature decide to furnish it, may not help the commission much.

Employers who honestly attempt to observe equal rights in hiring will continue to do so, records or no records. Those who don't will probably try to circumvent the commission by falsifying records or failing to keep them and risking a challenge.

A parallel may be drawn with the old argument used by the opponents of firearms registration: "When guns are outlawed, only outlaws will have guns."

The above column was written a year after the summer of '68, when civil rights and "black power" were at their zenith. The term Negroes was still the mainstream name for African-Americans, archaic as it sounds now.

■ ■

Thomas "Tony" Hill showed uncommon perseverance in advancing an anti-war bill in a Republican-dominated Ohio House where top leaders vowed it would never even be assigned to a committee. It was assigned to a committee, got two hearings and was nearly brought to a vote of the full House. The reasons? Noisy public pressure over the Vietnam War, and the Kent State University shootings only one month earlier.

Rep. Tony Hill Gamely Fought the Establishment on Vietnam

United Press International, June 11, 1970

COLUMBUS (UPI)—One of the most fascinating pieces of legislation to come before the Ohio General Assembly this year was a bill designed to prevent Ohioans from being forced to fight in undeclared wars.

Whether or not you support U.S. involvement in Indochina, this bill, sponsored by Rep. Thomas E. Hill, D-Cleveland, had thought-provoking possibilities. It is dead now, laid to rest by the House Rules Committee after a struggle that brought the bill further than Hill had ever dared hope.

Hill will also be gone, defeated in a bid for re-nomination at last month's primary election. But the bill is likely to be back next year unless the Vietnam conflict ends or unless the U.S. Supreme Court rules on the constitutionality of the president's committing troops without a declaration of war.

The proposal, drafted after a new Massachusetts law, merely seeks to allow Ohio to join Massachusetts in seeking a federal court test of presidential power to commit troops.

"We seek a constitutional ruling on the extent of the president's war-declaring power," said Steven Worth, an associate professor of political science at Northeastern University, who testified on the bill.

"We do not question the president's legitimate role in the exercise of foreign affairs. We merely question what we feel is an improper exercise of that part of our foreign policy which rests constitutionally in the Congress.

"In the entire history of American constitutional law, the courts have never once either explicitly or by inference affirmed the presidential usurpation of that part of the complex of foreign policy powers which commits the nation to war. We are seeking through this legislation one constitutional avenue under which the Supreme Court must make that decision."

House Republican leaders, not anxious for their chamber to become the focus for a debate on the Vietnam War, bottled up the bill on two reasonable grounds:

- The Ohio General Assembly is not a proper forum for deciding a matter in the hands of the federal government.
- Massachusetts is taking the issue before the federal courts, and Ohio should wait for that decision.

The answer by proponents of the bill to reasoning of this type is simple: the Ohio General Assembly should give state residents an opportunity to participate in a decision on such an important issue.

"The legislatures must get involved," said a young manufacturing executive testifying before the House Judiciary Committee on the bill. "I've seen you work for hours on raising dog license fees from $2 to $3, and have fought, like many of you, to keep myself from falling asleep."

If the Vietnam War is really as unpopular as many believe, the citizens of Ohio should be able to look to their legislature for help in altering control of its conduct, according to proponents. They should be able to participate by joining Massachusetts in court action.

To hear the matter out and vote on it in the halls of the General Assembly would clear the air once and for all. It would help restore some of the powers that many state legislatures are allowing to slip from their grasp.

Perhaps most important of all, it would show the young people that the system is interested; that they can take their problems to state government and get at least a sympathetic ear.

States working in unison wrote the Constitution on which America is founded. Through hard work together today, they may continue to guide the country in important decisions.

Of course Hill's bill didn't pass, and he was never heard from again politically after he left the House and went back to Cleveland. But the ghost of his proposal rattled its chain in 2003 when another Cleveland lawmaker, Dale Miller, sought to keep Ohio service personnel from being sent to Iraq, another unpopular battlefront.

■ ■

Organized Labor Protecting Women; Some Don't Want It

United Press International, June 16, 1972

COLUMBUS (UPI)—The state's largest and most powerful labor organization, riding herd on senators from both parties last week, managed to preserve what is left of Ohio's female protective labor laws, at least for the present.

Failure of the Senate to follow the House in voting for repeal of the protective laws was another setback for women's liberation groups, whose proposed Equal Rights Amendment to the U.S. Constitution is going nowhere fast in Ohio this year.

The Ohio AFL-CIO, which opposed repeal of the protective laws unless three special amendments were inserted, patrolled the Senate last Tuesday as the measure was sent to the floor by the Republican-dominated Rules Committee. The bill was never called up for a vote, and the following day it was nestled back in the shelter of the Rules Committee.

"They knew they were going to lose because they didn't have the horses," said Frank W. King, president of the Ohio AFL-CIO. "We hope we had some influence."

The legislation dates back to 1970, but serious movement did not occur until the Ohio Supreme Court ruled last March that protective laws for women working for firms employing 25 or more persons were in conflict with sex discrimination prohibitions in the U.S. Civil Rights Act of 1964.

Shortly thereafter, House Republican leaders with the help of some maverick Democrats passed the repealer bill by two votes.

The repealer applies to all female protective laws, including those applying to firms under 25 persons and doing business within Ohio.

It requires equal pay for substantially the same work performed by women and forbids an employer to require a woman to work more than 10 hours a day or 50 hours a week without consent.

It also repeals, at small companies, breaks for women such as separate lunchrooms, a mandatory half-hour lunch period, a ban on lifting more than 25 pounds repeatedly, chairs with back supports, and special posting of work schedules.

Organized labor wanted to insert a minimum wage of $1.60 for all workers, apply the hours limitation to men and forbid any worker to lift more than his or her capacity.

These amendments were narrowly defeated in the House, but labor had a record vote on them.

In the Senate Commerce and Labor Committee, organized labor nearly had one of their amendments passed—only voluntary work after 10 hours a day or 50 hours a week for both men and women.

This would have been fine with women's organizations, who have said they want equal treatment.

Ironically, the committee accepted a "sexist" amendment from Sen. Howard C. Cook, R-Toledo, eliminating men from the benefit. Labor was off the bill and women's liberationists lost.

Republican Senate leaders apparently were ready to push the bill through, along with several other major bills on Tuesday's calendar.

But unlike in the House, the Democrats held solid with King, and some Republicans evidently backed off.

The GOP apparently was unwilling to risk record votes on the Democratic amendments and the bill itself.

So it will be awhile before small firms in Ohio have women blast furnace operators, stag club employees or freight elevator operators.

The female protections seem quaint now, but they were in demand in 1972. For the fate of the Equal Rights Amendment, see the next column.

■ ■

This is a doubled-edged column. It provides a flavor of the debate on same-sex marriage in Ohio in 2004, and gives a good thumbnail summary of a similar hot-button issue of the early 1970s—the Equal Rights Amendment.

Constitutional Amendment on Marriage Won't Draw Drum-Beaters in Legislature

The Columbus Dispatch, March 1, 2004

If you think a constitutional amendment prohibiting same-sex marriages is going to be a slam-dunk, or even has a strong chance of passing, guess again.

Take Ohio, for example. The amendment to the U.S. Constitution proposed by President Bush already has the first strike against it in the Buckeye State, assuming it gets through Congress, which is no sure shot, either.

None other than the chief sponsor of Ohio's recently enacted Defense of Marriage law, Rep. William J. Seitz, says a constitutional amendment is premature.

"This is like saying in 1972 that we needed a constitutional amendment to outlaw abortion," said the suburban Cincinnati Republican. "The (U.S. Supreme) Court didn't even rule on Roe vs. Wade until 1973."

Seitz thrives on details of the law. When he winds himself up and makes a froggy-voiced pitch to his colleagues in the House chamber, he casts an E. F. Hutton spell: everybody stops what they're doing and listens. It's a teaching moment.

Seitz made an impassioned plea for House Bill 272, defining marriage in Ohio as between one man and one woman. He said it was necessary to prevent same-sex couples from demanding legal recognition in Ohio through marriages solemnized in other states. A majority of lawmakers agreed.

A constitutional amendment is unnecessary, Seitz said last week. He said no case on discrimination against homosexual couples has reached the federal court system. Until the U.S. Supreme Court finds same-sex marriages constitutional and eligible for the same benefits accorded heterosexual marriages, the Constitution needn't be changed, he said.

However, Seitz said, if the high court rules in favor of gay couples, he'll be the first one to support a constitutional amendment.

Seitz might be gone from the legislature because of term limits by the time Bush's proposal gets to Ohio, if it ever does. But the state's experience with a similar constitutional amendment 30 years ago is worth exploring.

The issue of equal rights for women boiled over in the early 1970s, and states were passing laws to end discrimination in various phases of life, chiefly employment.

Congress passed the Equal Rights Amendment, prohibiting any discrimination on the basis of sex, and sent it out to the states to be ratified. Rep. Donna Pope, a Parma Republican, was the first to sponsor it in Ohio, in 1972. It went nowhere.

Separate resolutions were started in the House and Senate the following year. The Democrat-controlled House quickly adopted the one sponsored by Rep. Michael P. Stinziano, a Columbus Democrat. But there was resistance. It got 56 votes, just six more than required.

The Senate was a problem. There were three female senators, but one was against the Equal Rights Amendment. Many women thought they already had it over the men and were afraid of losing special status.

For example, they didn't want to be eligible for the military draft, and they feared they would lose their natural advantage in court when it came to alimony and child support. Just as large groups of women journeyed to the Statehouse to promote the amendment, there were protests by housewives, Catholic women and parent-teacher groups. Passions ran high on both sides.

One woman told the Senate committee the amendment would "violate the sanctity of the family" and cause domestic trouble. Sound familiar? Didn't we just hear about violating the sanctity of marriage?

Sen. Harry Meshel, a Youngstown Democrat, scoffed at such predictions. "Men will still scrub floors, work two jobs, wash dishes and drive the wife and children around," he said. "The ERA is just recognizing the dignity and individuality we all have as men and women." Well, OK. He was wrong about driving the wife and kids around.

The resolution actually was defeated in Senate committee, but Stinziano's version was resurrected and passed, 20-12, on Feb. 7, 1974. It took two years of struggle, and even then there were attempts to rescind. Ohio was the 33rd state to pass the amendment. Only two more passed it, not enough, and it died in 1982. Granted, the Bush amendment is about stopping something, which may be more popular than expanding people's rights. But it won't break any speed records on the legislative track.

Ohio voters passed a constitutional amendment banning the recognition of same-sex marriages in 2004, but it was basically ignored by government entities in extending benefits to same-sex couples.

■ ■

This column exemplifies how the post-term-limits, conservative legislature of the early 2000s frothed over hot-button issues at the expense of more substantive matters.

Gays, Guns, Lake Erie: Legislators Get Down to the People's Business

The Columbus Dispatch, December 15, 2003

Last Wednesday was a busy day for libertarians in the Ohio legislature. It was a day to get back to the times when men were men, and they married women, not other men.

They owned their piece of the land and, by God, the government folks better keep hands off. Cuz if they didn't, them property owners would get out their guns and chase 'em away.

Yep, the legislature turned back the hands of time—200 years in some cases—and reinforced each of those three great principles, all in the same day. In some ways, maybe it's about time. The debate over marriage is much ado about nothing. Some advertise it as the Defense of Marriage Act. Others see it as the Denial of Benefits Act.

House Bill 272, which cleared the Ohio House overwhelmingly, reinforces Ohio's policy that marriage, legally defined, is between a man and a woman. This is in case folks come in from other states and try to claim the government owes them the legal benefits of marriage from a same-sex union. It has nothing to do with religious rites but only nails down Ohio's law to avoid a Massachusetts-type situation. The Bay State has been ordered by a court to legalize same-sex marriages.

The benefits portion of House Bill 272 affects only employees of the state of Ohio and possibly state universities who are in same-sex or unmarried relationships. Local governments and private companies may continue to offer benefits to whomever they wish. But the state could refuse to pay survivorship benefits or grant child custody to an employee's domestic partner.

The bill still has to go through the Senate. Then it would go to Gov. Bob Taft, who would do something with it, but nobody could say what. Some thought they knew what Taft would do with House Bill 12, permitting Ohioans to carry concealed weapons, but they didn't. The libertarians got as close as they could to pleasing Taft with a version of the bill that cleared the House and Senate by wide margins, but the governor found fault and said he'll veto it.

That would invite legislators from the governor's own Republican Party to defy him and override the veto.

Proponents of the bill say it's their right to protect themselves and their families. Sen. Eric D. Fingerhut, a Cleveland Democrat, said the measure would deprive his wife of her right to know whether a gun-toter is passing through the neighborhood where their toddler is playing.

Fingerhut's point: If individuals carried openly, which they can, his wife would be able to move the child away from possible harm. What he didn't say is that someone might be walking through the neighborhood right now with a hidden gun. Somebody else might have contagious flu. How would she know when to move the child?

Perhaps the best theater was provided by Rep. Timothy J. Grendell, R-Chesterland, who was protecting landowners on the Lake Erie shore from the government. Actually, the government has been taking a strip of their land, leasing it back to them and taxing them. That's not what our forefathers envisioned, and House Bill 218 eliminated that.

But the state does have an interest in recreation along the shore, and Grendell's bill would reverse a 200-year-old doctrine of public right-of-way, according to the Ohio Environmental Council. Under the bill, the low-water mark of the lake will be where the state's ownership ends and the landowner's begins. He agreed that if the lake recedes enough, the resident could own land all the way to Canada.

But Grendell also laughingly pointed out that if the water rises, the public may be able to fish in the property owners' basements.

The unasked question: Shouldn't these people who are so concerned with protecting a five-foot strip of land in their back yard be cooperating with the state on an erosion-control program? If the lake continues to eat away at their property, they won't have any left to protect.

It does lawmakers good to exercise their brains and jaw muscles over some of the classic issues involving individual rights instead of the normal fare of naming a portion of a highway after Drew Carey or declaring the turnip the state vegetable.

Now, if we can get two men to get married while wading in Lake Erie and carrying concealed handguns, maybe we can have a legal test of all this.

Ohio voters adopted a constitutional amendment declaring that marriage is between a man and a woman. The legislature passed a law permitting concealed weapons to be carried by qualified individuals. And in 2008, voters adopted a constitutional amendment affirming private property rights bordering public waterways.

■ ■

Ten Commandments Debate Brought Out Best in Lawmakers

The Columbus Dispatch, May 24, 1999

There's an old saying that when there's nothing to debate, the legislature will debate about nothing. Periodically, lawmakers will flap their gums over whether to make the Scioto snail the official state mollusk or to designate Rt. 44 between Cow's Tail and West Handkerchief the "Cootie Edgar Memorial Highway."

So when Rep. Dennis Stapleton of Washington Court House brought House Concurrent Resolution 17 to the floor last week, the alarm went off: Prepare for Out-of-Control Pontificating!

It seems that the Ohio Valley Local School District in Adams County built four new high schools, and a local ministerial association paid for marble tablets inscribed with the Ten Commandments to be placed near the entrance to each school.

Now, the school board has been sued by the American Civil Liberties Union, which wants the tablets removed because they bring religion to the schoolroom door.

Stapleton's resolution expresses the legislature's support, understanding and sympathy to the school board members in their legal battle.

A waste of time? An unnecessary intrusion into a local matter? Some legislators thought so. But others believed they had a right, even a duty, to weigh in for God and the school board.

To their credit, the lawmakers expressed themselves in a courteous and civil manner during the 50 minutes of debate. Passions were high, yet respect was shown for everyone's opinion as the resolution was endorsed, 81-15.

On the surface, it seemed foolish. Why should the Ohio House of Representatives stick its nose into an Adams County issue, especially since it can't affect the outcome?

Rep. Bryan C. Williams, R-Akron, who supported the resolution, conceded the court case probably will be lost.

Rep. Ann Womer Benjamin, R-Aurora, called it a "feelgood measure" and termed it "meddling." She chided the resolution's supporters who are constantly carping at the government for usurping parental rights. They should oppose government intervention this time, she said.

Rep. Peter Lawson Jones, D-Shaker Heights, said no one could argue with the value of the Ten Commandments, but he asked his colleagues to think about others who might be different.

"For a moment," said Jones, "let us put ourselves in the shoes of somebody . . . who might be a Muslim . . . or a Buddhist . . . or a Hindu." Jones said such people might feel alienated. They might feel like outsiders. Sound familiar? Where have we heard these words in the last few weeks?

Pushed to extremes, don't outsiders sometimes snap and do things that result in blood, death and tears? Is it worth going out of our way to provoke such alienation?

For Stapleton and others, the principle was the important thing. Higher even than the Constitution is the law of God, provided in the Ten Commandments. "Without the Ten Commandments, there's no power in that document," said Rep. Ron Young, R-Painesville, referring to the Constitution.

Stapleton engaged in some hyperbole when he quoted a listener to talk-radio host Laura Schlessinger: "How could God allow what happened in Columbine High School?"

"God isn't allowed in school," was Schlessinger's answer.

The truth is, God is allowed in the schools in the person of each of the students, teachers, administrators, secretaries, custodians, cooks and bus drivers. Orchestrated prayer or meditation in school is not going to magically change young people, and it may cause alienation.

However, Stapleton and his ilk are correct that the Ten Commandments are excellent ideals to follow for any human being—Christian, Jew, Muslim, Buddhist or Hindu.

The teaching of ethics and moral principles in the schools would help young people build the kind of society longed for by everyone and remembered, perhaps not quite accurately, by those who love to look backward.

Oddly, as a microcosm of Ohio, the House was practicing what it preached, once the members got past skewering the ACLU and needling the home-schoolers. It was not the carnival atmosphere that accompanies a highly partisan debate on a social or economic issue. Members looked directly at each other and listened to each other. It was the somber atmosphere reserved for serious occasions, as when a member is censured for an ethical breach.

Rep. Priscilla D. Mead, R-Upper Arlington, thought the House debated the issue like a family. "It was as close to intimate as you can get on the floor of a public body," she said.

Outside City Hall in Reynoldsburg, the hometown of Speaker Jo Ann Davidson, is a tablet of a different sort—a plaque bearing The Reynoldsburg Compact of Respect.

Adopted as the result of a community effort, the compact calls for "treating all persons in ways that I would like them to treat me" and "recognizing that each person is different and has an individual contribution to make to the community."

Not the Ten Commandments, maybe, but it wouldn't look bad at a school, either.

The reference to outsiders and alienated individuals in the middle of the column relates to the two students who had murdered a number of their fellow students the previous month in Littleton, Colorado.

■ ■

Damschroder's Moment-Of-Silence Bill Shouts for Dismissal

The Columbus Dispatch, October 29, 2001

Among the rash of new bills at the Statehouse to crack down on terrorists, punish hoaxers and promote patriotism is one that stands atop Mount Daffy.

Rep. Rex Damschroder wants to allow public schools to have a moment of silence in the classroom each day for reflection or meditation. Lots of luck.

If teachers could get a moment of silence in their classrooms, they'd be more than happy to use it for teaching. Then maybe some learning would take place, and we wouldn't be hearing these awful stories about how badly Ohio's public-school students lag their counterparts elsewhere.

That said, Ohio law already allows classroom teachers to set aside a period for meditation upon a moral, philosophical or patriotic theme. It does not require pupils to participate. So, what good does Damschroder's bill do?

The Fremont Republican's bill also prohibits schools from forcing students to participate in the moment of silence. Does that mean they would be allowed to disrupt it by making noise?

Lawmakers of Damschroder's stripe have gotten about as close as they can to restoring prayer in public schools without violating the Constitution.

Tinkering with the existing moment of silence or meditation program only may invite a lawsuit that would suspend the program. They would do better to turn their creative genius to other areas of social concern.

■ ■

Conservatives' Affinity for Divisive Issues Stymies All Other Work

The Columbus Dispatch, December 13, 2004

Single-issue politics, combined with term limits, have poisoned the well at the Ohio Statehouse. Conservatives have chafed through the years at the growth of government, the handcuffs placed on businesses, the moral decline of society and the independence of jurists who seem always to take the liberal view.

When Republicans took complete control of the Statehouse in 1995, they exercised a caution befitting their fragile mandate. Conservatives moved into positions of leadership, but they controlled their zealots, fearing the majority could be reversed.

Former Rep. Jim Buchy, a Greenville Republican and a principled conservative, put it best back then. "We're keeping them in their baskets," he said, likening the arch-conservatives to frisky puppies.

Republicans pursued a moderate agenda. They slowed the growth of government under Gov. George V. Voinovich. They enacted a policy designed to get Ohioans off the welfare rolls and into productive jobs, or at least into school or training programs.

Then some conservatives grew more restless, wanting their piece of the pie. House Speaker Larry Householder, after holding them at bay for much of the 2001-02 session, had to lengthen the leash gradually.

He and then-Senate President Richard H. Finan had to listen to the conservatives in their caucus and to allow them to influence legislation, and with good reason. People who get elected should be allowed to reflect the feelings of their districts in the policies that are developed.

Long-awaited legislation permitting Ohioans to carry concealed handguns became law after thorough debate. Householder allowed conservatives to tear apart Gov. Bob Taft's proposed budget and find the fat.

Now, the conservatives have become emboldened to the point where they are enforcing a litmus test: If you aren't against abortion, for gun rights, against taxes and against recognizing gay marriages, you are the enemy.

These may be important issues, but they are also inflammatory. They incite passions. Ohioans came out to vote in November, in part because of a red-hot presidential race and in part because they could weigh in on the issue of homosexual marriages.

Much of government is far less exciting. It's about providing services to help people with their everyday lives. It's about schools, jobs, roads, safety and health. It's about shielding citizens from the excesses of capitalism by regulating utilities, banks, insurance companies and various professional practices. It's about protecting the environment.

Well-rounded public officials are concerned with the big picture. They realize that extremists don't have the best answers. Capitalism is good when allowed to work, and when its practitioners don't get greedy and abuse it. Government should have a light touch unless the public interest is being ignored.

Republicans controlling the legislature have vowed to set priorities early next year as they deal with a budget that is underfunded by close to $5 billion. They say they will evaluate what government can be expected to do and what Ohioans are willing to pay for.

Good! This is public policymaking at its best. It's the big picture. What services do people want and what will they pay for them?

But the questions would be best debated by public officials who take the long view, listen to others and evaluate on a basis other than their own narrow interests. Unfortunately, some legislators would rather traffic in hot-button issues where everything is either black or white, and they represent the white. These issues lend themselves to simplistic solutions.

Because legislators are term-limited, these issues are right up their alley; they don't have time to deal with the complex issues, especially when the next election always seems to be right around the corner.

Constant chatter about the hot-button issues frequently pits one legislator against another, one group against another. The body of the legislature becomes fractured.

People wonder why the legislature is divided when Republicans control it all. This is why: It's hard to come together on extreme views. When public officials air extreme views, it's hard for them to come together and solve real problems.

Perhaps the new regime in GOP leadership will be struck by the holiday spirit and return in January with some of it. If not, 2005 could be a long and bitter year.

Post-mortem: Republicans lost the governor's office in the 2006 election because their candidate was too polarizing; they lost the House of Representatives in the 2008 election. The party began an internal debate over whether to focus on broader issues.

Chapter 4 The Good, the Bad and the Ugly

The following nine columns concern three poignant stories of individuals or situations, three examples of the "deals" that are cut at the Statehouse, and three stories about the "pay-to-play" environment in the 1980s and early '90s.

The Good

Hal Hovey Was One Special Bureaucrat

United Press International, January 5, 1973

COLUMBUS (UPI)—State government personnel rolls are replete with the names of employees qualified for mediocrity who put in their eight hours a day programmed hopelessly into a routine of the way it's always been done.

They are supervised by politicians who spend their time calculating their next move toward higher appointive or elected office.

This is why it is doubly sad for Ohio government that state Finance Director Harold A. Hovey, having worked himself out of job, is departing to become budget director of Illinois.

Hovey joined the administration of Gov. John J. Gilligan in 1971. He was 32, and his job seemed insurmountable. Some people laughed and said they sent a boy to do a man's job.

Hovey was faced with upgrading Ohio's multi-billion dollar budget and writing an acceptable tax package to finance it. This included the unenviable task of asking a reluctant General Assembly to enact the state's first personal income tax.

The young director did his job. His personal appearances in the legislative halls won points for the administration. Much of the budget-tax package was approved, and Hovey brought in talented young people to operate the state's appropriations machinery.

So last week, at 34, Hovey was literally washed up in Ohio government. He had nothing more to offer. "I went out to Illinois for a few days to help the new Democratic administration get set up," Hovey said in the Statehouse pressroom as he explained his resignation.

"When I came back, I realized it hadn't made any difference that I was gone," the director said. Everything worked without me. When they first offered me the job in Illinois, I said I wasn't interested. It would be hard, and I had it so easy now in Ohio. Then I realized I needed the challenge. I am basically crisis-oriented, and there's no longer any crisis in Ohio."

Hovey took a sheet of paper and began to draw parallel lines across it, one at the top and one at the bottom.

"When you first come to state government, your ability is way down here," he said, "and the opportunity for doing things for the people of the state is way up here." He pointed to the top line.

"As time goes by, these lines start to converge. You get better at your job, but the decisions you make seem to lock you in on a set path, and the chances of making changes become less and less."

Hovey drew the lines diagonally toward the middle of the paper.

"Then you hire talented people, and they begin to make important contributions, cutting down still further on your own usefulness."

Hovey drew some lines converging inside the original ones to make what looked like a pair of scissors.

"Finally, you reach a point where you are standing still." The lines met in the center. "That's where I am now. At the point where these lines cross, you're really not having any input at all. I am literally a bureaucrat who has worked himself out of a job."

Harold Hovey, a college graduate at 19, regarded as a genius in some quarters, so apolitical that he was not even a registered voter, let alone a Democrat, when he joined the administration.

His savvy on public finance probably saved Gilligan's fiscal program from total destruction in the legislature, and now he was packing up and moving to Illinois as casually as one would cross the street.

"Nice working with you fellows," called Hovey as he vanished from the pressroom.

James Leckrone, one of Hovey's deputies, was asked later what state government could do to hang onto valuable public servants. "Not a damn thing that I know of," lamented Leckrone.

If Hovey were to have drawn lines on the paper representing typical government, it would have been a circle, or perhaps a revolving door with no exit.

Hal Hovey, a longtime smoker with incurable cancer, checked out of life at age 60 in the same analytical way he had managed Ohio's budget. He studied books on cancer and calculated the cost of treatment. Then, having no health insurance by choice, he took the money he would have spent on his own care and established a fund. Proceeds from the fund were to cover non-medical costs such as transportation and child care for cancer patients 16 to 25 years old and for children up to age 19 suffering other chronic illnesses. Then he committed suicide.

The Hovey Fund is administered by the Candler Foundation in Savannah, Ga.

■ ■

Legislator Seeks Better Conditions for the Mentally Retarded

United Press International, October 9, 1977

COLUMBUS (UPI)—"My parents put me here," said Jim, a teenager chowing down on a meal of hamburger, French fries and stewed tomatoes at Orient State Institute last week.

"Where do your parents live?" inquired a visitor.

"Somewheres," he mumbled vacantly and resumed eating.

Jim, who is mentally retarded, was one of the few Orient residents able to communicate even vaguely with visiting newsmen, state legislators, and county mental health officials.

And he offered only faint clues as to what life is like for patients inside the state's largest institution for the mentally retarded.

The rest of the evidence must come from the employees and supervisors, or from what meets the eye when the doors are opened to outsiders. It is not pleasant.

Orient State Institute, which dates back to the 1800s and has some buildings 70 years old, is a sprawling 600-acre facility nestled in the hills of Pickaway County a few furlongs from Scioto Downs, southwest of Columbus.

Near the main road to Orient is a tavern which advertises "last chance" for beer. Traveling to the institution, it is truly the last chance for some 2,000 residents.

Many are severely and profoundly retarded, unable to be taught to perform even the most basic of personal living habits. They will never leave the institute alive and even if they did, they would require almost round-the-clock individual attention which their families apparently were unable or unwilling to give them.

So they spend their days sitting in chairs in dayrooms at the 50-year old "cottages" which resemble low dormitories or barracks. Many do not respond to anything going on around them. Some are diverted by constantly playing color television sets.

Those that can move wander idly about. The trainable residents are singled out for basic instruction at the pre-school level. A few are able to learn to perform menial tasks, such as counting bed sheets or cleaning dining facilities.

There is not enough hired help to look after patients, mop the floors, clean the latrines and wash the windows.

The workers seem pleasant and dedicated, but they are also frustrated. Some are in charge of several dozen residents at a time by themselves. They can do nothing except go from one to another.

There are flies and "boiling heat" in the summer, according to one employee, and chilling temperatures in the winter. Conditions are livable, but barely.

Near the cottages is the new $3.6 million health center, where the poor souls with medical as well as physical and mental deformities are attended. They receive more individual care in nicer surroundings than the majority of residents. Callous as it may seem, it is almost better to be sick.

The Rhodes administration is attempting to funnel more money into capital construction at OSI, to replace the ancient dormitories and improve living conditions.

State Sen. J. Timothy McCormack, D-Euclid, who arranged last week's tour, wants more of the residents moved to smaller community-based facilities.

The "Jims" of Orient may someday find a home in a community mental health center. But for those consigned to OSI for the rest of their lives, luxuriant conditions are a waste.

What they need are basically comfortable and clean facilities, nutritious food and attendants to look after them.

Orient is 1,700 below the desirable number of employees. The wisest investment for the state would seem to be raising pay scales and hiring enough people to do the often-thankless work.

■ ■

Oliver Ocasek: Big Man Left a Bigger Legacy of Helping Kids

The Columbus Dispatch, July 12, 1999

On the morning of June 27, about 130 people gathered on a sun-splashed green in the middle of the Monongahela National Forest near Parson, W.Va. Birds twittered and the American flag waved, with the Allegheny Mountains as a backdrop.

Young campers at the YMCA's Camp Horseshoe were there to celebrate with song, prayer and scripture the life of Oliver Ocasek, who had died just hours earlier at 73.

To Ohioans familiar with politics and government, Ocasek was a former state Senate leader from the Akron area. There was a time when he helped make the wheels of government turn.

To the campers, he was a faithful counselor who listened to them—listened to them—and tried to impart his recipe for living.

Ocasek begged adults in his final, cancer-riddled months to pay attention to young people and nurture them because they are the hope of the future. Were there more Oliver Ocaseks, there might be fewer Littletons.

As chairman of Ohio's Hi-Y Youth in Government program for 25 years, Ocasek came in contact with 11,500 bright teen-agers who visited the Statehouse to participate in a model legislature. He made government come alive for them and urged them to get involved. He said they could make a difference.

Another 1,500 youngsters received lessons in life from Ocasek over the years during the summer weeks he spent at the West Virginia camp. Sometimes, he'd leave camp at 4 A.M. for a meeting in Columbus, then return for the evening campfire and talent show.

David King, longtime director of the Hi-Y program in West Virginia, described the memorial in the forest glade.

Erica Campbell, a teen-ager from Cincinnati, gave the opening prayer and couldn't resist recounting what Ocasek meant to her in the two years she had known him.

Erica recalled that Ocasek would put on a beard and a burlap bag, carry a staff and play Father Time to remind the kids how fleeting time is and how they need to make something of themselves while they can.

Erica said Ocasek made her think about what she was doing with her life and how she could help her community. He challenged her and changed her life.

She read from the Book of Ecclesiastes: "There is a time for everything, and a season for every activity under heaven. A time to be born and a time to die."

Then Erica thought about Ocasek again.

"He's not here, but I am," King said she advised fellow mourners. "We've got to carry on and do the things he told us."

What Ocasek told the kids during his 50-year association with the Hi-Y program was to think about social responsibilities.

A bear of a man in his prime, Ocasek was a natural-born actor who preached good government in a loud, pedantic voice when he was on the political stage. With kids, he spoke quietly and earnestly. They were the children he and his beloved wife, Virginia, never had.

In Ohio, Ocasek moved in and around the Statehouse for almost 40 years, rubbing elbows with the great and the near-great. One time, he collaborated with the House speaker to block a powerful governor from delivering a State of the State address in the House chamber because he thought the governor would disparage the legislature.

At Camp Horseshoe, he was just Mr. Ocasek, taking delight in the activities, wearing an apron as he helped in the kitchen and appearing in camp skits, often as the foil for someone else.

Ocasek was a prime author of the formula that distributed the state's money to public schools. It was finally deemed inadequate by the courts, but schools made out better than they would have without Ocasek.

He had been in the Senate 16 years when he gained the leadership spot. In the "cleansing" following Watergate, he was the good-government guy overthrowing Sen. Anthony O. Calabrese, a Clevelander viewed as a practical politician and pal of the lobbyists.

After the 1980 Republican win, Ocasek got a taste of his own medicine. He was dumped by Sen. Harry Meshel of Youngstown because he didn't play the political game well enough.

But the political defeats suffered by Ocasek pale alongside the victories he scored with youngsters. At the end of May, Ocasek flew to Chicago to receive a lifetime achievement award, the highest that YMCA of the U.S.A. bestows. He had to be helped to his feet at the O'Hare Hilton, but he made an impassioned plea to his audience to listen to kids, to work with them and to get involved.

According to King, Ocasek said it's up to everyone to help young people focus on values and develop character, leadership and civic responsibility.

Then he talked about his dream for Hi-Y to have a leadership center in Ohio, just like Camp Horseshoe in West Virginia. At his death, he was helping the Y acquire 700 acres for the camp at Cave Lake in Pike County. There will be room for 30,000 young people to pass through each year.

"He liked to think big," said King.

The reference to "fewer Littletons" is to the shooting rampage by two troubled teens at a high school in Littleton, Colorado in April 1999.

■ ■

The Bad

The next three columns are about "deals"—a staple in the political world. Some work out, some don't. These were classics.

Collins-Wilkowski: The Ultimate in Tag-Team Backscratching

United Press International, July 26, 1975

COLUMBUS (UPI)—Backscratching is a common pastime in the Ohio General Assembly. It crosses party lines and knows no race, creed or station in life.

One political favor deserves another, and the name of the game is to get them done. Everybody's happy.

Usually the backscratching is difficult to detect. It's conceived in hallways and hotel rooms, behind closed office doors or in the recesses of cocktail bars. And it's carried off in a series of seemingly unrelated actions, often camouflaged in a web of parliamentary maneuvers.

That's why observers did a double-take last week when they saw, in broad daylight, what appeared to be the consummation of a backscratch involving two most unlikely pals—Rep. Arthur R. Wilkowski, D-Toledo, and Sen. Oakley C. Collins, R-Ironton.

Here's what happened:

Wilkowski, an urban-area liberal, had a master plan for developing a rapid transit system in Ohio, including an intercity rail line through his hometown.

Collins, a rural area conservative, was interested in a bill eliminating the ban on legislators receiving pay for other public jobs, say, Lawrence County school superintendent, to which he has been appointed.

What to do?

Wilkowski and Collins are two men who like to get things done, so they cheerfully went about each other's business.

The Toledo Democrat carried the "Collins Bill" through the House. It cleared the Senate and was quickly signed by Gov. James A. Rhodes.

Collins' wish was fulfilled, but he soon showed he is not one to forget a friend.

Wilkowski ran into trouble with a constitutional amendment aiming to permit the state to finance his rail plan. The proposal was defeated in the House in April when Republicans maintained it would put the state into the railroad business.

It was finally reworked, sent through the House and over to the Senate, where it cleared the Transportation Committee.

Normally, majority Democrats manage their House colleagues' bills on the Senate floor, making sure they are properly explained and claiming part of the credit.

Not this time.

Who popped to his feet to carry Wilkowski's rail resolution but Oakley Collins, fully prepared to defend it to the death.

Collins said that unless the constitutional change was made before next February, Ohio would lose $18 million worth of federal money to rebuild the railroads, grain and coal would have no way to market and industrial development would come to a grinding halt.

He even brandished a letter saying that Rhodes had "no objection" to the proposal, despite the fact that the governor prefers an alternative rail plan and hopes to clear the November ballot for his bond issues.

Collins' floor leader, Sen. Michael J. Maloney, R-Cincinnati, cringed at the performance, muttering that the constitutional amendment would get Ohio into a "bottomless pit" of operating bankrupt railroads and that $18 million was "not enough to lay track from here to Chillicothe."

"Suppose next year the auto industry gets in trouble?" growled Maloney. "Do we subsidize them, too?"

Shortly thereafter, the resolution passed handily. Collins went to the rear of the Senate chamber, where he was clapped on the back by a smiling Wilkowski. The pair shook hands and Collins, grinning broadly, flashed a clenched fist.

Both later denied passage of the Collins bill and the Wilkowski resolution had any link.

Truth was, said one knowledgeable source who declined to be named, Collins was merely returning a two-year old favor performed when Wilkowski inserted an amendment into a pay raise bill for state legislators.

Either way, it made great copy! Collins and Wilkowski were two of the best practitioners of "the deal." Separate columns elsewhere in the book contain more about these colorful lawmakers. Maloney's logic near the end of the column recalls the federal bailouts of 2008-09. Wilkowski never did get his high-speed rail line.

■ ■

Whether it's drawing lines for the legislature or Congress, you couldn't make this stuff up.

Bizarre Districts Serve One Purpose: Re-Election

The Columbus Dispatch, March 9, 1992

There's a new smash drama in New York featuring two blue-skinned men who act out social commentary on a sparsely appointed stage. One of them holds up a small canvas, ceremoniously spits paint on it and calls it art.

Apparently state legislative leaders did this in a closet one dark night last week. Only they used a map of Ohio and called the result congressional redistricting.

That's the only way to explain the new U.S. House districts, which feature assorted zigzags and curlicues. The plan divides counties, and honors communities of interest as if joining Eskimos with Cajuns.

Consider the shape of these districts:

- The 6th District, occupied by Republican Rep. Bob McEwen of Hillsboro, looks like a huge, curved smoking pipe. It starts in the Dayton suburbs and goes through a slim corridor on the Warren-Clinton county line, then through another narrow pass on the Highland-Brown county line. It goes through Pike County and then balloons over much of southeastern Ohio, traveling as far north as Muskingum County, only two counties away from the eastern Ohio border.
- South of the 6th is the 2nd District, occupied by Republican Rep. Willis D. Gradison Jr. This district connects the eastern half of Hamilton County with the northwest corner of the county by a slim bridge, about two cornfields wide, across the top of the county. The rest of the county is in another district.
- The 18th District, occupied by Democratic Rep. Douglas Applegate of Steubenville, runs from Sea World, near Cleveland, through a narrow passage one township wide in Mahoning County, and then almost to Marietta.
- Rep. Michael Oxley, R-Findlay, if he wins again, will represent the people of Lima and Zanesville, two-thirds of Ohio apart.
- Rep. David L. Hobson, R-Springfield, will have Marysville, the eastern suburbs of Dayton and Lancaster.

Unfortunately, architects didn't spit the paint on the map. They might have gotten more sensible districts. Instead, they painstakingly drew the lines using census data, calculators and books full of political notes telling them whether people vote Democrat or Republican.

They tried to put 570,901 residents in every district and accommodate 17 congressmen and one congresswoman. They did not try to accommodate Republican Rep. Clarence E. Miller of Lancaster or two retiring Democratic congressmen. "You cannot please everybody in congressional redistricting," said House Speaker Vernal G. Riffe Jr., D-Wheelersburg, a key player in the drawing exercise.

By law, the mapmakers must draw districts of equal population and combine minority communities where possible. The rest of the mischief was caused by political backscratching, ambition and money.

Why? Because those who drew the maps allowed it. No law says the mapmakers have to listen to Congress members, but one of the early agreements was that incumbents in both parties would be protected.

Senate President Pro Tempore Richard H. Finan, R-Cincinnati, has negotiated some of the most complex issues in the state legislature, involving taxation, workers' compensation and waste recycling. Redistricting, he said, was the worst.

"In my 20 years (in the legislature) this has been the most frustrating project the leader has ever asked me to get involved in," said the co-chairman of the conference committee that produced the map.

The reason is that Finan and the other negotiators were harassed constantly by incumbents wanting favorable territory so they could win again, and again and again, without breaking a sweat. And the legislators listened to them.

Sen. Paul E. Pfeifer, R-Bucyrus, said it best. "When the whole process revolves around protecting everyone," he said, "it's like these districts are pieces of property in which the incumbents have a perpetual and permanent (interest) that they can somehow claim and pass on to the next generation."

The districts are even identified by the Congress member's name, in the possessive form, by the news media.

If it's not the incumbent being protected, it's the next in line of succession. There was plenty of talk about carving out a district that a Democratic or Republican heir could win in the future.

But the most cynical line-drawing of all was done not for votes but for money. Remember the mouth of McEwen's pipestem in suburban Dayton and Warren County? He had to have those areas because that's where his campaign funds come from. There aren't too many monied folk over in the Appalachian part of the district.

And up in Cleveland, Reps. Louis Stokes and Mary Rose Oakar pitched a battle over downtown Cleveland, dividing up city blocks including Tower City, BP America, National City Bank, Gateway, Playhouse Square and Erieview Tower.

How come? Not for the votes of the homeless people who might huddle in the doorways or sleep nearby. Nope. For the right to solicit the suits inside those buildings for campaign donations.

And you wondered why there are lifetime terms in Congress?

The blue-skinned mimes referred to in the opening line obviously turned out to be Blue Man Group, now a famous traveling act featured on television.

For those unfamiliar with Ohio geography, all but one of the districts cited stretched more than halfway across the state. Narrow corridors helped link the desired territory while complying with the equal-population requirement.

This was a bipartisan exercise. When one party controls the governor's office and both legislative chambers, the minority gets nothing. But then the majority squabbles within its own ranks.

Under the 1990 Census, Ohio lost representation. In such a case, those controlling the process decide which district will be absorbed into the others. Clarence Miller, a longtime conservative Republican congressman, was chosen to be sacrificed. He had to run in McEwen's district and he lost in the primary. Miller's cries of foul play went unheeded and he took the Legislature to court. He lost again and was forced to retire.

■ ■

Y2speakers: Agreement May Get the Bugs Out

The Columbus Dispatch, January 17, 2000

In the early 1960s, Philip K. Wrigley, owner of the Chicago Cubs, decided to replace his field manager with eight coaches having equal authority. The "College of Coaches" never worked well and was abandoned before the Cubs finally contended for the National League pennant in 1969.

Now, Ohio House Republicans are trying team management as they head into 2001, when four of their six leaders will disappear, including Speaker Jo Ann Davidson of Reynoldsburg, the glue holding the caucus together.

It's an experiment brought about by term limitations.

"Some of you may think we're presumptuous," Davidson conceded last week, as the caucus leaders announced that Reps. Bill Harris of Ashland and Larry Householder of Glenford agreed to put down their spears and shields and split the speakership in 2001-02.

Capitol observers never had seen anything like it: a legislative caucus making a spectacle of its internal doings. But then, Ohioans never have seen legislative term limits, either. It's doing strange things to the political landscape.

Yes, the Republicans are presumptuous that both future speakers will win re-election and the GOP will retain control of the House in 2001, so that Harris can be speaker for a year and Householder can take over in January 2002. But not too presumptuous. Maybe they're just planning carefully.

The real questions echoing through the Statehouse Atrium last week were: "Will the agreement stick?" "Can the team concept work?"

At first blush, the Harris-Householder pact appeared to have roughly the life expectancy of a plan for the 6-year-old Cuban boy Elian Gonzalez.

Most veteran lobbyists were tongue-tied when asked whether the agreement would hold. They either don't know or they were afraid their opinion would offend. Dennis L. Wojtanowski, an influential lobbyist and former House member, offered a cautious assessment: "If they (the Republican leaders) took the temperature (of Republican House candidates) around the state, it could very well hold up.

"The long-term question is, 'Will this become the prototype for future leadership?'"

Term limits mean most future speakers will have no more prior House experience than two terms, and they'll be lucky to be speaker for more than one session. Turnover will be common.

The office of speaker will be weakened, and perhaps leadership by committee will become the rule rather than the exception.

In announcing the Harris-Householder truce, Davidson pointed out that since 1995, she has not been a dictator but a team leader, so Harris and Householder are no strangers to that concept.

The test will come after the November elections when Harris and Householder see who their fellow GOP members are, especially those from the 25 open districts that are apt to send Republicans to Columbus.

Might one or the other see an opportunity to abandon the agreement and grab for the two-year term each originally wanted? After all, the real vote for speaker is not until after the elections and new members are seated in 2001.

Nuking the agreement could produce a caucus of smoldering rubble and a rare opening for Democrats.

"Larry might end up having to run for minority leader in 2002," said one lobbyist, referring to Householder's plan to be speaker in 2002, 2003 and 2004, as long as the GOP keeps the majority.

Davidson deliberately announced the truce in a highly visible arena, so all could see. Curse the individual who breaks the agreement.

"The words they spoke today, they'll have to live by," predicted Rep. Gregory Jolivette, R-Hamilton. "Communication will be the key."

A major reason for the truce was to give lobbyists, who provide money for the campaigns, some assurance of who will benefit from their donations.

They hesitated to contribute to Davidson, because she will not be there next session. Donating to either Householder or Harris carried 50 percent odds. If they guessed wrong, too bad. So the agreement, in Davidson's words, provides a certain amount of "continuity and predictability."

"It gives them a line of succession," she said.

Davidson also could foresee intraparty warfare, breaking along the traditional lines of conservatives vs. moderates. She has spent five years mediating that dispute. She said there was "absolutely" a danger that the Harris-Householder split would damage the caucus. "We went a long way to assuring that we will be able to operate as we have," she said.

Rep. Gary Cates, R-West Chester, who believes Householder could have won the battle and hoped he would, summed up the compromise:

"Anybody who comes to Columbus expecting to get their way all the time is not going to be very successful."

The agreement to share the speakership during the 2001-02 session did not hold up. Working below the surface, Householder secured enough votes to win the job outright after the 2000 election. He served two terms as speaker. Harris was appointed to a vacant Senate seat and went on to become Senate president in 2005.

Householder's successor, Republican Rep. Jon A. Husted of suburban Dayton, was anointed well in advance, but an attempt to install fellow Daytonian Jeff Jacobson as Senate president in 2005 was short-circuited by Harris. In 2009, Democratic Rep. Armond Budish of suburban Cleveland was named speaker after serving only one term in the House!

■ ■

The Ugly

Rose Goes Where Few Dare to Tread; Hints at Dem Extortion

United Press International, February 17, 1984

COLUMBUS (UPI)—Like Jack, the giant-killer, state Rep. W. Bennett Rose, R-Lima, came forth last week talking about what insiders have known for a good while but are afraid to say out loud—that Democrats controlling the Statehouse are shaking money from lobbyists like leaves off the trees.

Only Rose gave it some new names. He called it bribery, extortion and intimidation and said it ought to be punished by law.

Pretty heavy stuff for an assistant minority leader whose receding hairline has been a figurative target for the gavel of House Speaker Vernal G. Riffe Jr., D-New Boston.

Oh, Rose didn't mention Riffe by name. He talked theoretically about "a speaker in the year 2000, maybe it could be me." But everyone knew who he meant, and the way things are going, Riffe and the speaker in 2000 might be the same.

The Democrats have grown wealthy through contributions to the Ohio Democratic Party, to Gov. Richard F. Celeste's campaign arm, and to Riffe's money committees.

But everyone within shouting distance of the Statehouse concedes that Riffe is the premier fund-raiser around, and the figures prove it. He can raise a quarter-million dollars by staging a birthday party for himself, or a celebration of his longevity record for being speaker of the Ohio House.

The next event is a leap-year party on Feb. 29—it comes only once every four years, so ante up accordingly.

Three Riffe fund-raising committees already have $375,000 posted for the 1984 legislative elections, and they've just begun!

What Rose finds invidious is the fact that the Democrats seem to be making the government's business a function of campaign donations.

There is an understanding on the part of lobbyists that their bills will pass or fail depending on whether they contribute to the cause, whether it be the Democratic coffers or to the defeat of statewide ballot issues, like Issue 3, repeal of the income tax increase.

This can be done because the Democrats have such total domination in the Statehouse. It can be done by the Celeste administration, it can be done by majority Democrats in the Senate and it can be done by Riffe.

Riffe's reputation as a strong speaker is undeniable. He has been quoted as saying: "Nothing moves around here unless I say it does."

The lobbyists know this. The lobbyists friendly to Democrats know it, so they contribute to stay in good with the speaker. The neutral lobbyists know it. They contribute to keep up with the others.

And the Republican-oriented lobbyists have been made painfully aware that if they don't join the parade, they'll be frozen out of the action with no recourse.

The ironic thing is that the same things would happen if all this money weren't pouring in: The Democrats would work their will. The money merely allows the Democrats to perpetuate themselves in office.

And so when Rose mentioned bribery, extortion and intimidation last week in connection with the current situation at the Statehouse, and urged victims to "Have the courage to step forward," he was invited to give some specific examples. Rose demurred, saying someone might get in trouble.

When Riffe found out about Rose's charges, his face reddened "If he said that about me, he's a damn liar," said Riffe, putting on his best speaker's scowl.

As luck would have it, Rose was nearby, and Riffe challenged a reporter to find out just who he meant.

So, with the two standing side-by-side, Rose's charges were repeated. Was he referring to Riffe?

"No," said Rose.

"See?" said Riffe.

There were looks of amusement. It's not easy dealing with a giant without a little humor.

It took another 10 years, but all this led to a scandal that toppled the Democrats, as described in an upcoming column. See also columns on the abuses of one-party rule.

■ ■

Ohio Senate Panel's Hair-Splitting Ruling Puts a Price Tag on Government

The Columbus Dispatch, May 9, 1994

In an 18-page hair-splitting opinion issued last week, a group of state senators effectively brushed off charges that financial consideration plays a part in the way the people's business is done at the Statehouse.

The Senate Legislative Ethics Committee cleared of legal violations all fellow senators who accepted honorariums for attending a pair of events sponsored by lobbyists in 1993.

One of those senators, Eugene Watts of Galloway, was mailed his check because he couldn't be at the June seminar held in Columbus by Cleveland-based McDonald & Co. Securities. He also received checks from three different lobbyists at a May get-together at the German Village home of lobbyist Paul Tipps.

The three Republican and three Democrats on the Ethics Committee said their colleagues violated neither the law nor the Senate code of ethics at the time. They said, however, that Watts was "careless" to deposit his $500 check and give McDonald its money back only when reminded seven months later that he hadn't been at the event.

The opinion was technically correct. But the tortuous path leading to the conclusion indicates that the committee was groping for a way to let its fellow senators off the hook.

The opinion puts the matter to bed just in time for next Thursday's inauguration of a Joint Legislative Ethics Committee and new ethics rules. What's past is past. Let bygones be bygones.

There can be no question that in 1993, honorariums, or speaking fees, were legal for state legislators. The lawmakers had to report annually on the receipt of any honorariums exceeding $500. This is why a $500 speaking fee was so standard.

Janet Lewis of Common Cause/Ohio believes certain kinds of honorariums amount to bribery or improper compensation, that is, a salary supplement for a legislator performing his or her official duties.

Lewis also said honorariums are illegal when they are given by an individual or organization "doing business with or seeking to do business with" a government agency, in this case the legislature.

Lewis's citations did not apply in these cases, said the ethics panel, but it arrived at that conclusion only after a semantic struggle.

The committee said that when the General Assembly rewrote the ethics law in 1986, it carefully constructed the law so proper honorariums could not be considered bribery.

For bribery to occur, the committee said, there must be a purpose or intent to corrupt or improperly influence the legislator in the discharge of his or her duties. The term "improperly" was underscored, leaving room for "proper" influence.

So to commit bribery, the committee said, the public official would have to "knowingly" accept something of value in return for a direct result in the performance of his or her duties.

"Making a speech, presentation or appearance at a private event or function is not, as a matter of law, among the official duties of a senator," the panel wrote. "In the case of the McDonald seminar, there is not a single fact to suggest that a single element of a bribery offense was present."

What are the official duties of a state legislator? The Ethics Committee said they consist of introducing and voting on bills and amendments, attending committee meetings and going to floor sessions.

Any normal legislator would fall down laughing at that limp definition. Most hours in a lawmaker's day are spent directing staff work, talking to constituents and responding to their complaints and, yes, listening to lobbyists. So appearances at seminars, free or for pay, are part of a state senator's job.

The ethics panel overruled Lewis's contention that McDonald was doing business with the legislature when the honorariums were passed out.

"McDonald, an investment banking firm, was not regulated by, doing business with, or seeking to do business with, the General Assembly," the panel wrote. "A general interest in bills and resolutions pending before the General Assembly does not constitute 'doing business with' . . . the General Assembly. Although registered with the Joint Committee on Agency Rule Review . . . McDonald had no interest in any legislation pending before the General Assembly in 1993."

Oh, no?

House Resolution 6, a $200 million parks and recreation bond issue, was one piece of legislation that might have captured the interest of an investment banking firm.

Records show that proposal passed the House on June 24, 1993, and the Senate on June 30. The McDonald receptions for representatives and senators were June 22-23. The conclusion is yours.

Legal wordsmiths notwithstanding, the gears at the Statehouse are well lubricated by good fellowship and money, sometimes for results but always for opportunity.

To construct such a strained defense for fellow lawmakers is to continue to feed the idea that it's OK for good government to have a price tag attached.

Ten years earlier, a prominent Republican lawmaker alluded to possible bribery in the pay-to-play system, as referenced in the previous column.

CAMPAIGN = COMPETE; GOVERN = COOPERATE

Politicking and governing are two different things. Smart elected officials know when it's time to quit the campaign and get down to the business of governing. But some can't get out of the campaign mode, often to their detriment.

This column shows what happens when campaigning is the end game. The best legislation often happens when lawmakers put away their campaign toys and work with each other. It is tempting to carry on the campaign. But mature officials know when the election is over. They reach out to the other side and try to forge agreements, sometimes on complex legislation. When politicians harp on inflammatory single issues, you know that nothing very constructive is going to get done.

Election Likely Didn't Put End to Brawls in the Legislature

The Columbus Dispatch, November 11, 2002

Picture, if you will, the grizzled cowpoke who has just been thrown crashing through the swinging saloon doors, landing in a heap on the dirt street. He struggles to his feet, clutching his midsection, which bears a bootprint. He spits blood and a couple of teeth, readjusts his nose, wipes some grit from his forehead, whaps the dust out of his hat, puts it on and limps back into the saloon.

There to welcome him is his tormentor, a large, muscular cowboy with huge hands and a face of granite. What to do? Does the crippled cowpoke take a punch? Offer to shake hands? Just stand there? Turn and run?

Such is the dilemma of Democratic state legislators. It could be either House members or senators, but for purposes of our discussion, the beaten-up cowpoke will represent the House Democrats and the muscular ranch-hand will represent the House Republicans.

Hours after the thrashing, Republicans were opening the saloon door and inviting Democrats back in to help mop up the spilled drinks, sweep the broken glass and set to rights all the overturned chairs and tables from the barroom brawl that was called an election. "Our door is open," said House Speaker Larry Householder, emphasizing that there's a time to campaign and a time to govern. "That was about campaigning," he said of the knock-down, drag-out fight of the past six weeks that netted Republicans three extra seats in the House and one in the Senate. "This is about taking care of the people of Ohio."

The Republicans took some Democratic seats and defended their own mainly by painting the Democrats as taxers and spenders. Those with legislative records were scolded for past votes for taxes. Prospective newcomers were chided for what they would do.

Several incumbent Democrats lost because they voted against the state budget and all its programs. They were fair game for TV ads that said they opposed programs for senior citizens, health care, education and agriculture. Householder said he warned the Democrats they were committing political suicide by voting no on the budget. They didn't believe him, and he stuck them with it.

What happens now? The Democrats are in an even deeper minority. Do they turn their backs again and risk getting tattooed for no votes on the next budget? Or do they grudgingly cooperate and get stomped again, anyway?

It seems like the GOP ads against "taxing" Democrats will run no matter what. After all, the votes against the budget were votes against taxes, because the Republicans had to raise taxes to balance their budget. But that didn't matter when it came to the campaign ads.

Householder says the Democrats "played political games" in 2001 when the budget was being written and later rebalanced. He says they never approached him with any realistic requests about what they wanted in return for their votes.

Householder and Sen. Doug White, an Adams County Republican who is expected to be the next Senate president, say they want to work with the Democrats. But they emphasize that the "working with" will be on Republican terms. Under no circumstances are they going to let the Democrats play political games or call the tune, or they'll throw them through the swinging doors again.

This scenario is backed up by new Republican majorities of 62-37 in the House and 22-11 in the Senate. But the expanded GOP edge puts in play a new dynamic. Conservatives have reached a high-water mark within the Republican ranks, and they will insist on receiving their share of passed legislation. In fact, any overtures toward the Democrats will annoy the conservatives, so the fighting may be within the Republican caucuses.

Look for a massive exercise in cutting government programs to appease the conservatives. Then, when the maximum reductions have been made, the lawmakers will begin looking for new revenues. Because Gov. Bob Taft has insisted that any major tax increase go to the public ballot, it will have to have Democratic support. Why? Because no partisan tax package would stand a chance. Even a bipartisan one might not pass.

The campaigns are over but the barroom brawls might continue.

The Democratic cowpoke ended up offering to shake hands, but the gesture was ignored by Republicans. For the next four years, the minority party in the legislature was relegated to the scrap pile. But Democrats came out of exile through the ballot box. They captured the governor's office in 2006 and the House in 2008, largely because of Republican arrogance and scandal. By 2009 it was two-party government at the Statehouse. How long that would last was anyone's guess.

■ ■

One of the titles suggested for this book was: "Let's Kill Each Other So We Can Work Together." Not bad. They do a good job of killing each other during the campaign; working together—not so much. What happens? Read on.

Domination of One Party Has Led to Abuses of Ohio's Political System

The Columbus Dispatch, June 28, 2004

The Bill Clinton syndrome is alive and well in Ohio. In TV interviews promoting his book last week, the former president said he became involved with White House intern Monica Lewinsky "because I could." This is why we read so many newspaper stories these days about ethical and sometimes criminal misadventures by those involved in politics and government in Ohio.

It's not that these are necessarily bad people. Indeed, when former House Speaker Vernal G. Riffe Jr. was slapped with a fine in 1996 for failing to report income properly, the judge said publicly that Riffe was an honorable man who made a mistake; that his other accomplishments should not be forgotten.

But when one political party rules the roost, the checks and balances go soft. Those aligned with the majority begin to push the envelope because they can. We have a Republican governor and Republican-run agencies. We have a Republican-controlled legislature and Republican-controlled statewide elected offices. That means the attorney general and the auditor are Republicans. Is this the fox watching the henhouse or what? Even the Supreme Court is dominated by Republicans.

That's why you read that:

- Certain members of state retirement system governing boards spent pensioners' money on extravagant furnishings, bonuses and travel, and allowed themselves to be wooed by prospective vendors with family trips, golf and entertainment.
- Gilbane Building Co. of Rhode Island is accused of providing golf, meals and lodging to influence the awarding of Ohio school-building contracts.
- An American Electric Power corporate jet was used to fly in Chief Justice William Rehnquist for the dedication of the Ohio Supreme Court building.
- Campaign fund-raisers and consultants for Ohio House Republicans played political hardball and may have crossed the line in some of their activities.

Yes, these matters have been under investigation by authorities ranging from the Ohio Ethics Commission to the FBI. And in some cases, a Republican officeholder has spurred the inquiry.

Secretary of State J. Kenneth Blackwell, already alien to some of his fellow Republicans, has not been bashful about pursuing allegations against the House Republicans. Some think it has more to do with his feud with Speaker Larry Householder and his quest for the governorship in 2006 than with an altruistic desire for law and order.

But the fact remains: Left unchecked, those in power will venture to the edge and sometimes beyond what is proper, because they can.

We don't know whether allegations are true about the fund-raising, candidate-recruiting and lobbying tactics of Brett Buerck and Kyle Sisk, who worked for the House Republicans until earlier this month.

But the seeds had been planted and the soil tilled before Buerck and Sisk came on the Statehouse scene.

Riffe developed the caucus fund-raising system that helped perpetuate Democratic rule of the House for 22 years. Once Republicans took over, they perfected the system of using campaign money to keep themselves in power. They wrote a campaign-finance law, but it had the loopholes that we now see being exploited. Campaign money can be hidden from public view, shuttled from one entity to another. Caucuses can raise boatloads of money, especially the majority caucuses.

Lobbyists complained, even before Householder became speaker, about the proliferation of fund-raisers. They said they were mugged for donations, week after week, in a pay-to-play system. You might weep crocodile tears for them. Poor babies.

The system is unhealthy. The activities may or may not be illegal, but practitioners have pushed the boundary until it bulged. Some are saying, "Let's stop these evil practices." But are they really serious?

Republicans have promised to make corrections in the campaign-finance law. They had all of 2003 to do that. This year, they decided to limit the reform to judicial campaigns so it would cover the races for the Supreme Court. They blew that, too, adjourning for the summer without doing anything.

Because they could.

Footnotes: None of the multi-agency investigations turned up any criminal violations by Buerck or Sisk. Republicans passed a campaign finance bill in early 2005 but it did little to curb the abuses. Democrats completed the turnaround at the Statehouse, capturing the governor's office in 2006 and the House in 2008.

Republican supporters of Governor James A. Rhodes in Akron, 1967. Left to Right: David Eugene Waddell, Summit County GOP Chairman; Ray C. Bliss, Republican National Committee Chairman; Governor Rhodes; former Vice-President Richard Nixon; Norman Auburn, president of the University of Akron. *Photograph by W. Richard Wright, used by permission of The University of Akron Archives.*

State Sen. Robert T. Secrest, D-Senecaville, whose political career spanned 46 years, enjoys a cigar at his desk on the floor of the Ohio Senate in 1969. *Photo by Charles Hays. Reprinted, with permission, from* The Columbus Dispatch.

A group of protesting students on the Ohio State University campus attack a man, apparently a plainclothes policeman. The scuffle started when police tried to break up a student roadblock. It was typical of the unrest of the late 1960s and early '70s. Published April 30, 1970, five days before the Kent State shootings. *Reprinted, with permission, from* The Columbus Dispatch.

John J. Gilligan, left, the Democratic nominee for governor in 1970, and John Glenn, who ran for the U.S. Senate the same year, share a bumpy ride on the Giant Slide at the Ohio State Fair in August 1970. They are smiling in this photo, but their relationship became bumpy in 1973 when Gilligan, as governor, refused to appoint Glenn to a vacancy in the Senate. Glenn later won on his own. *Reprinted, with permission, from* The Columbus Dispatch.

Frank King, chairman of the Ohio delegation to the 1972 Democratic National Convention in Miami, could not control his fractious delegation and, to the ridicule of the nation, had to repeatedly announce: "Madame secretary, Ohio passes!" on rollcall votes. The delegation was split almost evenly between supporters of Sens. Hubert Humphrey of Minnesota and George McGovern of South Dakota. *Reprinted, with permission, from* The Columbus Dispatch.

Many of the women (and men) who came to the Capitol to support the Equal Rights Amendment in February 1973 stayed in corridors, on stairs and in the rotunda (background) after they couldn't get into the small hearing room. *Reprinted, with permission, from* The Columbus Dispatch.

Sen. William B. Saxbe, known for his independence and irreverent sense of humor, posts a sign in his kitchen, May 1974. He got the sign on a trip out West. *Reprinted, with permission, from* The Columbus Dispatch.

State Sen. Stanley J. Aronoff, a Cincinnati Republican, drives his fellow Cincinnatian, Democratic Sen. William F. Bowen, past the Statehouse in an antique car in March 1975. The two were sponsoring a bill to exempt antique cars from installing pollution control equipment. *Photo by Charles Hays. Reprinted, with permission, from* The Columbus Dispatch.

Gov. James A. Rhodes, center, in dark-rimmed glasses, listens to a reporter's question, flanked by House Speaker Vern Riffe and Senate President Oliver Ocasek. They were explaining the state's response to a natural gas shortage during a severe cold snap on Jan. 27, 1977. At the top left corner of the photo is Sen. Harry Meshel. *Photo by Tom Sines. Reprinted, with permission, from* The Columbus Dispatch.

Ohio State football coach Woody Hayes, left, and Richard Nixon, joyously salute a pro-Republican crowd at a 1977 rally on the Ohio Statehouse steps. *Photo by William Blackstone. Reprinted, with permission, from* The Columbus Dispatch.

Sen. Ted Kennedy, left, confers with Lt. Gov. Richard F. Celeste, who ran unsuccessfully for governor in 1978. *The Dispatch* reported that Kennedy campaigned for Celeste at a Democratic rally in Cleveland but spent almost equal time promoting his national health insurance plan, which was still pending 30 years later. *Photo by Glen Cumberledge. Reprinted, with permission, from* The Columbus Dispatch.

Republican presidential candidate Ronald Reagan, right, gets a big laugh as Gov. James A. Rhodes tells why he decided to endorse Reagan on that day in April 1980. "Because yesterday was too early and tomorrow is too late," was the answer to a reporter's question. Reagan borrowed heavily from Rhodes' campaign strategy in Ohio. *Reprinted, with permission, from* The Columbus Dispatch.

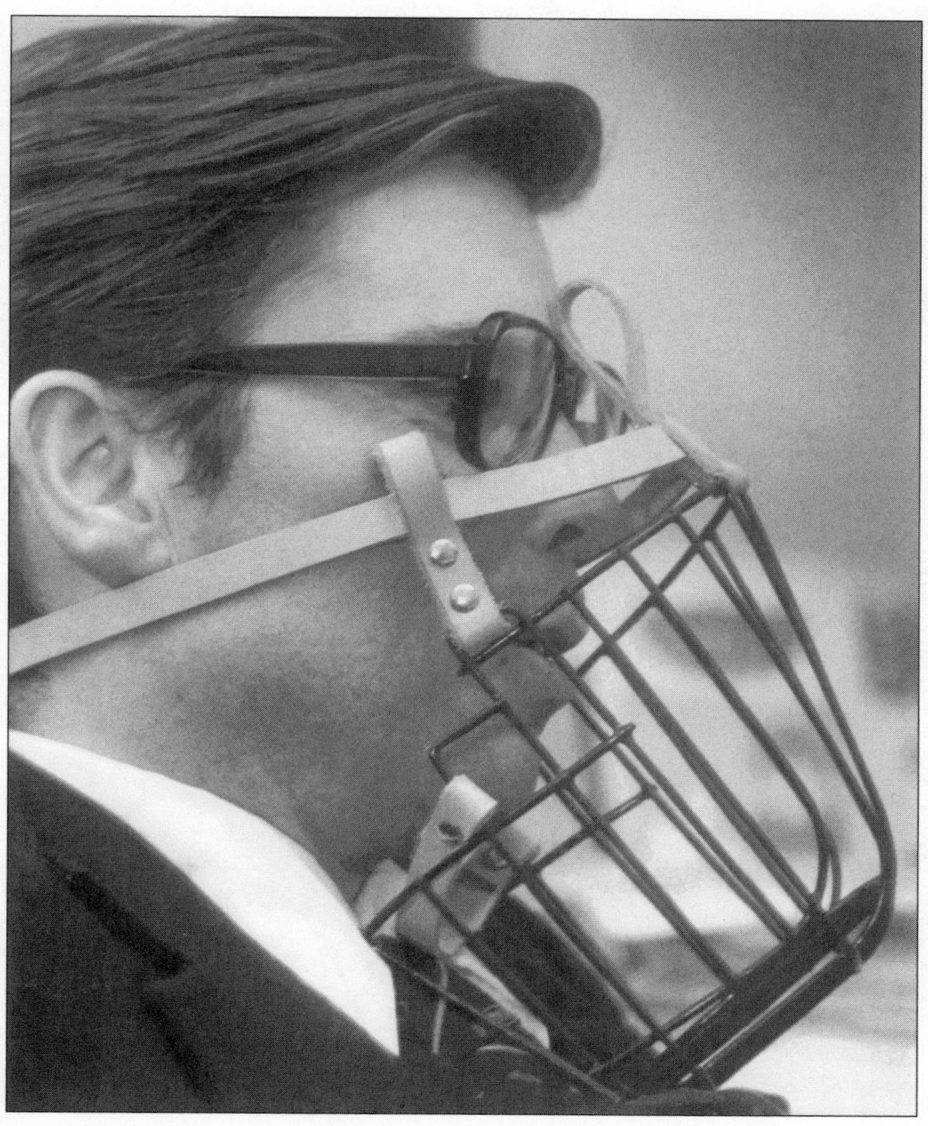

State Rep. William G. Batchelder, R-Medina, considered the Doberman of conservatism in the Ohio House, donned a muzzle February 24, 1983, to protest a Democratic gag on debate over a $300 million income tax increase. *Photo by Mary Circelli Borders. Reprinted, with permission, from* The Columbus Dispatch.

Ohio Gov. Richard F. Celeste bends to hear Democratic vice presidential candidate Geraldine Ferraro's words during applause at the International Brotherhood of Electrical Workers hall in Columbus on September 11, 1984. *Photo by Tom Dodge. Reprinted, with permission, from* The Columbus Dispatch.

Gov. George V. Voinovich and First Lady Janet Voinovich, longtime sweethearts, share a kiss at the grand reopening of the restored Statehouse, a three-year project honchoed by (at left) state Sen. Richard Finan, a suburban Cincinnati Republican. To the right is Lt. Gov. Nancy P. Hollister, who later would be Ohio's first female governor. *Photo by Lynn Ischay. Reprinted, with permission, from* The Columbus Dispatch.

Governor Robert Taft, left, and the author, at the author's retirement party, April 13, 2005. *Photo by James D. DeCamp, courtesy of Lee Leonard.*

GOVERNMENT

Chapter 5
The Governors

James A. Rhodes

Rhodes Hits Timely Topic: Ban Sex Involving Fellow State Workers

United Press International, June 19, 1976

COLUMBUS (UPI)—Late last week, Gov. James A. Rhodes rolled another hot potato into the fires of the upcoming campaign in which he hopes to help Republicans recapture the Ohio House and make gains in the Senate.

So far, the governor has flogged the Democratic-controlled General Assembly for overspending, creating bureaucracy, causing future tax increases and doing nothing to promote industrial expansion and jobs.

The latest salvo was less conventional but perhaps just as effective in putting the Democrats on the defensive. He proposed a bill forbidding the hiring of government employees for sexual purposes and making it unlawful to force a government employee to submit to sex for job preservation.

Rhodes has a knack for capturing the public's imagination with his proposals and statements, and this one appears to have all the ingredients to suit his purposes.

What is the hottest political topic of conversation? Sex on the payroll. Where has it been discovered? In Congress, the legislative branch of the federal government.

The transfer to the state level seems simple. If the issue is raised often enough, people may begin to question whether it exists in the Ohio General Assembly. "It was a timely subject," grinned Frederick Mills, the governor's top legislative aide, when asked why Rhodes proposed the bill.

Timely for talk, perhaps, but hardly for action. The legislature is in adjournment until at least September. Moreover, Democratic legislative attorneys point out, the law already affords protection for harassed government employees.

And as for hiring sexual performers or hiding public funds for sex, Robert McDavitt, aide to Senate President pro tempore Oliver Ocasek, D-Akron, observed that the legislature, unlike Congress, can't afford the luxury. There's too much work to be done and not enough money. "We live in a glass house," said McDavitt. "There's no opportunity for that."

Both McDavitt and Rick Pfeiffer, counsel to House Speaker Vernal G. Riffe Jr., D-New Boston, said the bill was an "insult" to the legislature. They indicated they will ignore it and conduct their legislative campaigns on positive issues.

Earlier this month, Rhodes accused the legislature of a lack of action on the important issues of the day. "You have done nothing," he told the lawmakers in a "State of the State" message.

McDavitt and Pfeiffer have prepared a detailed performance record of the 111th General Assembly, including enactments on consumer protection, responsible spending, energy development, labor, property and business tax reductions, education, health care and election reform, among others.

McDavitt also said Rhodes himself will be made an issue in legislative districts. "The guy's got no legislative programs," said McDavitt, pointing out that aside from the sex legislation and his four bond issues, the governor has proposed only three other bills in two years outside of the budget. "He's doing nothing."

"The issue is Jim Rhodes, and the only hope the public has against that huckster and salesman downstairs is a veto-proof legislature," McDavitt said. But the two legislative aides recognize the governor's uncanny ability to gain public attention through devices like the sex in government bill.

"It just means we'll have to work that much harder," said Pfeiffer.

The reference to sex on the payroll in Congress was to U.S. Rep. Wayne Hays, an eastern Ohio Democrat, whose blonde, comely secretary, Elizabeth

Ray, was alleged to have been unable to type or take dictation. Once the powerful chairman of the House Administration Committee, Hays left the House in disgrace but was elected two years later to the Ohio House.

This column was included to showcase Rhodes's resourcefulness, especially in an election year when Democrats controlled the legislature. 1976 was not a Republican year, and the Republicans did not recapture the Ohio House as Rhodes had hoped. Legislative elections usually are decided by the issues, quality candidates and available campaign money within each district, not by painting the legislature with a broad brush.

■ ■

Reporters often had to clean up Jim Rhodes's quotes so they made sense. He talked in such a way that the public would not have understood what he meant. On this occasion, however, it was time to let the recording tape speak for itself.

Rhodes Unedited: If It Weren't Recorded, You Couldn't Believe It

United Press International, May 2, 1980

COLUMBUS (UPI)—There is nothing Gov. James A. Rhodes likes better than to merchandise the state of Ohio, especially its parks and recreational facilities, for natives and out-of-staters alike.

So Rhodes was at his wild and woolly best last week, putting down other states, winking at reality and uttering non-sequiturs as he helped the state Department of Economic and Community Development launch its campaign to attract summer vacationers with an "Ohio's For You" promotional.

Here's the way it went, with a few added observations or explanations to make sense out of it. Believe it or not, the governor's quotes were taken from a tape recording of the press conference.

Rhodes was asked if he often tours Ohio to set an example as governor.

"I am the only governor in the history of the state of Ohio that has visited every museum, every cultural center, every state fair and everything that we have, attractions, in the state of Ohio, including the Giant and the Monster."

True. Rhodes has cut the ribbons on many of them. As for being the only governor in the history of Ohio to visit them, it's no contest. He's been the only governor, period, since they've been completed.

Rhodes was asked if he plans to visit Florida this summer.

"I will not go to Florida," he bristled. "I visit my relatives. I have a daughter, a grandson and a son-in-law."

It was observed that he frequently travels to Florida, where he has a condominium on Millionaire's Row near Fort Lauderdale, home of his daughter and her family. By now, the governor was visibly nettled. "I visit my own relatives, right here in the state of Ohio, close by. (His relatives live in Upper Arlington.) I'm the only governor that has visited every ski lodge . . . and every ski (that's right) and snowmobiles. . . in the state of Ohio. I visit every place in the state of Ohio where there's action." He does, mainly on political campaigns.

Then the governor proudly defended Ohio's recreational facilities against the rest of the country's. Ohio's no doubt stack up favorably, but Rhodes was in full stride by now, and he mixed his puffery with some uncharacteristic bad-mouthing of other states. "What we have in the way of parks and recreation and lodges . . . When you go to any other state, or the surrounding states, or the Tetons, or any of the national lodges or anything like that—they're all tool sheds!

"We're the only place that they have an indoor swimming pool outdoors (that's what he said!). We have more activity in some of our lodges than they have in Yellowstone National Park.

"You cannot in the summertime get in. We have the finest lodges in America. We have more recreation per square mile than any other state. So what we get is an abundance of people. Our trouble is, in the southern part of the state, people from Kentucky coming into our lodges, they like to see how a good one looks like."

To remedy the problem, the governor said Ohio is building three more lodges. One is to be near Akron, but he couldn't remember where the others would be. So if it's activity you want this summer and the cost of gas is getting you down, stay in Ohio. But if it's rest and relaxation you crave, go to a tool shed in some other state.

The "Giant" and the "Monster" were rides at Ohio amusement parks.

Rhodes actually knew a lot about Ohio from traveling around. But he vacationed often in Florida, and you can see from the column that reporters enjoyed baiting him about that. Years earlier, they had caught Democratic Gov. John J. Gilligan secretly vacationing in Michigan while touting Ohio's advantages. Here, the baiting was tried on Rhodes, yielding the hyperbole for which he was so famous.

■ ■

This was at the bottom of a multi-item column. It is included because it shows the nerve Rhodes had. Abe Zaidan, a reporter and columnist for the *Akron Beacon Journal*, once described thusly the statue of himself that Rhodes had placed on the Statehouse grounds: "A tribute in bronze to his brass."

"Doctor" Rhodes, the Fireman ... Or Is It the Arsonist?

United Press International, September 18, 1981

... For pure cheek, it was hard to top Gov. James A. Rhodes, who went to Cincinnati last week to receive a Doctor of Laws degree (goodness knows he's doctored enough of them).

Rhodes told onlookers his new budget and tax plan shows he is the "fireman" who dashes into the inferno to save people while everybody else just stands around. The governor said the state was figuratively on fire "and there was someone inside to be saved and I was the only one to go inside and save them, and there was many of these people who just wanted to hold the hose."

Longtime students of Rhodes, after they had regained their composure from laughing, recalled they also have an analogy about the governor that involves fire, but in this one Rhodes is constantly running around starting brush fires so he can put them out.

Concerning the state's financial crunch, the governor has slept through the early fire alarms, then stood on the hose or turned it on anyone else who tried to extinguish the flames. Now he's going to throw a bucket of water on the blaze and hope it goes out before the 1982 election.

The forgoing took place during a state budgetary crisis that was Ohio's worst until 2009 arrived. Rhodes tried mightily to get out of raising taxes, but eventually he had to.

■ ■

James A. Rhodes and Joseph T. Ferguson tormented each other politically for years. The next two columns show the relationship of these two adversaries.

Joe Ferguson Lands a Political Grenade on the Head of His Nemesis

United Press International, October 4, 1974

COLUMBUS (UPI)—State Auditor Joseph T. Ferguson and former Gov. James A. Rhodes may be miles apart politically, but they have their similarities.

Both were reared in poor surroundings in the southeastern quadrant of Ohio. Both fought their way up the political ladder, paid their dues and built up a long list of IOU's. Both are past retirement age and are on or trying to get back on the public payroll.

And both are well-schooled in the old politics. They have memories that span decades along the political timeline. A bad turn is not easily forgotten.

Rhodes, a 65-year old Republican, can be seen every day trying to avenge his descent from the governor's office which began in 1969 and culminated in rejection at the polls in a 1970 Senate bid.

But today's story is about Ferguson, the 82-year old Democratic auditor who has run for state office in every decade since the 1920s and is on his last lap.

Twenty-two years ago, Rhodes ended Ferguson's 16-year grip on the auditor's office. He rebuffed a challenge by Ferguson for the same office four years later.

Ferguson never forgot. When he ran again for auditor in 1970, he vowed to reporters he would dig into the Rhodes administration and expose all the corruption.

A part of the results of Ferguson's labors came forth last week in a rather startling way. Ferguson produced an audit report on the Southern Ohio Correctional Facility (SOCF) at Lucasville. It concluded that Rhodes had the prison located in Scioto County to fulfill a political promise, and that it cost the state an extra $7.8 million and 10 years' use of the facility.

The report itself is a masterpiece of detail. It is about three inches thick and contains deeds, soil sample reports, water supply contracts and transcripts of conversations between government officials.

It must have taken thousands of man-hours to compile. Ferguson's office isn't saying how many, claiming state agencies aren't charged for the audits.

But Ferguson's top personal examiner, Thomas R. Clink, and three other examiners started working on the audit July 1, 1972.

The essence of the report is that the prison should have been located at London, Grafton or somewhere on the level land in northern Ohio near the population center and transportation lines.

Unfortunately, this has been concluded in practically every study ever done on the Lucasville penitentiary, including the governor's own task force on penal institutions and the special investigating unit which went in after two guards were shot to death in the summer of 1973.

It has been generally agreed upon that although Lucasville is a "white elephant," nothing can be done but to live with it and hope for good administrators.

Most audit reports confine themselves to bookkeeping, purchasing and other fiscal operations, and on this one it must be said in fairness that the Ferguson report scored the (Democratic) Gilligan administration for sloppy practices at Lucasville. But why dredge up the old question about location of the prison? "This was our first audit on Lucasville, and we always go back and get a historical perspective any time we make our first audit," Clink explained.

Then if it was the first audit of Lucasville, how come it was not done earlier? "This is normal."

Then how come the state Lottery Commission audit was published Sept.10, only a few months after the commission began work? The auditor's office explains that the examiners met with dead ends and blind alleys at Lucasville, and that only after "Mr. Ferguson told them to get it done" and began to personally supervise did it get finished.

The timing couldn't have been better. It got finished March 18, was approved Sept. 25 and was filed Oct. 1—six days before Ferguson suspended further audit reports for fear of political implications during the campaign.

Oh, yes. Before the report was certified last week, it was leaked to a major Ohio daily newspaper for maximum impact.

It was Ferguson's way of bringing another old chestnut out of the fire for Rhodes to juggle while he runs on the ticket opposing Ferguson's son. And it was a nice way to pay back an old IOU.

For an example of how the apple doesn't fall far from the tree, read the next column and see what political traits Joe Ferguson passed on to his son. One was the tenacity of a bulldog.

■ ■

The dialogue toward the end of this column was made up, but the rest is fact.

"Remember Kent State": Tom Ferguson Continues Feud with Rhodes

United Press International, December 10, 1982

COLUMBUS (UPI)—The political world often spins in a different orbit from the real one, and political feelings can run deep.

Just how deep was demonstrated a week ago, when a man resembling state Auditor Thomas E. Ferguson entered the auditor's office on Sunday morning to run a political errand, placing in a fifth floor window a large sign reading: "Remember Kent State."

The significance of that Sunday morning errand was that several hours later, across the street on the Statehouse grounds, a monument would be unveiled honoring Gov. James A. Rhodes for his record 16 years of service as governor.

Rhodes happens to be the same governor who, 13 years ago, ordered National Guard troops onto the Kent State University campus to quell disturbances. Four students ended up being shot and killed, and nine others were injured.

Thomas E. Ferguson, like his late father, Joseph T., also a Democratic state auditor, has no use for James A. Rhodes. The feeling is mutual; the feud has worked two ways. It is Ferguson's contention that Rhodes has tried for years to cover up and bury the Kent State issue, the latest example being a proposal that Kent State be merged with the University of Akron as a giant northeastern Ohio institution with a new name.

Rhodes was one of the few Republicans who could beat "Jumpin' Joe" Ferguson, and he did so twice in the 1950s. Ferguson never forgot. When he made a comeback in 1970 as auditor, he vowed to unearth a scandal about Rhodes. But he never did.

So it fell to son Tom to carry on. "He can't obliterate history that way," Tom Ferguson was quoted as saying about the proposal to merge the universities.

With a little imagination, one can almost picture the scene at the Ferguson residence Sunday morning a week ago, the day Rhodes' monument was to be dedicated:

Mrs. Ferguson: "Where are you going, dear? You never get dressed up on Sunday morning."

Ferguson: "I've got to go to the office, honey."

Mrs. Ferguson: "What's the matter? Somebody pilfering the treasury again?"

Ferguson: "Naw. I got a little business to take care of."

Mrs. Ferguson: "But you promised to read the comics to the kids."

Ferguson: "That can wait. This is important."

Mrs. Ferguson: "What's that sign under your arm?"

Ferguson: "Just a little message for an old friend."

Mrs. Ferguson: "Well, who is it?"

Ferguson: "You ask too many questions. It's Rhodes."

Mrs. Ferguson: "I didn't think he was a friend of yours."

Ferguson: "He is today. I'm going to help him dedicate his monument."

Mrs. Ferguson: "I see what that sign says. You're not going to help at all. Why don't you leave the old man alone? Let him have his monument."

Ferguson (departing): "I can't. A little voice keeps telling me to do it."

So the sign appeared in the office window, but it was removed by a building security guard long before the dedication ceremony.

The monument is now in place, and the question is which will last longer, the statue or the Ferguson-Rhodes feud. Smart money is on the feud.

Actually, the statue still stands, although it was moved off the Statehouse grounds during a Democratic administration and is now in front of the State Office Tower bearing Rhodes's name on East Broad Street. Tom Ferguson cheerfully attended a 90th birthday party for Rhodes in 1999, so the feud had mellowed.

■ ■

John J. Gilligan

Gov. John J. Gilligan is a One-Termer

United Press International, Oct. 8, 1971

COLUMBUS (UPI)—During last year's election campaign, many political observers were willing to bet that the winner of the gubernatorial race would be a one-term governor.

Now they are sure of it.

Some feel the governor has his sights set on higher offices, but that's not the reason.

The "Goodbye Gilligan" bumper stickers have started to sprout, but that could happen to anyone. Even an "income tax" label could be shed through proper public relations.

The underlying reason for ascribing one-term status to Gov. John J. Gilligan, observers say, is that while nothing has been accomplished during his nine months in office, he has taken the position of a man bobbing for apples with his mouth full.

They cite these two examples, and others, to back up the viewpoint that the governor is slowly dragging himself across an unbridgeable chasm, even from members of his own party, by reaching for the moon:

- Gilligan threw a record $9.1 billion budget and an unprecedented 1 to 8 percent personal income tax in front of the legislature last March and told lawmakers: "The choice is yours. You must decide." When they decided against it, he failed to bargain or offer any counter-proposals until practically forced to do so by the Republican-controlled General Assembly.
- The governor, after accusing GOP legislators of hatching their own tax proposals "in Statehouse cloak rooms" without fair public hearings, produced and directed behind closed doors a legislative reapportionment plan designed to purge the General Assembly of his foes and turn control over to his friends in just one year. It may yet backfire.

"I never saw anybody deliberately try so hard to make old friends into new enemies," said one Democratic senator who described the reapportionment plan as "political myopia."

There were even some who said Gilligan was trying to handpick next year's legislature to suit his own views by tailoring districts for fresh Democratic faces at the expense of incumbents.

If Gilligan's apportionment tactics have been heavy-handed, his tax-budget attitude could be described as aloof.

The governor has never shown any desire to roll up his sleeves and get down to informal face-to-face bargaining with Republican legislative leaders—the kind of constructive negotiating that produces settlements.

Any talks have been stilted and non-productive, with the governor leaving it up to the Republicans.

"In all the talks we've had, I don't think he's ever called me anything but Mr. Speaker," said House Speaker Charles F. Kurfess, R-Bowling Green, whose friends call him "Chuck."

"He'd do a lot better if he used a little honey and not so much vinegar," said Senate President Pro Tempore Theodore M. Gray, R-Piqua.

In short, the governor might be doing better by accepting half a loaf, and by avoiding actions which alienate members of his own party.

Even last week, he poured some more fuel on the fire by vetoing bipartisan legislation to take control of the Emergency Board out of the hands of the executive branch.

In 1967, Raymond P. Shafer was inaugurated governor of Pennsylvania with control of one legislative chamber. He proposed a 1 to 3 percent income tax, the state's first, and would not accept less.

Four years later there was no income tax, Shafer had destroyed constructive relationships with his party's legislative leaders, and he went back to being a private citizen. Similar handwriting is starting to appear on the walls of the Ohio Statehouse.

This turned out to be a prescient appraisal after only 10 months of Gilligan-watching; he lost his 1974 bid for re-election, but not by much. And when his four-year record was reviewed, he actually had accomplished a lot.

As Sen. Gray pointed out, Gilligan's bedside manner left something to be desired. He had strong opinions and did not suffer fools, as shown in the next column.

■ ■

Blunt Governor Pulls No Punches, Ignores Political Fallout

United Press International, August 18, 1972

COLUMBUS (UPI)—After watching Gov. John J. Gilligan in office for 19 months, Statehouse denizens have learned at least one thing about the man—ideals will overrule political instincts every time.

Before he was even elected in 1970, Gilligan dared to campaign on a platform proposing a state income tax. He won, with the help of some blundering on the part of Ohio Republicans.

Then, to the horror of all Republicans and some Democrats, the governor actually had the nerve to ask the General Assembly for the dreaded income tax, coupled with a proposal to more than double state spending for public welfare.

Pure political poison, perhaps, but Gilligan stuck to his guns and got some semblance of his program through. He still is faced with another budget battle and an income tax repeal movement, but he is standing firm against the cries of "Goodbye, Gilligan."

Not long after he took office, Gilligan unveiled his infamous "Ohio Plan" which was to require college students to pay back the cost of their education once they began to earn enough money.

The kindest reaction this proposal received was a horselaugh or two. College students, who had carried the torch for Gilligan during the campaign, suddenly began to refer to him in terms they normally reserve for Melvin Laird.

A year ago, when the state was slowly slipping toward bankruptcy because of the protracted budget-tax battle, Gilligan decided to tighten the belt.

One yank closed the state parks, and screams were heard from Hueston Woods to Conneaut. Gilligan learned of the power of outdoorsmen and some new bumper stickers were spawned, but the governor still maintained caring for the mentally ill and poor and elderly were more important than camping out.

Last December, the governor threw caution and the favorite-son concept out the window and jumped on Sen. Edmund Muskie's presidential bandwagon.

Gilligan was warned what would happen if he backed a loser, but he said he believed Muskie was the best man for the job; that Ohio Democrats were tired of being "coerced and co-opted" by favorite sons and backroom politics, and that he would worry about losing later.

Last month, Gilligan finally put on a George McGovern button, still declaring Muskie would have made the best president.

Now, the governor has done it again. Last week he gave his personal support to the boycott of California and Arizona iceberg lettuce.

The boycott, urged by Cesar Chavez's United Farm Workers Union, is a favorite item on the agitation list of McGovern supporters. But it has not made much of a splash in Ohio and would not appear to make many points for Gilligan with the voters.

Why did Gilligan stir up the issue, drawing adverse reaction from the Ohio Farm Bureau Federation? "Cesar Chavez convinced him it was the right thing to do," said Robert C. Tenebaum, the governor's press secretary.

Wasn't Gilligan jumping into an issue on ideological grounds without testing its popularity?

"That's just the point," Tenebaum said. "He does those things."

The governor has slightly more than two more years to keep on doing them before another election rolls around, and it is doubtful he will stop even during an election campaign.

Gilligan didn't stop, even during an election campaign, and he lost in 1974 to Republican James A. Rhodes, who knew how to appeal to Ohio voters. Although the lettuce boycott was of interest in Ohio only to migrant farm workers, Gilligan thought it was right so he supported it.

The reference to Melvin Laird early in the column: Laird was President Nixon's defense secretary who supported the military draft.

■ ■

Gilligan's Candor Costs Him in Narrow Upset by Rhodes

United Press International, November 8, 1974

COLUMBUS (UPI)—Ohioans, acting collectively, have opted for a coalition government. They will try it out for at least the next two years to see how it works.

The governor's office was turned over to Republican James A. Rhodes in Tuesday's election, while the Ohio House maintained its Democratic complexion and the Senate went Democratic for the first time since 1960.

Thus, a virtual standoff was set up. Rhodes won't be able to get anything through the legislature without talking and compromising with legislative leaders. And being one vote short of over-riding a veto in the House, the Democrats won't be able to enact liberal legislation by the carload. They, too, will have to meet their adversary halfway. This is not how it has been in the Statehouse for the last four years, and perhaps the voters sensed it.

Gov. John J. Gilligan was not one to jawbone with legislative leaders, either his own or those of the opposite party. He sent his programs upstairs to the legislative chambers and insisted upon them.

Most of the time, the governor was successful. Senate Republican leaders made some alterations but let most of the major legislation pass through.

The result was that liberal proposals unheard of in Ohio annals were enacted. There was a state income tax; record increases in workmen's and unemployment compensation; a liberalized abortion law; Sunday (liquor) sales and horse racing; creation of new government bureaucracies; civil rights legislation; prison furloughs; strip mine reform. The list could go on and on.

There were suspicions that if Gilligan won this time, the government would be run by organized labor. By electing Rhodes, voters have conveyed a message to Ohio government—slow down. They also have indicated they would feel more comfortable with Rhodes.

There are tremendous differences between Gilligan and Rhodes and the job they have tried to do for Ohio.

Rhodes, as depicted in one of his television commercials, believes if you give a fellow a job and a school for his kids to go to and a park for his family to visit, and then keep your hands off him, he will be happy.

At least half the people bought his arguments that state government was spending too much, wasting money on frills and public relations, not supporting the schools, driving industry away and harassing everybody.

Gilligan, on the other hand, believes government should lead the way and be a guiding light for the concerns of others; to do for people what they cannot do for themselves.

"They spend money to put on television some of the best commercial advertisements telling people 'you've got to grab for everything you can get in this life,'" Gilligan said in a reflective mood recently.

"All we've been saying the last four years is 'How about thinking a little about the elderly or the mentally retarded.' But it's like holding up a candle in a wind tunnel. Who's going to redirect our intentions? Who's going to distract us from this madness?"

To a certain extent, the Gilligan administration has redirected attention during the last four years, but now it looks like it will be back to the bread-and-butter issues of jobs, highways, vocational training and reduced government spending.

The Gilligan people regard Rhodes as a "fossil" and a "Neanderthal." The Rhodes people regard Gilligan as a free spender and wild-eyed liberal.

There may be room in the hearts of Ohio voters for both men. Each of them got about half the vote for governor.

Rhodes served a third and fourth term, but he had a two-year standoff with the Democratic legislature and never duplicated the progress of his first two terms. Much of his time was spent fighting with Washington on energy and environmental matters, detailed elsewhere in this book.

By the time Democrats regained the governor's office, the Reagan era had begun, and Gov. Richard F. Celeste had to move toward the center of the spectrum.

■ ■

Richard F. Celeste

This episode took place in an era when the press erred on the side of caution when dealing with the personal foibles of candidates and office-holders. Today, the allegations about Gov. Celeste would have been on the Internet in a nanosecond, and then would have been picked up by the mainstream media.

How the Celeste Morals Story Went Public

United Press International, June 7, 1987

COLUMBUS (UPI)—For years, reporters on the Statehouse beat had heard stories of Richard F. Celeste's personal indiscretions. They had heard them frequently enough and from credible sources to make them believable.

But nobody ever wrote about them.

They did not write about them when Celeste ran for governor in 1978, when he ran for governor in 1982 or when he ran for governor in 1986.

The reason they did not write about them was that 1) nobody could prove they were true and 2) Celeste's personal habits did not seem to affect his ability to govern Ohio.

Now, somebody has written about them and turned the Statehouse topsy-turvy. How come?

James Duerk, and aide to Celeste's prime political adversary, Republican James A. Rhodes, had a very short answer when asked last week, but it was the right answer. "Gary Hart," said Duerk. "Jim Bakker."

Rhodes, who beat Celeste narrowly in 1978 and lost to him by a landslide in 1986, had collected through his many tentacles and earpieces extending into the state government a dossier on Celeste's personal foibles.

The Republican candidate for governor had the gun cocked and ready to fire at Celeste in 1986, but he couldn't find anybody willing to pull the trigger for him.

Rhodes would hint broadly at press conferences that Celeste's personal background could not stand close examination. "Nobody ever questioned my morals or the integrity of my family," Rhodes would say. Asked if that meant somebody questioned Celeste's morals, he would reply: "Nobody ever questioned my morals or the integrity of my family."

And nobody took the bait to write about Celeste's personal life. Rhodes then tried to portray his opponent as siding with homosexuals and Nazi-sympathizers.

Frustrated at his inability to capture the public with those issues, Rhodes declared to reporters that scandal apparently was out of vogue.

But it popped into fashion last month when former Colorado Sen. Gary Hart was driven from the presidential race by a series of stories about his personal indiscretions.

Meanwhile, the evidence mounted that Celeste was going to enter the Democratic presidential sweepstakes himself.

The governor and his hometown newspaper, *The Plain Dealer*, had been in a running battle for months. The newspaper felt that "the governor from Cleveland" had been a disappointment. Its reporters and columnists felt he had deceived them and downright lied on occasion. Celeste and his people felt the *Plain Dealer* was "out to get us."

In view of the new "Hart" rule of politics and journalism—that personal indiscretions by presidential candidates were fair game for the news media—the Cleveland newspaper prepared a story on Celeste's alleged escapades. It held the story.

But on June 1, the governor denied at a press conference that he had any Hart-type problem in his background that would preclude him from running for president.

That was like waving a red flag in front of the *Plain Dealer*, which knew differently. Celeste was not going to step casually over that land mind on his road to the White House without somebody tripping the detonator. And if the *Plain Dealer* didn't, the national press corps would.

The resulting explosion changed the complexion of Ohio's participation in the 1988 presidential race and changed the nature of the relationship Celeste, his administration and other politicians will have with the Statehouse press corps.

Celeste's chances for national office, now or in the future, are up in the air. But as one veteran politician observed, Celeste's first job must be to make sure he does not lose control as governor, where he has to spend 3 ½ more years.

The rest of the story ... Two reporters were sitting on the sidelines at a Celeste press conference in his Cabinet Room. One held up a quarter and dared the other to ask THE question. "Governor, are there any Hart-like problems in your background that would preclude you from running for president?"

"No," said Celeste, when he should have said, "That's a private matter and it's none of your business."

Dick Celeste had all the tools to run for president and to be the president. He was every bit as qualified as Bill Clinton. Unfortunately, he shared Clinton's Achilles heel.

■ ■

Celeste Developed a Message for the Presidential Campaign That Never Was

United Press International, Aug. 2, 1987

COLUMBUS (UPI)—Gov. Richard F. Celeste says that if he's to run for president, he has to have a message that will set him apart from the myriad other Democratic candidates.

Well, Celeste apparently has developed that message and it's a good one. He tried it out 10 days ago on the National Urban League in Houston.

Fittingly, it was an address that could have been made by the late President John F. Kennedy, and it contained elements of the "I have a dream" speech by Martin Luther King.

Using the themes, "What We Could Be," and "Yes, We Can," the governor talked about the need to eliminate racial injustices and poverty, making everyone a winner.

Celeste appealed to the traditional Democratic coalition, including liberals, and he spoke of the progress Ohio has made in education training and labor-management cooperation under his administration.

The governor wound it up with a poignant story from his Peace Corps days about a nearly-blind volunteer in Senegal who taught nutrition and reading to the natives, and who saw herself, the Africans and her own country in a new light through the experience.

She called it "The gift of new eyes," and Celeste said that if Americans cooperate constructively, perhaps they can receive "the gift of new eyes" to build a better world. Clearly, he wants to be the leader in cultivating that vision.

Not forgotten were the barbs to be flung at the Reagan administration by any Democrat who is to be successful in 1988.

Celeste accused the administration of dividing the country into haves and have-nots, mortgaging the future and taking the easy road.

"Instead of cooperating in a common vision, they've asked us to doze off and dream of the good old days," said the governor.

"Ronald Reagan and his administration have given us the poverty levels of the 1960s, the civil rights attitudes of the 1950s, the farm policies of the Dust Bowl and the religious intolerance of the Spanish inquisition.

"They've appointed people to key government posts whose hearts wouldn't make it through metal detectors in the airport. People who believe that the way to serve the president of this great nation is to keep the Congress and citizens and the chief executive in the dark."

Great stuff for a campaign. But then nobody ever claimed Celeste wasn't a great campaigner or a man with a vision. He has a way to go, though.

At a reunion of the Class of 1957 of an upstate New York high school last month, none of those asked could identify the governor of Ohio.

A professor of political science from San Diego came the closest. "He's the one with the peccadilloes," offered the professor, apparently recalling news stories about the governor's personal indiscretions. Not a good sign.

One man, active in local politics in New Jersey, was told Celeste was planning to enter the crowded Democratic presidential field. "Forget it!" he suggested.

Celeste has heard this advice over and over again, but there's no evidence he will take it. He has a vision, and he may not soon get another chance to carry it out.

Hmmmmm. "Yes, We Can!" Didn't we hear that one about 20 years later? And didn't it work? Discounting the peccadilloes, Celeste came off as almost a white Obama. The crowded Democratic field in 1988 was reduced to Massachusetts' Michael Dukakis, another big-state governor, who lost to Republican George H. W. Bush. Celeste never got another chance to carry his vision higher, although he was probably more qualified than Bill Clinton, who beat Bush four years later.

■ ■

Celeste Has Left Mark On Ohio Government

The Columbus Dispatch, January 14, 1991

As Richard F. Celeste leaves office as Ohio's 64th governor today, the political leadership of the Buckeye State will take a turn in the road and never return.

"I think it's the end of an era," said state Rep. Judy B. Sheerer, D-Shaker Heights, as she watched Celeste deliver a stirring final address to a joint session of the General Assembly last week.

"Dick became the spokesperson for a point of view that came out of the Democratic activism of the 1960s," said Sheerer, who knew Celeste as a part of the New Democratic Coalition in Cleveland in the late 1960s.

Celeste's activism began at Yale University in the late 1950s.

As a senior, he was elected president of the National Methodist Student Movement and appeared before a congressional committee testifying against the military draft.

Later, he was among the first of the rabid Kennedy Democrats, organizing Youth for (John F.) Kennedy in Cleveland.

Still later, he served the Kennedy administration as executive assistant to the U.S. ambassador to India.

Still later, he was director of the Peace Corps.

Meanwhile in Ohio, Republican James A. Rhodes was governor, if not king. Bricks and mortar. "Profit is not a dirty word in Ohio." There's not a social ill in the world that isn't caused by lack of a job. No new taxes. Lock 'em up and throw the key away.

Jim Rhodes stood for the opposite of Dick Celeste's ideals, and vice versa. Democrat John J. Gilligan was a liberal stand-in during a four-year Rhodes hiatus at the start of the 1970s, but he lacked the political skills to win another term.

After another eight years of Rhodes, Ohio was finally ready for the likes of Celeste, even though Celeste had to mask his liberal stripes.

Though he disliked what Rhodes stood for, Celeste learned something from Rhodes: how to get elected.

And he put that knowledge to use, demonstrating peerless campaign strategy and techniques, and operating from Rhodes's longstanding premise for success—tell people what they want to hear.

Celeste was now a liberal in Rhodes clothing. And although his managerial skills were lacking and he made some mistakes in judgment, he tried to do his best to make government responsive to people—always within the confines of protecting his political future.

Fiscal stability was achieved under Celeste. Balanced budgets passed on time, and they developed a small savings account as well.

The number of state employees remained almost constant, despite the popular conception that he was bloating the government.

Only after his last election was past and he couldn't run again for awhile did his liberal tendencies sneak out again. He called for another tax increase, this time to benefit education. He condemned racism, which he said abounds in Ohio and throughout the country. And in his last two weeks, he sprung from jail two-dozen women convicted of violent felonies, and saved another eight convicted murderers from the electric chair because he opposes the death penalty.

While Celeste was governor, the number of women and minorities in high-ranking state government positions doubled. Women now represent 28 percent of the people in high-ranking office and blacks represent 17 percent.

"He has done more for African-Americans than all the other governors combined," Sen. William F. Bowen, D-Cincinnati, the highest-ranking black state legislator, said last week.

Sheerer was right. There may never be another Dick Celeste as governor of Ohio, unless it's this same Dick Celeste.

There will never be another child of the '60s as governor, unless he or she carries a Golden Buckeye card. George Voinovich is 54, Celeste's age, but he was doing different things in the 1950s and 1960s.

Voinovich wasn't taking part in sit-ins and teach-ins and war protests. He had a different agenda, and he'll have a different agenda as governor.

As near as anyone can tell, Voinovich wants to streamline state government to a lean, mean fighting machine, and to be known as "the education governor" when he gets through.

But let it be known that Voinovich studied at the feet of Rhodes, learned from him, received campaign money from him, hired his driver as a cabinet member and can still pick up the phone and call him, a block away, for advice.

And this is the 1990s. Profit still is not a dirty word. It's the end of an era.

Dick Celeste went on to become president of Colorado College and said he was never happier. George Voinovich charted his own course and made the government more responsive to the taxpayers. The next governor to approach Celeste in terms of philosophy was Democrat Ted Strickland, elected in 2006.

■ ■

George V. Voinovich

Any time the governor of a major state exhibits some popularity, as George Voinovich did with his record re-election margin in 1994, he or she gets on the short list of potential candidates for president or vice president. The local media encourages the speculation because it makes for good stories, or columns such as the following:

Voinovich's Decision Reflects His Longtime Independent Streak

The Columbus Dispatch, August 5, 1996

Lt. Gov. Nancy P. Hollister can rest easy now. No more panic attacks every time she thinks about heading out to the Governor's Mansion in Bexley in January when Gov. George V. Voinovich goes to Washington.

Voinovich is not going to Washington. At least, not yet.

The governor let the world know last week that he's not interested in being on the Republican national ticket with citizen Bob Dole. Democrats said it was a no-brainer: He doesn't want to take a cruise on the Titanic.

Some cynics have speculated that Voinovich found out early that he would not be Dole's choice when the former Kansas senator announces his running mate this week in Russell, Kan., or next week at the Republican National Convention in San Diego. So Voinovich said in effect, "They can't fire me; I quit."

There are stout denials all around, including from Voinovich himself. It's really quite simple, according to the official line. The governor wants to finish the two years and five months left in his term and then run for the U.S. Senate in 1998. He doesn't want to be vice president.

Whatever: Voinovich was typically low-key when reporters were summoned last week to hear about the vice-presidential decision. There was no script, no fanfare. Voinovich began talking about the work of lawyers who prosecuted rioting inmates at Lucasville. When he finished, an awkward silence ensued.

"So you don't want to be vice president," ventured one reporter. Voinovich seemed caught off guard. He began tentatively, as if he had not rehearsed his lines and had forgotten his message. Soon, however, he was in gear, so much so that he even cracked himself up with one line.

"Couldn't this be perceived as jumping ship?" asked one reporter.

"It can be perceived any way you want to, but the fact of the matter is that I never was on the ship," said the governor, laughing heartily.

Not on the ship? Everyone had Voinovich on the list of possible running mates for Dole. He was the first governor to support Dole for president, and he was a loud cheerleader for him in Cleveland and other parts of Ohio, lending him his own campaign machinery.

All signs pointed toward Voinovich as one of the favored few for veep. But the governor says he was oblivious. "I paid no attention," he said.

This is part of the mystique of George Voinovich. He keeps his own counsel, follows his own agenda and plays by his own rules. He is never on the ship when you think he is. But he always floats to the surface.

He was not on the ship when he was mayor of Cleveland and Ronald Reagan was president, because Voinovich had a plan for Cleveland and Reagan wasn't helping. The mayor said so, publicly.

He was not on the ship in 1986 when Republicans begged him to run against then-Gov. Richard F. Celeste, whose scandal-pocked Democratic administration made him ripe for plucking. Voinovich said he wasn't finished being mayor, and he left it to three other Republicans to figure out how to lose to Celeste. They did.

And he's not on the ship when something bad happens at the Statehouse. It's always somebody else's fault. We're gonna fix it, but don't look at me. It was Celeste's fault or the legislature's. Or media exaggeration.

So Voinovich is charting his own course. Oh, he'll help push the Good Ship Dole when it comes to Ohio this fall, but he's got his own life raft, ready to get on with the rest of his political career if the ship goes down.

It is admirable that Voinovich wants to finish the job of being governor. Many politicians would be dazzled by an invitation to the national ticket and maybe to the White House. The governor wants to go to Washington, but evidently not until he finishes his current job.

Voinovich has sensed the letdown that accompanies state administrations toward the end, especially when the leader is headed somewhere else. "That extra zest, the special kick at the end of the marathon is very needed to get the job done," the governor said. "I want to stay with it and get it done."

Sometimes, the special kick is stolen away by lame-duck status or the governor's ambition for another office. Voinovich may find his "kick" blocked in 18 months or so, when he is a lame duck campaigning for the Senate, but for now he seems to want to accomplish more, especially in education.

"He really gets fired up when he thinks about the projects," said press secretary Michael Dawson. "They're what make him tick."

You would think Voinovich would want to go back to Cleveland, but he may be following the path cut by the late Frank J. Lausche, the Cleveland mayor who became governor and then senator.

Voinovich believes he has the stature and know-how to lead the Senate toward policies of returning power to the states. "I feel strongly I could make a difference," he said.

After that, who knows? Maybe he'd be finding somebody to be his national running mate.

As it turned out, Voinovich got elected to the Senate in 1998 and 2004. He took stands against the Republican Bush administration periodically and tried without much success to get power returned to the states and Ohio dollars returned to Ohio. He often alienated conservatives, thus diminishing his chance of ever having to choose a national running mate. And early in 2009 he announced he would not seek a third term, saying he wanted to finish his final two years in the Senate productively, without the distractions of raising money and campaigning. Typical Voinovich.

■ ■

Sometimes, satire is the best way to get across a point, as with this parody about Gov. George Voinovich.

'More With Less' May Have Been Too Much for Governor's Unhappy Campers

The Columbus Dispatch, March 1, 1993

Gov. George V. Voinovich rounded up his cabinet and staff last week and took them on a retreat to Mohican State Park.

The governor said he wanted to assemble everyone at an isolated location and talk about the big missions of his administration: management, education and jobs.

"It's a way of getting your whole team together for 18 hours away from the phones," said press secretary Mike Dawson.

Sure, Mike. You don't have to tell us. Richard F. Celeste, the previous governor, used to go on retreats, too.

Celeste would gather up his advisers and groupies, and head up the road to Mohican. Rumor had it that they burned exotic candles, chanted mantras and listened to old LPs of Pete Seeger and Bob Dylan.

"We body-paint," said Celeste's irreverent press secretary, Paul Costello, when asked if these rumors were true.

Not so with the Voinovich clan. We spied on them.

To save the state gas money, they hitchhiked. Then they pitched tents so they wouldn't run up the heating bill in the lodge. Sleeping arrangements were poor. Superintendent of Public Instruction Ted Sanders could only get 6 feet of his lengthy body inside the tent. The other 7 inches were outside in a snowbank.

Moreover, Sanders and his tentmate, Board of Regents Chancellor Elaine H. Hairston, began to argue loudly about which had taken more budget cuts: primary and secondary schools, or the colleges and universities.

Soon, the entire encampment was in turmoil. Shouts of anguish echoed through the hills as cabinet members squared off against one another. "We took more cuts," said Natural Resources Director Frances S. Buchholzer. "In a pig's eye!" retorted Agriculture Director Fred Dailey. "We did."

Development Director Donald E. Jakeway had a headlock on Donald Schregardus, director of the Environmental Protection Agency. Pillow fights broke out. Clothing and sleeping bags were torn. Rabbits and deer scurried into the woods in fear.

Finally Voinovich called on Adjutant General Richard C. Alexander to stop the mayhem. Alexander gave the signal, and a large mortar was set off. That got everyone's attention.

"Get to bed!" ordered Voinovich. "We have work to do in the morning."

At daybreak, a National Guard bugle sounded reveille, and breakfast was served. But first it had to be gathered.

The campers foraged for roots, berries and Mueslix. They collected twigs for the fire to brew tea from sassafras leaves. The faint of heart, and stomach, sneaked away to Dunkin' Donuts.

Then it was time for calisthenics. The governor led everyone in the nose-to-the-grindstone exercise, followed by pencil sharpening and a snappy game of "Pin the Pink Slip on the State Employee."

The first workshop was supposed to teach the team how to pronounce and define paradigm. "It's pronounced PAIR-uh-dime," instructed Voinovich. "Anyone know what it means?"

"Twenty cents?" volunteered Budget Director R. Gregory Browning.

"No, you idiot," responded the governor. "No wonder we can't get our budget in balance without raising taxes. It means model. When I say we need to develop a new paradigm for delivering government services, I mean a new model."

"Then why don't you say it?" Corrections Director Reginald A. Wilkinson muttered under his breath.

Voinovich led a session on "Advanced Shoe Polishing: the Spit Shine" and his wife, Janet, taught "Garments Made Easy."

The feature presentation was chief of staff Paul C. Mifsud, conducting a seminar entitled, "How to Deal With Aggressive Lobbyists: Yield to Them."

Before heading home, the Voinovich crew gathered around the campfire, extended their arms into the center of the circle, grasped hands and recited the cheer:

"Two bits, four bits, six bits, a dollar.

"If you save one, be sure and holler."

As they broke up, Judith Y. Brachman, director of aging, showed Voinovich an old jar of body paint she'd found under the snow. "Just leave that here," instructed the governor. "We'll need it at the next retreat if we accomplish the rest of my mission."

■ ■

Adroit Voinovich Deftly Defuses Controversy Over Central State

The Columbus Dispatch, July 15, 1996

Attention, Bob Dole. Did you catch Gov. George Voinovich's act last week? Puts out a nasty brush fire at Central State University. Tames Jesse Jackson. Think that's the stuff of which vice presidents are made?

Whether or not Voinovich makes the final cut for the Republican vice presidential nomination, the governor once again displayed considerable political skills in handling a ticklish situation.

The disclosure (for the umpteenth time) of financial mismanagement at Central State and the shutdown of wrecked dormitories had all the makings of a racial conflagration.

But by week's end, with the help of Ohio Senate Minority Leader Ben Espy, D-Columbus, and most other black elected officials, a start was made on putting the predominately black university back together under responsible oversight.

Central State was the "project" of the late state Rep. C. J. McLin of Dayton and former Sen. William F. Bowen of Cincinnati, two important black lawmakers who saw that CSU received special supplemental bonuses. The annual bonuses were perpetuated by legendary House Speaker Vernal G. Riffe Jr. and McLin, one of the craftiest politicians at the Statehouse.

In fact, the only serious challenge ever made to Riffe's domination came on a 1977 power play by the black caucus, headed by McLin. The issue was support for Central State. Riffe won, but ever after that, Central State was an "untouchable" when it came to financial support.

Every few years, the Ohio Board of Regents would come to the state Controlling Board and report that Central State was in financial trouble of its own making. Every time, the university would be bailed out, usually on the promise that it wouldn't happen again. But it always did.

Now, it seems, the string has run out. McLin, Bowen and Riffe are gone. So are the other lawmakers who would paper over the problem. So are the governors, James A. Rhodes and Richard F. Celeste, who were willing to throw state money at the university near Dayton and tell it to run itself.

When Voinovich learned of the latest crisis at Central State, the temptation might have been to call a press conference, rail against the mismanagement and exploit the natural resentment against favored treatment of a black institution.

But Voinovich has been through enough sticky situations to realize that this was not the time to hot-dog it. He had to reach out behind the scenes for a consensus solution to the problem.

Central State is Voinovich's "affirmative action" in higher education. Remember that Voinovich, in the face of opposition from many of his Republican friends, favored helping minority firms secure government contracts with a special set-aside. He also supports a black-oriented state university.

However, word leaked out of the governor's office that Central State might be closed. Maybe communications got muddled. Maybe they meant the dormitories would be closed, which they were. Maybe the governor's office wanted a hard spin on it.

At any rate, it got the attention of the Central State folks and the black community. Some reacted well; some did not.

Espy and Sen. Jeffrey D. Johnson, D-Cleveland, president of the Ohio Legislative Black Caucus, immediately called for the resignation of the Central State trustees and went to work on a solution to the problem.

They chose to cooperate with the governor, but they also held out for the strongest possible black-oriented university at Central State, refusing to accept two-year or commuter-school status.

The Central State community took a defensive posture—protesting, denying reality and blaming the state for a lack of funding. Espy and Johnson were more realistic. They knew if Central State was to stay open, they would have to work with the governor.

Civil rights leader Jesse Jackson swung from the lip and threatened to turn Central State into the "Birmingham" of 1996. But by the time he had met with the governor, his rhyming rhetoric had given way to a photo op brimming with the spirit of cooperation. Jesse had been Voinoviched.

A less-shrewd politician attuned to radio talk shows would have snubbed Jackson and taken the hard line, just what Jackson was looking for. Welcome to Birmingham.

"Politically it was very smart," conceded Espy, who believes he and Johnson helped persuade the governor to ease up on Central State. "He can't do anything to inflame the black community," said Espy, pointing out that Voinovich is running for the Senate in 1998 and draws far more black votes than most Republicans.

It's worth noting that Voinovich didn't just drop off the turnip truck when it comes to dealing with minority concerns. He survived 10 years as mayor of Cleveland.

Aides deny the suggestion that Voinovich had one eye on Washington as he reacted to Central State. "He handled it in the way he handles every other situation—in a very systematic way," said press secretary Michael Dawson.

But if Bob Dole was watching, it couldn't hurt.

Of course George Voinovich was not Bob Dole's running mate. But the forgoing column typifies the way Voinovich handled racial politics and being governor.

■ ■

Robert A. Taft II

Unbudging Taft Should Have Used Tact in Legislative Budget Skirmish

The Columbus Dispatch, December 8, 2003

Gov. Bob Taft is a puzzle. Sometimes he's so wishy-washy that you can't tell whether he stands for anything. Other times, notably during turf wars with the legislature, he puts his foot down so hard it goes through the floor.

He can be cagey and coy when asked to take a position on legislation, but the governor stands firm on the separation of powers between the legislative and executive branches. Not sexy stuff, but important.

For years, lawmakers have tried to impose spending directives in the state budget, and they've gotten away with it. Not with this guy. Time after time, he's vetoed the directives, especially when they have affected his ability to balance the budget.

Last week, the tug-of-war over closing state institutions to balance the budget came to a head. Sparks flew. Senate Bill 4, an innocent attempt to stop abuse of mentally retarded and developmentally disabled clients, is the focus of the battle.

Senators annoyed with the governor's plans to close two developmental centers inserted a provision requiring legislative input before any closings.

In the House, where feelings are even more hostile over the closing of Lima Correctional Institution, the legislative input was extended to any prison closings.

A joint conference committee later restricted the legislative oversight to the Department of Mental Retardation and Developmental Disabilities facilities, and the bill was passed last week.

Taft had warned senators in March that he would veto any such provision, and he repeated that warning last week. He's facing an override, because the House passed the bill 92-3 and the Senate approved it 32-0.

At first blush, the legislature's provision seems harmless enough. Senate Bill 4 would require the governor to notify the legislature 10 days before a public announcement of intent to close a developmental center.

The legislature's research arm, the Legislative Service Commission, would then have 90 days to conduct a study of the costs involved and the closing's effects on residents, staff and the local economy, among other things.

A five-member panel including two private sector executives and a representative of the state employees' union would use the study to make a recommendation. The governor could follow the recommendation or ignore it, but he would have to state his reasons in writing.

Sen. Steve Austria, a Republican representing the Springfield area where Springview Developmental Center is, said the administration's reason for closing it—to balance the budget—was bogus. He said the institution will not be closed until after the current budget period.

Rep. Merle G. Kearns, a Springfield Republican, said that when legislators were consulted after the fact, no amount of reasoning would change the administration's mind.

"The governor wouldn't budge," Kearns said. "He wouldn't even visit Springview."

Sounds pretty harsh. What would be the harm of a legislative review?

Robert Jennings, communications director for the Department of Mental Retardation and Developmental Disabilities, said his agency determined in late 2002 that two centers would have to be closed to live within the department's budget. He said an extensive review was made, including the age of the centers, their proximity to other centers and the cost per resident. The families of clients were consulted, he said.

"Everyone at Springview has made a choice where they want to go," he said, adding that 16 of the 86 clients have been placed.

To disrupt the process now with a legislative review would unsettle the emotionally fragile Springview clients and raise fears that other centers might close, the governor said late last week.

"It could potentially provide false hopes," said Taft spokesman Orest Holubec.

Although the closing won't take place for two years, delaying the proceedings would have a negative effect on the next budget.

The hard feelings arose at the Statehouse because legislators weren't consulted before a decision was made and minimal consideration was given to the impact on employees of the centers.

It might not make sense to reopen the discussion of Springview, but in the future, legislators need to be brought into the mix early.

Taft may be right on principle, but he ought to have the political sense to communicate better with lawmakers. You can get more with honey than with vinegar.

The irony here is that Taft was a member of the Ohio House for three terms—long enough for him to appreciate how governors should deal with lawmakers. In 2005 and 2009, the budget constraints were even more severe, but the forgoing is an example of Taft's stubbornness.

Chapter 6
THE LEGISLATURE

While other areas of the book also deal with legislative matters, this chapter has five columns showing what the Ohio General Assembly was like in several different eras. Four columns highlight the lobbying that goes on in the legislature and another dozen are devoted to Statehouse characters including the legendary House Speaker Vern Riffe, who merited his own section.

The Legislative Process

Ohio's Legislature Becomes Full-Time Operation

United Press International, August 1, 1969

COLUMBUS (UPI)—Statehouse denizens like to tell you that the biggest mistake ever made in these parts was air conditioning the House and Senate chambers.

Before air conditioning, the story goes, the legislature used to adjourn at the first gasp of sultry Columbus summer air.

Modern technology fixed that, and now the lawmakers can stay here in comfort well into August. In fact, they spend so much time here that they're even thinking of constructing a new state office building.

They reason that once the administrative agencies move out of the Statehouse and into the new structure across the street, there will be plenty of space for some nice new offices for—guess who—members of the General Assembly.

The forces behind this plan may be correct in pressing for individual offices for legislators, more space, better equipment, more stenographic help.

After all, this type of progress in the business world has made our nation the most advanced and comfortable place on earth to live and work.

But one representative has an interesting theory that such progress in the legislature may have reached the point of diminishing returns. He is Rep. Thomas B. Rentschler, a Republican from Hamilton, and this statement he made on the House floor last week should give you a faint clue as to how he stands on spending for the benefit of lawmakers:

"See that chandelier up there?" he said, pointing to a large circle of sun-lamp type fixtures hanging from the ceiling of the ornate chamber. "That cost $75,000, and they won't even turn it on anymore because when they did, there were too many sunburned heads."

Rentschler is of the opinion that the more the legislators spend on salaries and surroundings for themselves here, the longer they'll stick around each year to enjoy it and justify their existence. "My fear is that if we make the legislative quarters so attractive, we will stay here all year," he said.

Rentschler says the legislature should have wrapped up its 1969 business last April, and he blames the members for letting too many minor things get in the way of major work. "The fellows around here, in order to get re-elected, are constantly worrying about Aunt Minnie's welfare check or about somebody's 16-year old getting a driver's license," he said. "The legislators have forgotten the three branches of government. We are not the people's ombudsman. We are not here to intercede in administrative matters."

Rentschler wants the legislature to convene, perform its business and get out of town so the members can go back to their full-time jobs at home.

"We are turning into professionals and not a citizen's assembly as the legislature originally was intended to be," he said. "The more professional we get, the more we are going to be looking after our own skins and the more we are going to perpetuate ourselves. And the longer we stay here, the less contact we will have with the people back home."

This, Rentschler says, is what has happened to congressmen. He says they have lost touch with the outside world; that candidates for Congress are seeking a job and not public service.

"Give us a nice bed to sleep in, make it attractive to be here, and we're not going to operate efficiently," he said. Few of Rentschler's colleagues, with an eye on a private office, telephone, filing cabinet and secretary, can see it that way.

This was written at the time that the legislature was changing. Until this time, sessions convened for six months in the odd-numbered year and perhaps not at all in the even-numbered years. The lawmakers had their desks in a common "bull pen," shared telephones and used the steno pool to type their letters.

Rentschler was prophetic. The all-year session of 1971 made Ohio's a full-time legislature. Each member got an office, a secretary and a legislative aide. The office tower referred to early in the column was built in 1974 and by 1989, the House of Representatives had its own office tower.

Later, term limitations were supposed to bring back the citizen legislature. They did not. Legislators often treated their position as a job and a stepping-stone to higher office. When they did escape Columbus, it was not to return to their civilian jobs—it was to raise money for the reelection of themselves and their party's colleagues.

■ ■

The idea of term limits didn't originate in the '90s. Here's a column from 20 years earlier.

Two-Term Limitation Proposed for Lawmakers

United Press International, August 30, 1974

COLUMBUS (UPI)—In case you're not aware of it, there's a New American Revolution brewing.

It's constitutional, peaceful, orderly and firm, according to its sponsors, and "it just might work." It will take only one day—Nov. 5, Election Day.

Simply stated, the plan calls for something recommended for years as a solution to poor government performance—throw the rascals out.

Only the version espoused by the New American Revolution, a Washington, D.C., citizens' lobby group, calls for both the rascals and the good guys to be done away with.

Tony Hodges, a 34-year old former pilot for Hawaiian Airlines, breezed through Ohio last week on behalf of the organization urging the defeat of any incumbent congressman or legislator who has served two or more terms.

Moreover, Hodges urged the defeat of any candidate who wouldn't support a state constitutional amendment limiting elected public officials to two terms.

Hodges, a pleasant, Ivy League version of Ralph Nader, presents a logical, rapid-fire argument for his case in language spiced with expressions left over from his college days in the late 1950s.

"When you go to Congress," he begins, "the No. 1 rule is to shut up. They tell you to shut up for 10 or 12 years, and by that time, you've forgotten what it was you wanted to say when you got there. Either that, or you've been compromised by the special interest groups who tell you what to say."

Hodges complains that incumbents get re-elected 93 percent of the time, chiefly because they have all the campaigning resources on their side—like publicity, free mailing and other advantages.

He believes government is like "a barrel of bad apples, rotten and getting worse," and that the bad ones only contaminate the good new ones that come in every two years.

"What we propose," he says, "is to tilt the barrel on its side, very gently, remove as many of the rotten apples as possible, clean the inside of the barrel and fill it with clean fresh apples. If we do that often enough, the apples won't get rotten again."

Hodges is sincere. His goal is lofty and his purpose laudable. But the method is a trifle drastic. Limiting a lawmaker to two terms, while muffling the potential for corruption and opportunism, would rob him of the chance to make meaningful contributions to government.

It takes one term to learn the system and several years for any depth of understanding about how government is trying to solve problems.

"Nonsense," says Hodges. "Experience means nothing more than whom do you cuddle up to." And he argues that researchers and lawyers attached to the legislatures and Congress can furnish the information for neophytes "representing the people" to write good laws.

If that's true, we might as well set up a bank of computers in the legislative chambers. They could write laws reflecting their constituents' opinions as determined by frequent polls. They wouldn't tarnish or corrode.

No, the problem isn't getting rid of the rotten apples. The people do that every once in awhile. The hardest part is cleaning the inside of the barrel—that is, strengthening and modernizing legislative procedures—to reduce or reverse the rot.

Although not as revolutionary as the two-term limit, upgrading procedures is making slow progress. It will no doubt receive a boost in the post-Watergate atmosphere and may provide a more permanent solution to the "bad apple" problem than simply throwing them out.

Procedures were not upgraded in the Ohio legislature, although they were streamlined starting the following year when Vern Riffe became House speaker and developed caucus fund-raising into a high science. Riffe's 20-year reign caused Ohio voters to impose eight-year term limits in 1992 and they took effect at the end of 2000. See other columns on campaign finance and one-party-rule abuse.

■ ■

The concept of the "Big Three"—the few making decisions for the many—actually started as the "Big Five" in the late 1970s when Gov. James A. Rhodes brought the four House and Senate leaders—two from each party—together to find a solution to the school-funding problem. As we see in the following column, the gathering later was streamlined to cut out the minority.

Statehouse Oligarchy of Three Irks Minority-Party Legislators

The Columbus Dispatch, April 4, 1994

The civics books say it works like this: A bill is introduced, undergoes hearings with pro and con testimony, receives thoughtful amendments and thorough debate, passes both the House and Senate and goes to the governor.

In Ohio, it works like this: A bill is prepared behind the scenes by Gov. George V. Voinovich, House Speaker Vernal G. Riffe Jr., D-Wheelersburg, and Senate President Stanley J. Aronoff, R-Cincinnati, or reasonable facsimiles of them. The bill is introduced. It has swift, perfunctory hearings in each chamber, but no changes are allowed to upset the pact made by the Big Three. Then it gets voted on and is returned to the governor.

Sure, there are lots of exceptions. But on many major state-policy issues, when the Big Three want to do something with little fuss or muss, democracy goes out the window and "The Agreement" is brought into play.

So it was last week with an 800-page reappropriation of extra state funds achieved through savings. Minority Senate Democrats were hot about it, and one sounded off. "I want to see a book on how a bill becomes law," said Sen.

Joseph J. Vukovich, D-Youngstown. "You open it up, and there's a picture of the governor and Aronoff and Riffe. And below them it says, 'When they say so.'

"Isn't that the way it used to work in Russia?" asked Vukovich, who once suggested the other chamber be renamed "The Ohio House of Representative" to denote Riffe's authoritarian ways.

House Bill 715, the pre-negotiated bill sent to the governor last week, appropriates $126 million of a projected $197 million savings this year. Some legislators wanted to put the money in the state's savings account; others wanted to send the windfall to Ohio's school districts.

But Riffe and Aronoff, or their representatives, met with Voinovich's fiscal experts and carved up the proceeds. Yes, they took suggestions from minority-party legislators. But basically it was an administration bill tailored to majority-party legislative whims before it was even brought out of the closet.

Riffe and Aronoff defend this process, saying it saves a lot of wear and tear. The majority parties are going to prevail, anyway, so why muddy things up and prolong the agony? They say that if an appropriations bill is laid open for public debate, it will be loaded up with pork because every legislator and lobbyist will want something. The budget will come unbalanced, and Ohio's credit rating will be damaged.

And why does it continue—this process of a government run like a business instead of a democracy? Because power is divided. The Republicans have the Senate, and the Democrats have the House. In stalemates, compromise is logical.

A second, and more-unhealthy, reason is that over the last 20 years, caucus fund-raising has been perfected to keep the same majorities in power in the Senate and House. The strong stay strong. Lobbyists know where to check in to get things done. The system is perpetuated.

Vukovich recalled last summer, when the closed system was used to assemble a workers' compensation reform bill. He said the result was such a farce that it ended up in court. Lawmakers had to come back and correct what they had passed. "If this stuff is such good legislation, why are they afraid to let it see the light of day?" asked Vukovich. He likened the process to an automobile assembly line. "Halfway down the line, the transmission falls off, so we throw it in the trunk and say, 'Let the dealer or the owner worry about it.'"

In other words, the blueprint's in place and you can't make changes in the middle. Ironically, the majority Senate Republicans didn't bear the brunt of the heat from their Democratic colleagues. Instead it was the Democrats' House brethren. The Republicans were willing to let the Senate Democrats plug in a few harmless amendments, but Riffe said any changes would violate the agreement.

Vukovich was infuriated. "We make them teach Social Studies for the proficiency test, and then we ignore it," he said. "You're supposed to have a House, a Senate and a governor. Why do we have a charade of . . . three people meeting in a closed room to tell everybody else what they're going to do?

"We could have Albert Schweitzer here (as a member) or the village idiot. What difference is it going to make when you have leadership making all the decisions?"

The next test of the system will come in May, when the $1 billion capital-construction project list comes rolling out. Senate Democrats already are talking about going over to the House to get their pet projects included early. But the way they talked about Riffe last week, they may not get much there, either.

"The System" may be coming to an end. Riffe is retiring after this year, and if the Republicans take over the House, the balance of power will be upset. Then the Democrats will be lucky if they get the crumbs under the kitchen table.

Postscript: Not only did Riffe retire, the Democrats lost the House in the 1994 election. But that did not end the concept of the "Big Three." It continued under Voinovich and a Republican-controlled legislature, and was carried to an extreme under Gov. Bob Taft, when Democrats were completely excluded from input on major bills. This one-party rule was abused and eventually the pendulum swung back to the Democrats in 2006 and 2008.

■ ■

Columns on legislative illogic, bizarre procedures and pork could be written almost every week. This one is particularly illustrative.

Aroma of Pork Fills Statehouse as Big Spending Bill Trots Ahead

The Columbus Dispatch, May 27, 1996

Michael A. Fox, a bulky lawmaker from Hamilton, was anesthetizing his colleagues in the Ohio House of Representatives last Friday with a speech about one of his favorite subjects—wiring school classrooms for computers.

Fox, a Republican who blends a conservative political philosophy with a nose for pragmatism, had hoped for more support from local boards of education to put $150 million for SchoolNet into the capital budget.

"Where are the school boards tonight?" asked Fox.

"Sleeping," shouted one House member who would rather have been in bed than listening to floor debate on the $1.87 billion two-year capital construction appropriation at 2:55 A.M.

That's the way it went with House Bill 748, the long shopping list of construction projects that some people cynically refer to as "pork." It passed about 10 minutes later with one vote to spare, and the scenario will be repeated this week in the Senate.

Why were the lawmakers debating a major spending bill after midnight under the soft, bedroom-level lighting in the temporary chamber in the ancient Ohio Departments Building? Because minority Democrats were angered that the bill had been assembled in private by top Republican legislative leaders and the administration of Gov. George V. Voinovich.

The Democrats wanted to slow the process down and try to get some leverage. So they refused to provide the votes for a procedure that would have allowed debate to finish the previous evening. Republicans didn't want the bill to lie around and shed votes during the Memorial Day weekend.

The Voinovich administration had to hold down spending this year because the state is reaching its limit for outstanding debt. Capital projects are funded by borrowing.

Still, there is mounting pressure to keep up with construction needs for prisons and higher-education facilities.

Several years ago the state started down the road of helping fund "community projects," including sports stadiums and arenas, and major urban areas continue to come begging for that money.

The administration put $37.8 million in House Bill 748 for stadiums, risking opposition from rural lawmakers who complain that their districts would never share in that largesse.

The Voinovich administration also found room for $270 million for primary and secondary education—a record for a capital bill normally reserved for projects at college campuses, mental hospitals, prisons and parks.

Wonder why? Because a lawsuit claiming inadequate school funding is hanging over the state's head like "the sword of Damocles," to quote state Budget Director R. Gregory Browning.

Even so, the $150 million for SchoolNet Plus, a program to wire every kindergarten through fourth grade classroom in Ohio for computers, was well below the $250 million promised last year.

The Ohio Board of Regents suffered in silence as its $577 million request was pared to $539 million. Rep. Otto Beatty Jr., D-Columbus, said he calculated that the actual figure will be $502 million because some of the community projects are charged to the universities' quotas.

The board, which normally yelps at any cuts in its request, sometimes loudly, apparently was warned against making a fuss this time. Top regents officials were nowhere in sight when crunch time came, and were nervous about making any public comment.

As the bill emerged from the privacy of leadership discussions, the Voinovich administration and the Republican legislative leaders had the ticklish task of building a majority of 50 votes in the House.

They were relentless in their pursuit of votes. House Speaker Jo Ann Davidson, R-Reynoldsburg, called members in, one by one, and tried to find out what they needed in return for their support.

She chose Democrats who were in "safe" districts not subject to Republican challenges this fall. Any "targeted" Democrats were not likely to cooperate anyway. One, Rep. Frank S. Sawyer, D-Butler, sniffed at an offer of an $800,000 project. "I'm not selling out for that," he said. "I'm at least a $2 million man." There was no such offer, and Sawyer opposed the bill.

The Republicans worked over members of the Finance Committee, salting the bill with pet projects to lure votes. Even after the bill hit the floor at 12:30 A.M., GOP leaders fanned out to gain likely converts among their own membership.

In the end, they offered a "master amendment" containing little bacon bits—projects ranging as low as $40,000 to snare votes.

Rep. Richard Hodges, R-Metamora, may have fallen for a last-minute $500,000 award to the Holy Trinity School in his district. Likewise, Rep. Lynn E. Olman, R-Maumee, received $50,000 apiece for the Maumee Youth Center and the Maplewood Market Project in Sylvania.

Nobody liked the process, or the witching hour for the vote, but they chalked it up to the necessities of politics.

The procedural vote that the minority Democrats squelched would have waived the constitutional requirement that bills be considered in each chamber on three separate days. Republican leaders, in a hurry to pass the pork, got a jump on the third day by convening a post-midnight session. The fear of going home for the Memorial Day weekend was this: Lawmakers can be talked out of voting for things when they're back home among their constituents.

■ ■

To All New Legislators: Leave Your Individual Thinking Caps At Home

The Columbus Dispatch, January 6, 2003

If you're a brand new state legislator in town for the start of the new session today, and you think you're going to be Mister Sterling, you can disabuse yourself of that notion right now. And the sooner, the better.

In the age of reality TV shows, the new NBC offering on the life of a senator promises to be more like fantasy TV shows. The promos have the fictional Sen. William Sterling vowing to "shake up the system," saying, "I'll do things my way."

Many Mr. and Ms. Sterlings have joined the Ohio legislature. They quickly find out that the system is bigger than they are and the only shaking they'll be doing is with the hand of their leader as they humbly murmur, "Yes, sir, you'll have my vote on that."

Legislators do the bidding of the House speaker or Senate president—and thank them for the privilege. If they don't, they may find themselves on the Exterior Relations Committee, locked out of the party caucus and sitting at a desk in a broom closet next to the underground parking garage with a second-hand computer and no secretary. And that's if they're in the majority. If they're in the minority, they might as well mail it in.

Another thing, newbies: get a phone with speed re-dial. You'll be using it a lot to call your acquaintances to raise money. Plan to start doing that oh, about right after you've finished unpacking the boxes in your office. Time's a-wasting. The election's in November 2004.

Whatever you raise, plan on giving 80 percent of it back to the caucus. Because today, it's all about working as a team and preserving the majority. Take a back seat, Mr. Sterling. You're too much of an individual. It's not happening that way any more.

Priscilla Mead is the latest casualty of the legislative system in place at the Statehouse. The Republican senator from Upper Arlington quit midway through her first term because she feels unable to be the legislator she wants to be.

"This is an ideal place for somebody who relishes caucus politics and savors the campaigns as they have come to be," Mead said last week before cleaning out her office. "I'm not a hardball player, and I don't want to become hardened."

Mead, who served eight years in the House before joining the Senate, enjoys immersing herself in issues. She views herself as a coalition-builder who is good at getting people on all sides of an issue to come up with solutions to problems. She was a leader in the ticklish negotiations on a bill deregulating electric utilities in 1999.

Mead said she was able to do that job in the House but has discovered less opportunity in the smaller Senate where, she said, caucus politics dominates even more.

"It's a less collaborative body," she said. "It's much more individual."

Mead said in the Senate, the committee chairs are more influential and to become a committee chair, you have to raise money for the caucus. She said she is capable of raising enough money to defend her Senate seat but is reluctant to spend the time needed to raise money for others.

Mead played the game up to a point. Term-limited in the House in 2000, she ran for the Senate because then-President Richard H. Finan wanted her to. He had lost every female in his caucus, and Mead would provide needed experience gained during her House service.

Some folks think lawmakers violate the spirit of term limits when they move back and forth from the House to the Senate. Mead merely encountered a system that would not, she felt, let her be a legislator and, as former Rep. Patrick A. Sweeney used to say, "wrestle in the mud of public policy."

Instead of concentrating on issues and problem-solving, Mead says, senators are fixated on their next opportunity, whether it's running for Congress, returning to the House or becoming a county official.

"There's pressure to move forward every eight years," she said. "It's a game of limitations. They say, 'If somebody else has it, then I have to go after it.'"

Mead wasn't exactly Ms. Sterling, but she didn't blindly follow her leadership, either. She went against the grain in opposing the right to carry concealed weapons and in empowering elected local officials, not appointed health czars, to govern smoking bans in public places.

And it bothered her that the legislature wouldn't take the eminently sensible step of enhancing the statewide emergency response network to pinpoint the location of cellphone callers, as 41 other states have done.

"The world has changed," Mead said last week. But the Ohio legislature isn't changing for Mr. Sterling or anybody else, so Mead is taking her leave.

■ ■

Lobbying

Lobbyists Happily Pay to See Hated Lawmaker Decked

United Press International, Nov. 13, 1985

COLUMBUS (UPI)—They came to see Charlie Butts get his clock cleaned but what they got was a lot of lip and a no-decision.

About 100 Statehouse lobbyists paid $75 apiece to see state Sen. Charles L. Butts, D-Cleveland, who enjoys a reputation as one of the most unpopular legislators in Columbus, fight former world heavyweight contender Earnie Shavers.

"The Main Event," a fund-raiser for Butts' 1986 re-election campaign, was staged in the basement of the Trinity Episcopal Church across the street from the Statehouse.

"I came to see Charlie Butts get knocked on his rear," grinned Vincent Squillace, a lobbyist for the Ohio Homebuilders Association as he approached the makeshift ring of red-and-blue ropes.

Vendors roamed through the crowd, offering hot dogs, peanuts, beer and soda from carriers hung around their necks.

Lobbyists chanted, "We want Earnie!" One said a pot of money was being collected to award Shavers "if he coldcocks Charlie."

State Rep. Robert E. Hagan, D-Madison, the ring announcer clad in half a tuxedo, billed the fight as "the greatest since the Willard-Dempsey fight in Toledo."

"We staged this in a church so it would be easy to go upstairs and administer the last rites," said Senate Democratic Leader Harry Meshel of Youngstown, a personal friend of Shavers who arranged the match.

Gray-haired and bespectacled, the 43-year old Butts drew loud boos as he entered the ring, garbed in a red silk "Ohio" robe, to the piped-in "Theme from Rocky."

It was evident the fix was in when referee Larry Price announced the rules: No hitting before the break, after the break or between breaks, no hitting anyone with glasses, and no hitting below the belt.

Butts removed his robe and displayed a pair of three-foot-long white trunks hitched up under his arms.

Except for a few menacing gestures by both fighters, it was all downhill from that point. The wildest applause went to a bikini-clad girl who carried the "round" cards around the ring.

"You got to go at least three rounds, Charlie!" yelled a lobbyist. But after a few seconds of chasing, the fight was declared over without a blow being struck. Butts was safe and his campaign chest a little fatter.

This was one of the more creative events to raise money for a legislative campaign, although state Sen. Doug White, a gentleman farmer, once got lobbyists to pay to see him ride a bucking bronco. He got thrown, and his wife made him promise not to do it again.

■ ■

This column represents a textbook primer on how to lobby legislators—always be close to the action, make your wishes known and, oh yes, don't be shy about contributing to campaigns. Even then it doesn't always work, but it helps. The professor is Pat Sweeney, a veteran legislator who earned his stripes and was unafraid to say what was on his mind, even if it offended some. Here, he scolded the private detectives at a committee meeting in full view of the public.

Chickens That Cluck Loudest Save Eggs from State Tax Man

The Columbus Dispatch, July 29, 1991

On an oppressively hot and humid Saturday, July 6, Ira Gaffin sat quietly and patiently in a rickety straight-backed chair just off a main corridor of the Statehouse, guarding a heavy wooden door that was shut.

Behind that door, an Ohio House-Senate conference committee was reassembling the state's $27.2 billion budget, trying to make the expenditure pieces fit the revenue pieces.

Gaffin, a private citizen but a former Ohio Senate staff member, had one aim: to restore a 50 percent cut in the House appropriation for a hemophilia study program. He waited alone outside the door, save for two or three news reporters. About 2 P.M., he was approached by Sen. William F. Bowen, D-Cincinnati, a member of the conference committee and a defender of human services. "You can go home, Ira," Bowen said softly.

Gaffin soon left, confident his program was protected. But he returned the day the committee's report was made public. "It's never really safe to go home," he smiled.

And that's what the nurserymen, security guards, private detectives and lawn-care services, among others, found out about the legislature in general and closed-door conference committees in particular.

They learned this lesson the hard way: If you don't weigh in and speak up at the Statehouse, you're liable to get your tail feathers plucked and handed to you.

House and Senate leaders, along with Gov. George V. Voinovich, were looking for ways to raise money to plug a hole in the budget. They took the line of least resistance. They extended the state sales tax to a variety of services, and you had to be paying close attention to know whether you were included.

One member of the Ohio Association of Private Detective Agencies, at the group's convention in Cleveland, accused the lawmakers of a "sneak attack" on his industry.

"We were submarined, and it was done on purpose so (the tax) could get pushed through before we could raise hell," the member told Rep. Patrick A. Sweeney, D-Cleveland, chairman of the conference committee.

"You identified it exactly," Sweeney replied.

Then the chairman, a veteran of 25 years in the legislative wars, told members of the association the facts of life about self-protection at the Statehouse. He told them they have to use their detectives' tools and then do a little play-acting.

"It's your fault for not having participation down there to watch," he said.

Sweeney said lobbyists representing amusement rides, film companies, television stations and chewing tobacco averted taxes by finding out they were on the list and aggressively fighting back.

"I think you have to get to us," Sweeney told the detectives. "I think that the squeaky wheel . . . if we don't hear from you and if there's not anger out there . . . nobody's upset.

"Believe me," he continued, "if you don't put the tears on the cheek and the anger in the voice like you're doing tonight, and routinely and strongly throughout Ohio, you're going to be a victim."

Sweeney told the detectives that when groups "scream and complain" about the possibility of a tax increase, the legislators will "run away."

"The TV guys came down real hard on us" over a proposed extension of the sales tax to films distributed for television, he said.

"We're a representative body," said Sweeney. "We react to what we hear and what we feel. Your anger has to be sustained and brought to the level of those that are going to make those decisions. If you don't do that, people are going to get comfortable with the fact that you agree with the taxes.

"Some of your clients . . . should be part of that chorus," advised the chairman. "If the voice is raised, it gets listened to."

One professional lobbyist says the budget conference committee was among the most difficult he's seen in terms of obtaining information about who was at risk.

"It takes time and hard work," said Columbus attorney Thomas R. Winters, a former insider at the House of Representatives, who checked in that crucial Saturday to help protect Bob Evans Farms (they got taxed) and the Ohio Council of Retail Merchants (they escaped), among others.

One group that took Sweeney's advice literally made an impression but received nothing extra for its time and effort. Welfare demonstrators chanted loudly against cuts in general assistance, blocked a Statehouse door and tried to chain it shut.

Several were roughed up and carted off to jail by Ohio Highway Patrol plainclothesmen, and the lawmakers treated general assistance just as they had planned anyway.

In addition to screaming and complaining, Sweeney might have noted, legislators react best to people who befriend them, butter them up, wear pleasant aftershave and drop a few pesos in the old campaign fund every so often.

■ ■

Many panelists and luncheon speakers at national legislative conferences induce sleep. When one comes along to deliver a pointed elbow to the ribs of the lawmakers, it's worth a column.

As Legislators Gather, Lobbyists' Lures Conflict With Speech on Ethics

The Columbus Dispatch, August 3, 1992

The words shot out of Barbara Jordan's mouth like sharp-tipped arrows aimed at state legislators assembled from all over the country to enjoy one another's company, Cincinnati's charm and the overtures of heavy-hitting corporations that want things done and undone.

The former Congress member and spellbinding orator from Texas had just finished wrapping education, citizenship, responsibility and ethics into a neat package of ingredients for preserving democracy.

Now she stared out at the hundreds of people at the National Conference of State Legislatures luncheon and assigned them to make it work.

"Public trust—ethics," she said. "Public servant—*you*, servant. *We . . . are . . . servants*." The words had almost enough volume to reach Montana, Arkansas and other locations where the lawmakers have now returned.

And they may need to hear the echoes as they go back to work. For though Jordan's words hit home during that dramatic moment in Cincinnati, they may have been drowned out quickly in the surrounding corporate cacophony.

The legislators were wooed at every turn by utilities, petroleum companies, tobacco and beer companies, communications giants, retailers and health-care and insurance companies. They were beckoned to play golf, eat at Cincinnati's finest restaurants and pay attention to the corporate agenda as they hiked through an enormous "trade exhibit" that took up almost half a city block.

Thoughts of being a servant must have been remote as they received the red-carpet treatment, dining on prime beef and Alaskan king crab, and sipping from a selection of several dozen fine California wines.

True, there were plenty of worthy seminars in which the lawmakers exchanged information about higher education, school financing and government efficiency. But there also were roundtables on the wine industry and how to help it.

Sen. David E. Nething of North Dakota, a veteran of 26 years in his legislature and a former president of the NCSL, could see no harm in the close proximity of lobbyists, far from the people at home.

"The good legislators know that if you can't take their food and eat it, and take their wine and drink it and then vote against them the next day, they're not much of a legislator," said Nething.

The North Dakota senator said his district is so small, population 13,000, that he can't hide from his constituents. "The thought that some lobbyist is going to get to Dave Nething is repugnant to my constituents," he said.

Carolyn Oakley, a state representative from Albany, Ore., pointed out that few Oregon lobbyists traveled to Cincinnati, so she wasn't in danger of being coopted. However, Oakley said she did have lunch with one of the trade-show exhibitors to find out more about the purchase of services for the Oregon lottery.

"We are here because we want to expand our knowledge," she said. "We want to get more information to take back home. I enjoy the interaction with the lobbyists. I can tell a lobbyist 'no' and for the most part they understand. You can still be friends with these folks."

Nething said new legislators tend to keep lobbyists at arm's length. "The new ones are a little squeamish," he said. "Pretty soon they'll find out how valuable lobbyists are."

That may be the answer to the most frequently asked question about term limits—what should the limit be? About the time the legislators start finding out how valuable the lobbyists are.

Jordan told the lawmakers if they are serious about keeping the public trust and preserving democracy, they can begin by upgrading education for everyone in their states. Knock, knock, Ohio. Anybody home?

She said that education is the cornerstone for an enlightened democracy and that everyone is entitled to it. "Some say universal education for everybody dilutes the quality of education," she said. "You . . . must . . . say . . . no!"

In the end, Jordan told the lawmakers that if they're serious about serving the people, they need only a simple code of ethics—the Golden Rule.

"Your constituents expect you to look after their interests before you look after your own," she said.

The reference to "Knock, knock, Ohio" was a reminder that a lawsuit had been filed the previous year against the state's system of funding schools. The system was found to be inadequately and unfairly funded by the Ohio Supreme Court in 1997. Lawmakers put more state money into the system, but by 2008, state funding was moving in reverse.

Ironically, Jordan's warning to legislators about ethics took place about a year before a pay-to-play scandal broke over the Ohio legislature, resulting in a new ethics law that was far more complicated than the Golden Rule and drastically altered the relationship between legislators and lobbyists.

Sen. Nething of North Dakota apparently was unaware of the age-old Statehouse maxim: "Whose meat I eat, whose wine I drink, his will I do."

■ ■

What, No Pity for Lonely Lawmakers?

The Columbus Dispatch, January 8, 1996

As 1996 begins, state legislators and lobbyists are counting the days until the three-year restoration of the Statehouse is completed and the House and Senate can move their sessions back to the original chambers. The forecast is for repossession by early autumn, and it can't come soon enough for most erstwhile Statehouse denizens.

Since 1993, the Senate has been meeting in what was known as the Statehouse Annex, on 3rd Street, and the House has occupied temporary chambers in the Ohio Departments Building, at 65 S. Front St.

That puts a long two blocks between the House and Senate, which were accustomed to staging their theatrics less than 40 yards apart.

The fact that legislators are out of sight of each other and the lobbyists has contributed to the general social paralysis on Capitol Square. Another factor is the 1994 ethics law that has thrown cold water on lobbyists entertaining legislators.

Believe it or not, the legislators made themselves so scarce to lobbyists in 1995 that the best place to catch them for a bit of conversation was at their fund-raising breakfasts or cocktail parties.

"The one place you can socialize is at a fund-raiser for legislators," said Jim Henry, the veteran lobbyist for the Ohio Council of Retail Merchants. "We used to blow them off because we had something else to do. Now we go because we know most members of the caucus are going to be there and we can socialize with them. The political fund-raiser sponsored by a legislator has become the Galleria watering hole where you meet everybody."

The Galleria Tavern, now defunct, was at one time the focal point of legislative nightlife. Now, said Rep. Frank Sawyer, D-Butler, what little socializing there is takes place at Christopher's, atop the Riffe Center; the Guest Quarters, across the alley on Front Street; and Damon's on Nationwide Boulevard.

When legislators and lobbyists were asked late last year about the effect of the new ethics law, an overwhelming number of them replied, in one way or another, "It's not as much fun anymore."

The ethics law, the physical separation and career planning brought about by the impending term limits have combined to take a lot of the fun out of legislating and lobbying.

"I think the cameraderie is gone," said Gordon M. Scherer, a Cincinnati lobbyist and former legislator. "I think the collegiality has suffered, particularly in the House, where there are more (office) doors than in the U.S. Congress. It's more difficult to get access."

"It just doesn't happen anymore," agreed Sawyer, referring to the legislator-lobbyist socializing. "I don't feel I know the new members. With nobody buying their beers now, I think legislators are going to McDonald's, grabbing a burger and going back to their rooms."

Sawyer is not the only one who doesn't know the new members. Some lobbyists say the freshmen run away from them or slam doors in their faces because they've been warned they can get in trouble by fraternizing with lobbyists.

"The new people have this idea that lobbyists are underhanded and can't be trusted," said Cynthia Snyder, an independent lobbyist representing a variety of health-care groups.

"The new legislators are almost petrified to spend time with lobbyists," agreed Vince Squillace, president of both the Ohio Lobbying Association and the Ohio Trade Association Executives.

One is entitled to ask: "So what? What's so all-fired important about their social lives, anyway? Who said it's supposed to be fun in the first place? We don't send our legislators to Columbus to cavort with each other and with lobbyists."

The lobbyists will answer that question, thank you. They say that most legislators are away from home and need companionship at mealtime and in the evening. What harm is there in socializing for a few hours until it's time to go to bed, so you can get up and tie into that legislative agenda the next day?

William Weisenberg, the veteran lobbyist for the Ohio State Bar Association, points out that legislators are not reimbursed for their living expenses while in Columbus.

"What's wrong with having dinner with someone and picking up the tab?" he asked. "Basically, all we do is provide information and hope they believe us. It builds friendships. You learn about them. Sometimes building friendships helps you deal with them better."

Lobbyist Snyder sees "building relationships" with legislators as no different from what a company tries to do in the private sector.

Perhaps the difference is that the legislature is in the public sector, and it never was intended to be a business.

So folks can be excused if they shed no tears for the demise of the good times on Capitol Square. After all, they rarely get a chance to build a relationship with their legislator, unless they're married to one.

Lawmakers did indeed return to their original chambers in the Statehouse in July 1996, but the damage was done as far as socializing goes. The 1993 pay-to-play scandal followed by the 1994 ethics law limited how much lobbyists could spend on legislators. Later, term limitations prevented long relationships from being established. But lobbyists made up for it with unprecedented amounts of money contributed to legislative campaigns.

■ ■

Vern Riffe

The next six columns relate to the legendary Ohio House speaker who held that top leadership post for 20 years. When he was first elected by deposing A. G. Lancione, his fellow Democrat, expectations were that he would last one term. In the first column of the series, Riffe addresses the opening session of the House and vows to reassert legislative power. One of his foremost accomplishments turned out to be returning power to the legislative branch of government.

New Speaker Vern Riffe Wants House on Equal Footing with Governor

United Press International, January 11, 1975

COLUMBUS (UPI)—Democrats wasted no time in exercising their newfound power in the Ohio General Assembly as the 111th session opened last week, but they found time to offer some clues as to how they plan to use it in the future.

One tipoff came in a speech given by Rep. Vernal G. Riffe Jr., D-New Boston, after he was installed as the new House speaker.

Riffe said the Democratic majorities would attempt to assert themselves as at least an equal power to incoming Republican Gov. James A. Rhodes.

Other hints were offered as Gov. John J. Gilligan presented his final budget proposals and legislative Democrats made plans to spend another $91 million in surplus funds to increase state school subsidies.

The indications were that the Democrats will be unafraid to spend money without waiting for direction from the incoming Rhodes administration.

Riffe issued the keynote:

"The governor-elect, while receiving a plurality of the votes cast in his race, did not receive a majority of the votes," he said in reference to Rhodes' 49 percent tally.

"In contrast, the Democrats in this House received a clear majority of the votes cast in House elections, while the Democrats who ran for election to the Senate did likewise. Additionally, the total vote for Democrats running for this House exceeded the total vote for the governor-elect.

"Given these facts," Riffe continued, "I believe the people of this state expect the Ohio General Assembly to be at least an equal with the governor in leading the government of this state. I believe they expect this General Assembly to have its own ideas about how Ohio should be governed."

If the Democrats got this feeling from the November election, they also must have received a message that the voters want increased support for public schools.

They quickly announced plans to spend the $91 million for school subsidies, and the announcement came six months ahead of the end of the fiscal year. In the past, the Democrats were more cautious about spending anticipated surpluses.

Perhaps they could foresee Rhodes beating them to the punch. Their explanation was that Ohio's schools need a financial shot-in-the-arm to keep some from closing before June.

In his keynote speech, Riffe lifted a couple of pages from Rhodes' book. He talked about increasing aid to vocational education, a traditional staple of Rhodes' government.

And he said the Democrats will "take every opportunity to create new jobs," another Rhodes byword.

"We will make every attempt to assure that this state's working men and women stay on their jobs," Riffe said, "and we will make every attempt to assist in returning our state's unemployed to their jobs."

Receipt of the governor's budget alone was enough to push the Democratic lawmakers along the trail of increased spending, even if they hadn't offered the education appropriation.

Gilligan told the legislators there would be almost $1.5 billion available for new state spending, without additional taxes, because of the "elastic" income tax. This is like taking the lid off a jar of freshly baked cookies around a small boy. Once the lawmakers and lobbyists get the scent, it will be difficult to stop them.

And the Democratic spending plan will have a two-month foothold in the legislative finance committees before Rhodes even submits his own budget.

■ ■

Riffe Wields Power in Creating New University

United Press International, February 9, 1986

COLUMBUS (UPI)—"This is probably the most important bill you will vote on this year," said Ohio House Speaker Vernal G. Riffe Jr., D-New Boston, in a rare floor speech to his colleagues last week.

Riffe was not talking about a budget, a tax bill, an abortion bill or a death penalty bill.

He was talking about a bill to turn Shawnee Community College in his district at Portsmouth into a four-year state university, a proposal developed independently from the Ohio Board of Regents and without the blessing of that coordinating group for higher education.

While Riffe smiled and other House members guffawed, there was an underlying feeling of uneasiness. It was probably the most important bill they will vote on.

For Vern Riffe has demonstrated that he is peerless in the use of political power. That's why he has remained speaker for a record 11 years.

Some have learned the hard way what happens when you don't follow the speaker's lead.

Rep. David Hartley, D-Springfield, a promising young liberal, dared to vote "no" one time when Riffe was seeking re-election as speaker. Only after a couple of sessions in exile was he awarded a committee chairmanship.

Former Rep. Robert J. Boggs, D-Jefferson, spoke out one day about the hypocrisy of the tax policy being developed by Riffe and others. He was stripped of his committee chairmanship the next session and eventually fled to the Senate.

Most recently, freshman Rep. Michael Camera, D-Lorain, misbehaved and was not penitent. He was turned out of the fold, received no support for re-election and lost.

So when Vern Riffe stepped down off that rostrum and took the microphone to present his first bill in 13 years, the message was clear: "You better vote with me, podnuh, or you'll never get another bill through here again."

Now Riffe didn't actually say that. When somebody has power, it's unnecessary to display it openly.

Looking around the chamber at his fellow members, Riffe pointed out that since he has been in a position of influence, universities in Dayton, Cleveland, Youngstown, Cincinnati, and Akron have achieved four-year status in the state system.

"I've been a part of that, and I'm proud of that," he said. "We gave the young people of those areas an opportunity to further their education while at home."

Having heard that, no House member from those cities, or anyplace else in Ohio, needed an excuse to vote for Shawnee State University. Even the Republicans seemed mesmerized by Riffe's logic.

"Southern Ohio has got this one coming," said Rep. Waldo Bennett Rose, R-Lima, the assistant minority leader.

"I'm going to vote for this," said Rep. Michael A. Fox, R-Hamilton. "It's my way of saying thanks."

Rep. Robert E. Hagan, D-Madison, injected some humor when he suggested that football team at Shawnee University might be named the "Shawnee Speakers," with little gavels on their helmets. Everybody laughed, but it was the kind of laugh reserved for humor that is too close to the truth.

Shawnee State turned out to be a pretty good university, and southern Ohio indeed had one coming. But it took Riffe, who eventually made it to 20 years as speaker, to pull it off.

■ ■

Building Named After Political Legend While He Still Works There

United Press International, Sept. 25, 1988

COLUMBUS (UPI)—Statehouse observers were more than a little amused last week when Gov. Richard Celeste saw to it that the new $130 million state office tower was named after House Speaker Vern Riffe.

State Office Tower 2 was just completed on Capitol Square this past summer, and much of it is still vacant.

But Celeste, in a three-page memorandum to Ohio Building Authority Chairman Harvey Oppmann, whom he mistakenly addressed as "Harry" Oppmann, put in a strong plug for Riffe as the honoree. Oppmann and the Building Authority (board) quickly complied.

There is precedent for naming state buildings after living politicians, still in office.

Gov. James Rhodes, when he controlled the Building Authority, quietly had the first state office tower named after himself. The workers put the sign up while Rhodes was in China so it wouldn't look like he had anything to do with it.

Riffe, though a power in state capital circles, has labored in relative obscurity as a House member for 29 years and as speaker for 14—a record for Ohio. While he has several buildings and institutions named after him in his southern Ohio district, he has long hungered for statewide recognition.

Rhodes offered that recognition shortly before he left office in 1982. Riffe had helped Rhodes get a statue of himself erected on the Statehouse lawn with private money; now it came time for the return favor.

Rhodes proposed naming State Office Tower 2 after Riffe and Senate President Paul Gillmor.

But the tower, then in the design stage, became mired in controversy over the selection of a construction manager and the awarding of contracts for architects and engineers by the Rhodes-controlled OBA without competitive bidding. Sound familiar?

Riffe wanted no part of that noise, so he asked that his name be dropped from the project. So did Gillmor. Construction proceeded and, with a few bugs to be ironed out, the building is ready for occupancy.

Riffe says he had no idea Celeste was going to propose naming the tower after him, but he's honored. "I think it's an honor to have a state building named after you," he said last week.

For the record, Riffe also insists he never said he didn't want the building named after him. "I just said to take my name off that sign that was sitting in the middle of that vacant lot," he said.

Riffe said he "never had a thing to do" with Celeste's letter to Oppmann, a letter which goes into more detail than a governor would ever know about Riffe's political career.

"We are taking a historical perspective of what this man's contribution has been," said Debra Phillips, the governor's press secretary. "He's carved out his niche."

To be sure, Riffe has carved out his niche, and is still carving. When Celeste tries to get his final programs through the General Assembly next session, having named the office tower after Mr. Speaker isn't going to hurt his chances. And when Riffe attempts to run for governor in 1990, it's no liability to be a living legend, marked in stone, in Columbus.

It might not be a bad idea to let our leaders put down their carving knives before we start lionizing them with monuments.

The building ended up being named the Vern Riffe Center for Government and the Arts. Curiously, it was Riffe who suggested that the arts be added to the name so it wouldn't look like the building was solely a political nest.

The next column shows the author's contempt for further lionizing the speaker while he was still at work.

■ ■

This short but punchy column was the product of the author's outrage. It was not received warmly by its subject. Riffe, a certified Ohio political legend, led for 3½ more years before retiring.

Where's Line Between Honor, Pandering?

The Columbus Dispatch, May 21, 1991

What if Pete Rose had been elected to the Hall of Fame by the players before he retired?

That's not too much of a stretch from the situation at the Statehouse, where House Speaker Vern Riffe has been made a permanent part of the Capitol Square landscape during his active career.

The 31-story government office building and theater complex was named in Riffe's honor in 1989 and just last week it was decorated with a large bronze bust of the speaker in full battle pose.

The bronze Riffe, arms defiantly folded, hand gripping gavel, is glaring menacingly at an unseen adversary, ready to lower the boom as the speaker has so many times in the past.

Only last Wednesday, Rep. Ronald D. Amstutz, R-Wooster, was the recipient of that withering gaze from the real Riffe as Amstutz strayed out of bounds while debating an amendment on the state budget.

One day later, after House Democrats had pushed through their budget with something in it for everyone, Riffe was feted with the $77,000 sculpture, not paid for with public money but donated by friends and admirers.

Five weeks from now, many of those friends and admirers, plus hundreds of others, will assemble at the Aladdin Shrine Temple in northeast Columbus for the speaker's birthday party.

This time, they will contribute $400 apiece for the privilege of being seen and trying to ensure that Riffe extends his record 18 years as speaker by another two years, beginning in 1993.

Have the Riffe tower and the bronze bust now blurred the line between what is honoring a genuine legend and what is political pandering to one of the most powerful public figures in the history of Ohio?

Obviously, Riffe thinks not. At the sculpture's unveiling, he found it hard to express his feelings, first saying he was humbled, then proud, then humble again. "I believe that when you've been honest and fair . . . and you've done the best that you can do . . . then you feel very, very grateful," he finally decided.

The speaker also said he opposes anyone having political fund-raisers in the Vern Riffe Center for Government and the Arts because it's a state building. "I think it's wrong," he told reporters.

Nevertheless, Riffe's enshrinement, coupled with the way he controls the agenda at the Statehouse, definitely tilts the process against any adversaries, and democracy is supposed to give adversaries an equal footing.

The perception is that legends can't make mistakes. Riffe's building and bust confer an aura of invincibility. The Ron Amstutzes of the world don't have a chance.

What do people think when they read about lobbyists and political insiders canonizing a government leader while he's still doing the public's business?

It might be better, as Harry Truman once said, if nobody had a monument until his days are finished.

The answer to the question of what Ohioans would think of Riffe's premature beatification was, apparently, not much. They adopted term limitations for legislators the following year, based in part on Riffe's hammerlock on the House.

Pete Rose is still awaiting his induction into the Hall of Fame.

■ ■

Republicans, Long Suppressed By Riffe, Taste Power

The Columbus Dispatch, April 5, 1993

In the old days, Corwin Nixon, a horse trader from southwestern Ohio, would canter up the steps of the rostrum in the Ohio House of Representatives, shield his mouth with his hand and whisper in the ear of Speaker Vernal G. Riffe Jr.

Then Nixon, the minority floor leader, would return to his seat in the back of the chamber on the Republican side to watch the proceedings on the state budget.

Republicans would stand up, one after another, offering suggestions on how to change the budget. Mostly, those suggestions were treated like something that came out of a sewer pipe.

No matter how loudly the Republicans shrieked, the result was the same. House Majority Leader William L. Mallory, D-Cincinnati, would invariably move to lay the amendment on the table, and his motion would always pass. The Republicans were lucky Riffe didn't throw his gavel and hit them in the head for good measure.

How times have changed! Nothing cures the arrogance of power faster than an election where the Republicans secure 46 seats to the Democrats' 53, instead of the lopsided 61-38 breakdown of 1991-92.

Last week, there was the new Republican leader, Jo Ann Davidson of Reynoldsburg, up on that same rostrum in her lavender power suit, exchanging good-natured finger points with Riffe as they got their signals straight.

And the results were quite different. Even the hard-nosed conservatives in the Republican caucus found it difficult to say much bad about the $30.6 billion budget, though they voted against it.

Gov. George V. Voinovich's original outlay had been rewritten by the Democrats, but with plenty of input from the GOP members.

Debate was laid back. There were lots of smiles. When Mallory moved to table a Republican amendment the first time, there were gasps. He got only 51 votes, and he only tried it one more time. Republicans got two prime amendments into the bill, a rarity in recent years.

There was a time when the Republicans would outline their amendments a day ahead of the budget debate so they could get some press coverage; they knew they wouldn't get anything on budget day.

This time, the Republicans were so surprised at their own effectiveness they had to caucus to reflect on how to vote—whether to attack the budget as a product of the evil Democrats or embrace it as a compromise, bipartisan document.

Thirty of the 46 Republicans, including most of the 14 freshmen, decided to play the partisan card and differentiate between themselves and the Democrats.

There were plenty of opportunities for public relations during the debate, and both sides took advantage.

This is not new. One time in the 1970s, the minority House Republicans under Rep. Charles F. Kurfess of Bowling Green paraded a stream of attractive female House employees across the front of the chamber during the debate.

Dubbed "Charlie's Angels" by the media, they displayed charts and graphs on state spending to accompany the presentation of Republican amendments.

Speaker Riffe, the wily Wheelersburg Democrat, may have eased up on the Republicans this time, but he was not about to let them run away with the show. Riffe used the free-wheeling debate to showcase his own party's freshmen, deliberately setting aside speaking time for them in hopes they would capture some media attention. He did so even though only one of them had spent more than a token amount of time in the budget committee hearings.

Rep. Thomas W. Johnson, R-New Concord, the Republicans' senior finance man, poked fun at the Democrats and got away with it. "Mr. Speaker," said Johnson, "if we had all our freshmen speak and they took 10 minutes apiece, it would take two hours and 20 minutes to get finished."

Rep. Michael A. Fox, R-Hamilton, who has had a knack over the years for getting amendments in the budget because of his friendship with the speaker, offset the Democrats' public-relations effort.

Fox had three-ring binders with colored tabs made up at taxpayers' expense, detailing nine amendments he got in the budget, and circulated them to reporters.

Fox defended the expense of the notebooks, which he estimated at $2.95 apiece, saying his amendments on special education, medically fragile children and environmental-protection projects would save the state millions of dollars.

The photocopying cost not nearly as much as it cost to copy the 1,233-page budget, Fox said.

"For all the money I've saved 'em, they ought to pay for that and more," he said.

"I'm very proud of those amendments," Fox continued. "They wouldn't have been in there if I hadn't driven them. If folks like you don't know about them, I've got no chance of getting the message out. The whole idea is to try to get the darned things passed."

Now Fox and the others will look toward the Republican-controlled Senate to see if their efforts are treated as kindly as they were in the Democratic House.

It is not a slam-dunk that senators will treat House members of their own party kindly. Inter-chamber jealousies sometimes override party loyalty.

■ ■

This column, written under the pressure of deadlines involving the death of a Statehouse legend and a major legislative debate over school funding, is probably the clearest explanation of how Vern Riffe was able to remain House speaker for 20 years. His political acumen, in the author's opinion, may have surpassed that of Republican James A. Rhodes, who was governor for four terms.

Riffe Honed Legislative Skills on Old-Fashioned Tactics

The Columbus Dispatch, August 4, 1997

Ohio House members, unaccustomed to a good, old-fashioned hardball fight over a sticky political issue, expressed their irritation last week as Speaker Jo Ann Davidson, R-Reynoldsburg, tried to round up votes for school-funding legislation.

"Nine hours," grumbled one Democrat cooling his heels in the House chamber late Wednesday night while Davidson lobbied her individual members to raise 50 votes for school accountability and performance standards. "Vern would have had this done in 10 minutes."

"Vern" was Davidson's predecessor, Vernal G. Riffe Jr., the Wheelersburg Democrat who served as speaker for a record 20 years, long enough and expertly enough to merit a state funeral today.

"He would have pounded on the table and we'd be out of here," said House Minority Leader Ross Boggs Jr., an Ashtabula County Democrat.

State Sen. Michael C. Shoemaker, D-Bourneville, who sat through Riffe-led caucus meetings in the 1980s, agreed that Riffe was unsurpassed at swiftly extracting votes from wavering members on critical issues. "We'd say, 'What about the Republicans (providing votes)?' " related Shoemaker. "He'd say, 'We're in a position of leadership and, by (spicy word), we're gonna take responsibility.'"

Riffe would get his caucus unified. Then he'd get some votes from the Republicans. Not as many as his members wanted, but Republican votes, nevertheless. When his troops cried that the Republicans would use the issue against them at the next election, Riffe would reassure them: "Don't worry. We'll raise more money than they will."

"The Democrats were going to take the heat and Vern was going to defend them," said Shoemaker.

Nothing said here is meant to demean Davidson. She has skillfully managed her fractious caucus. She has a more difficult task than Riffe. Her caucus, even her leadership team, is more fragmented philosophically, and she couldn't use his power methods even if it were her style, which it is not.

The purpose is to review what made Vern Riffe successful in similar situations, and to see what built the legend—20 years on top of the mountain when nearly everyone was trying to topple him.

One of Riffe's methods was to involve the minority party in the solution to any major problem. That resulted in a better public policy and took away his adversary's weapons.

True, Riffe ignored his own advice in 1983 when the Democrats rammed through Gov. Richard F. Celeste's income tax increase with no regard for the Republicans.

In retrospect, Riffe said it was the biggest political mistake he ever made, according to C. Paul Tipps, the Columbus lobbyist and Riffe confidant.

How would Riffe have attacked a mega-issue like school funding? First, he would perform damage control and then he would solve the problem in a way that a majority of the public could buy.

Tipps said Riffe's style was to talk to as many interest groups as possible and settle on a solution that would "take the sting out of everybody's personal future."

Once Riffe decided on the best course, he would begin selling it back to the interest groups. He would convince them that the compromise was good for them, to the point that some began to believe it was their own idea.

And how did he do this? He found out their bottom line—what they absolutely had to have. "The first thing they ask you for is what they want. Then you have to figure out what they need," Tipps quoted Riffe as saying.

Selling legislators was different. With his own members, it was a carrot-and-stick method. Riffe had intimate knowledge, developed during years of studying human nature, of their wants and needs. When crunch time came, he exploited those pressure points.

He reminded wavering members of the times he helped them, which were numerous. If they were unimpressed, he hauled out the stick.

One variation of a biblical principle employed by Riffe: If you do not ask, you shall not receive. When he was in the House, Democrat Joseph J. Vukovich of Youngstown found this out the hard way. Exiled from his committee chairmanship by Riffe, he failed to ask for reappointment the next session because he thought he was still in the doghouse. He later learned the chairmanship would have been restored for the asking.

Why did they have to ask? Because once they asked a favor and it was granted, then they'd owe. And that's what politics is about, as former Gov. James A. Rhodes once said: "You do things for people and get them obligated."

If history lessons have been learned well, the school-funding solution will be bipartisan. The Republican solution is built on going to the ballot. They reason that letting the people of Ohio vote meets Riffe's test of a political solution that satisfies a majority.

But—and here's where Riffe had no peers—the Republicans failed to think beyond the next move. What if the people defeat the tax issue? Then the legislators will be faced with three bad choices: raising taxes themselves in an election year after voters have told them no, cutting government to shreds or waiting for the Supreme Court to order them to raise taxes.

Vern Riffe rarely, if ever, let himself get boxed in like that.

■ ■

Statehouse Characters

Speechifying Secrest Sparked Fond Remembrances

The Columbus Dispatch, May 23, 1994

For Bob Secrest, happiness was a fresh package of Mail Pouch, another round of drinks and a cluster of good friends with whom to converse.

Bliss was a speaker's platform bedecked with red, white and blue bunting on a patriotic holiday, a high-school band and an audience of war veterans, old-timers, school kids and just plain folks.

Bob Secrest never met a speech he wouldn't give, especially on Memorial Day, Veterans Day or the Fourth of July. "Gave five speeches over the weekend," the lanky, craggy-faced Secrest would proudly report to colleagues in the Ohio Senate when he returned from a holiday weekend in the early 1970s.

Only death could still the voice of the former member of Congress, whose public service totaled 46 years. On Friday, all the speeches were about Secrest as they laid his 90-year-old, well-traveled body to rest in his beloved Senecaville.

Despite rubbing elbows with the greats of Washington in the 1930s and '40s, Secrest "never forgot the little town he came from," nephew Joe Secrest said last week. "He'd give a Veterans' Day speech in the Senecaville Cemetery, and he'd look up the hill and say, 'There's where I came from, and there's where I'm gonna be planted.'"

Robert T. Secrest may have been the Ted Williams of the U.S. House. Williams, a Hall of Fame baseball player, missed four seasons in the prime of his career because of World War II. Secrest resigned from Congress at the same time to join the Navy.

As it was, Secrest served 20 years in Congress. Time after time, he got reelected, a Democrat fighting a Republican tide in southeastern Ohio. Had he not resigned in 1942 and again in 1954, this time to accept a presidential appointment, his continuous service would have matched that of some of the legends of the House.

Bob Secrest hated to fly, so he drove his car back and forth to Washington. But he wasn't some Congressman Claghorn from the sticks. He had a law degree and a master's degree in international administration from Columbia University. He was an intellectual without the affectation.

After losing his seat in Congress, Secrest won one in the state Senate. "He was Ohio's Will Rogers," said former state Sen. Oliver Ocasek. "He had common sense."

When Ocasek became the Senate Democratic leader in 1975, most of the Democrats were working at their desks on the Senate floor and used the steno pool for typing. Ocasek got each of his members a private office, a secretary and an aide. "Bob came into my office and said: 'Mr. Leader, I think that was the dumbest thing anybody has done around here. We've got aides to write our speeches, and so we have to read 'em. Now the sessions are going to last hours instead of minutes.'"

Secrest wasted no words on his fellow senators during sessions. The few bills he sponsored were to help veterans, senior citizens and rural folk, and he explained them briefly. "Vote!" he would shout when the debate droned on.

Speaking to the people was another matter. After all, they had elected him, and he felt he owed them his best. Secrest had learned the art of public speaking at Muskingum College, where he captained the debate team. He could have an audience in tears one minute and heaving with laughter the next.

Neal S. Tostenson, president of the Ohio Mining and Reclamation Association, recalls that Secrest addressed his group one Friday afternoon, then stayed on for a cocktail party and dinner. After dinner, he decided he wanted to make another speech, "and he told the same jokes!" said Tostenson.

Some of Secrest's best audiences were six or eight legislators, lobbyists and reporters late at night at the Neil House across the street from the Statehouse. The senator would spin yarns about Harry Truman, Lyndon Johnson and his other Washington acquaintances.

Full glasses and bottles would become empty and cover the tabletop. After last call, Secrest took personal care that they were all empty. The next day, he would arrive at the Statehouse at 8 A.M., as chipper as if he'd turned in with the birds.

Secrest smoked pungent cigars and chewed tobacco. They gave him a handsome brass cuspidor on his 70th birthday, but he continued to use the blue Maxwell House coffee can that he carried everywhere.

There's a granite bust of Secrest outside the courthouse in Cambridge. Sam Speck, a former Republican legislator from the area, said he watched one winter day as a patch of snow slid off the top of the bust and covered Secrest's face.

"This elderly, stooped-over woman with a shopping bag and a babushka on her head approached the statue, reached into her purse, pulled out a scarf and lovingly wiped the snow off his face," said Speck. "That says it all about the love that he inspired."

■ ■

Meshel Leaves Big Shoes to Fill As He Departs Senate

The Columbus Dispatch, April 26, 1993

When Harry Meshel left the Ohio Senate last week, he was in much the same position as when he entered it 22 years ago—a minority in a minority and tucked away in an attic office the thickness of a roof away from pigeon droppings.

But what a ride between the time he arrived as a city government guy from Youngstown and now, when he leaves—as a past president of the Senate and new chairman of the Ohio Democratic Party! And what a character!

The loss to the Senate is not the 100-hour-a-week senator who got curb cuts enacted for the handicapped to enter public buildings and tapped the state's liquor profits for industrial development loans. It's not the loss of a legislator who fought for retirement benefits for police officers and firefighters, and for collective bargaining for public employees. It's not the loss of a senator who helped establish a couple of medical schools and tried to protect the eastern Ohio coal-mine operators against too many government regulations.

No, the loss here is measured in terms of a character the likes of whom will never again lighten the Senate chamber.

"Harry's politics are personal and passionate in a day when politicians are packaged like underarm deodorant," said Senate Minority Leader Robert J. Boggs, D-Jefferson. "He's somebody who wears his politics on his sleeve. He's in your face."

During the farewell ceremony, several senators confessed to being intimidated by Meshel's rich baritone voice bouncing polysyllabic words off the chamber walls during debate.

"You had to get your dictionary out," recalled Sen. William F. Bowen, D-Cincinnati. There is no question that Meshel was a serious worker—a habit developed during his youth when he got his hands dirty stuffing ads in newspapers, operating a printing press and shoveling dolomite into a blast furnace from midnight to 8 A.M. at the Ohio Works of U.S. Steel.

He rose through the Senate Democratic leadership ranks to become Senate president, because he worked at it harder than anybody else. But he had fun, too—something he learned as a graduate student at Columbia University when he'd drop his business administration books and go to Bop City or Birdland to see Dizzy Gillespie, Miles Davis or Charlie Parker.

That's why the Senate spent more than an hour last week bidding him goodbye. And you needed to hear only the first sentence of his response to understand why.

"I have mixed emotions about leaving," said Meshel. "It's kind of like watching your mother-in-law go over a cliff in your new Cadillac."

"Harry's idea of a crime," said Senate President Stanley J. Aronoff, R-Cincinnati, "is an unopened bottle of Scotch."

"A half-empty bottle," corrected Meshel.

Sen. Robert L. Burch, D-Dover, recalled how annoyed Meshel became when the Senate passed a resolution restricting smoking to the rear of the chamber.

Meshel, who has since quit smoking, tried to amend the resolution to outlaw "noxious odors and body scents" emanating from offensive men's colognes on the Senate floor.

Sen. Richard H. Finan, R-Cincinnati, remembered that Meshel was so upset with a Republican tax bill once, he said the GOP wanted to "put a tax on everything except flatulence."

Meshel recalled his early days in the Senate when he and Aronoff went on a field trip for the Elections Committee. "We went to Beverly Hills, stayed in a mosque and covered the elections," he said. "I got Randolph Scott's autograph."

That's not the only autograph he got. Until he moved, Meshel's office was littered with autographed pictures of people ranging from Robert DeNiro to Johnny Bench to Ray "Boom Boom" Mancini, former lightweight champion from Youngstown.

Meshel loves to mingle with the fight crowd. He was a sort of adviser to former heavyweight contender Earnie Shavers and thinks nothing of jetting off to Las Vegas for a title fight.

One of his greatest kicks was to go to the White House for lunch when Jimmy Carter was president and he was chairman of a group of Democratic state leaders. "That night I'd be back at the East Side Civic Club in Youngstown drinking 35-cent beers," he said.

He has a building named after him at Youngstown State University, where he graduated years after discharge from the Navy in 1946, and where he has taught real estate and business.

"Harry could have been anything," said Boggs. He chose to be a senator, and a character.

Shipped off to Youngstown as he moved from the Senate were 75 boxes of plaques, books, photos, clocks, shovels and ribbons and the scissors he used to cut them.

Even Meshel, as he left, seemed to realize there are few with his rich and varied background to lend color and perspective to the legislative process. "There is a paucity of historical reference in this place, and it is getting worse," he intoned.

Go get your dictionary.

■ ■

Lottery's Father Passes Torch to Son in Ohio House

The Columbus Dispatch, February 10, 1997

If you blinked, you missed the passing of the torch from one generation to the next in the Ohio House of Representatives last week.

The 20th District seat, suburban Cleveland, shifted from father to son so seamlessly that few noticed. With no advance warning, Ronald M. Mottl, the father of the Ohio lottery, resigned and engineered the appointment of his son to replace him.

Within minutes, his eyes moist and his voice strained, Ronald M. Mottl administered the oath of office to Ronald M. Mottl for a 23-month interim term. The next day, Ronald M. Mottl was in committee pushing his father's bills as his own.

Most people in the 20th District, when they go to vote in 1998, will think they're voting for Ronald Milton Mottl, who's been on the ballot for a quarter century and has represented them at the Ohio Statehouse for 18 years.

But they'll really be voting for Ronald Michael "Mickey" Mottl (not Ron Jr., yet another member of the North Royalton family), a 23-year old aspiring law student.

Ron Mottl Sr., a conservative, independent-style Democrat and a loner in Columbus, accomplished a lot. He reduced the amount of an estate subject to probate, annoying his fellow attorneys. He railed against the banks, utilities and insurance companies, by name, for abusing consumers.

He got the legislature to enact, after one gubernatorial veto, death by lethal injection for convicted murderers. Capital punishment advocates were furious: too soft.

But Ron Mottl's political epitaph is the Ohio lottery, which provides about $700 million a year for Ohio's public schools.

Mottl haunted the Statehouse corridors and offices for 14 months in 1971 and 1972, literally pestering the lottery to passage single-handedly. In each chamber, his proposal was defeated and he had to start over. It finally passed, with the exact number of votes required in the Senate and with one to spare in the House. Once he got it to the ballot in 1973, the people approved it almost 2-1.

In the legislature, it was tough going. Rural lawmakers feared the wrath of the voters if they supported gambling. Mottl's own party leader, the late Sen. Anthony O. Calabrese, asked him: "How bad do you want the lottery?" The answer was, badly enough to vote for a $1,250 legislative pay raise, the only one Mottl ever supported.

Mottl cut deals with one legislator after another to bring the lottery to the brink of passage, but it was stonewalled in the House Rules Committee. "I'll never let your lottery out of Rules Committee," Mottl quoted House Speaker Charles F. Kurfess as vowing.

Then, an angel appeared in the form of James W. Shocknessy, the founder of the Ohio Turnpike and, like Mottl, a Notre Dame graduate. "He said, 'Ron, do you need any help? We Notre Damers have to stick together,'" Mottl related.

"Two weeks later, that bill was on the (House) floor. He had friends in high places."

Mottl was always a man on the move. He went to Congress for eight years and befriended the likes of Dan Quayle and Al Gore.

Defeated in a realigned district in 1982, Mottl returned to Columbus. Tired of staying in $28-a-night motels, he began driving back and forth to Cleveland each day, rising at 5:30 A.M. and dropping wearily into bed at midnight.

He burned up I-71, making the 130-mile trip in just over two hours and only getting one speeding ticket outside Columbus. Mottl averaged about 40,000 miles a year on his cars, but because his father-in-law is an auto dealer, he got a good trade every couple of years.

Mottl has always made quick getaways, bolting from the chamber after the last roll call and ignoring party caucuses. "I'm a guy that likes to get things done," he said. "Those things are a waste of time. All they do is sit around and gab."

"One thing I learned about Ron," said Speaker Jo Ann Davidson in bidding Mottl farewell. "Not to get between him and the door."

Most recently, Mottl has suffered from sleep apnea, a disorder that causes him to stop breathing up to 300 times a night. To keep his foggy mind alert on the morning drive to Columbus, he munches Golden Grahams, swigs pop and listens to sports programs on the radio.

At 62, Mottl doesn't look much different than he did 30 years ago, although gray has crept into his crewcut, wrinkles have invaded the baby face and his 244 pounds are distributed a bit differently on his 6-foot-3 frame.

He still looks like he could pitch a few innings, as he once did for the Schenectady Blue Jays of the Eastern League. In 1955, Mottl pitched 15 innings against Big Ten champs Ohio State and fanned 15 batters.

If suburban Clevelanders vote for Mickey Mottl enough times, he will be one of the most experienced House members because his contemporaries will be term-limited out of office by 2005, and he'll still have two more years. He could be the speaker. Fathers always want their sons to go further than they did, you know.

The brazen switcheroo backfired. Mickey Mottl was defeated at the next election by Parma-area voters incensed that Ron Mottl tried to keep his legislative seat in the family.

■ ■

Gregarious Oakley Collins Perfected Art of Politics

The Columbus Dispatch, November 7, 1994

With Election Day Tuesday, it's fitting to devote this space to the late state Sen. Oakley C. Collins, for whom every day was a campaign—a horn-honking, hand-waving, grinning and gripping jaunt through his home town of Ironton or wherever he happened to be.

Collins, whose 30 years in the state legislature between 1947 and 1987 ranked him as one of the longest-serving lawmakers in Ohio history, died last week at age 82. His colleagues recall him as one of the most charming and shrewd politicians ever to work at the Statehouse.

A bear of a man, Collins had wavy black hair, naturally white teeth and hands the size of boxing gloves with fingers. He liked to whack people on the back and tousle their hair. More than one senator howled upon receiving a good-natured greeting.

Collins, a Republican, favored navy-blue suits and peered through black plastic-rimmed glasses. He was immensely popular with folks along the Ohio River, even though many of them vote Democratic. His secret, as with all great politicians: Don't let party politics or ideology interfere with getting things done.

Collins worked closely with then-Gov. James A. Rhodes, a native of nearby Jackson, and Democratic Reps. Myrl H. Shoemaker of Ross County and Vernal G. Riffe Jr. of Scioto County. It was said that Riffe would secretly help Collins win.

And, oh, could Collins campaign! He would stride through a crowd, whether at the Circleville Pumpkin Show or a county fair, his huge hands a blur as he grabbed hands on both sides of him, his husky southern Ohio voice crying, "How's it goin', Chief?" or, "Good to see ya, Hoss!"

It was said that Oakley could dive into the Ohio River and shake three hands before he surfaced. The first thing he wore out on a car was the horn, folks said.

An eyewitness reported that Collins once worked a ferry between Ironton and Russell, Ky., near election time, knocking on car windows and greeting prospective voters. Some lived in Kentucky, but it was said they'd cross the river to vote for him before voter registration came to southern Ohio.

Collins, a school superintendent, honchoed the funding lines in the budget for primary and secondary schools. He formed an unlikely alliance with Democratic Sen. Oliver Ocasek, an erudite college professor from Akron.

"They had immense power," recalls Robert J. Boggs, D-Jefferson, now the Senate minority leader. "It was a symbiotic relationship. Oliver never liked to get his hands dirty, but he was the public speaker."

Collins made the deals; Ocasek made the speeches. Together, they funneled more money to public schools, both urban and rural. Collins always demanded more money for school districts in his area.

Some people believe the "equity" problem with Ohio's poor school districts is a direct result of Collins' defeat in the 1986 election, the same year Ocasek ran for Congress and lost.

Boggs remembers that Collins and Ocasek backloaded the two-year school appropriation to ensure more money the next time. In other words, if there was $1 billion to spend, they'd appropriate $700 million of it in the second year to boost the base for the next budget.

Collins did battle in 1971 with freshman Rep. Sam Speck of New Concord. Speck spearheaded enactment of a strip-mine reclamation bill that cost Collins' mining company a lot of money. Speck said Collins hated the law but remained his friend.

Later Speck, who had a doctorate in political science from Harvard, was outmaneuvered by Collins, whose political lessons came from rural school boards, Legion halls, farm fields and mine sites.

Speck amended the state budget to fund nine portable scales to keep trucks from overloading and tearing up the roads in southern Ohio. Collins was violently opposed to the scales as an interference with coal-truck commerce.

Speck and an ally were on the Senate-House budget conference committee with four Democrats. Four of the six votes were needed to remove the portable scales.

"There was no way Oak was going to get four Democratic votes," recalls Ohio Supreme Court Justice Paul E. Pfeifer, then a fellow senator, "but he did, by trading who-knows-what for them. That was an incredible demonstration of how he knew everybody so well. He knew their hot buttons."

Ben Rose was a freshman state representative from Lima in 1973 when Collins joined the House after getting reapportioned out of his Senate seat. "One of Oakley's principal negotiating tricks was to trade his vote as many times as possible," said Rose.

In other words, Collins would ask for colleagues' votes on a bill and promise to vote for a bill they wanted. Little did they know he was going to vote for it anyway.

For example, according to Rose, Collins was trying to kill a bill to replace county school boards with regional education resource centers. He told various House members that if they would vote to kill the bill, he would vote for a legislative pay raise.

"He traded his vote 15 times," marveled Rose. "Every time I'd see him, he'd cackle, rub his hands together and say, 'I got me another one!'"

"I always tried to help people," Collins said in late 1986. "Then I had some IOUs, you know what I mean?"

■ ■

Lobbyist Dudgeon Always Had Just the Right Word for It

The Columbus Dispatch, January 6, 1997

They called him "The Curmudgeon," but it only fit because few other words in the English language rhyme with Tom Dudgeon, the Statehouse lobbyist, commentator and kitchen cabinet member who died last month, leaving no apprentices to inherit his role.

There's *bludgeon,* but Tom never did that. Instead, he dissected stuffed-shirt politicians and bad ideas with wit and sharp, polysyllabic words buried in 3-inch-thick dictionaries, waiting, it seemed, for Dudgeon to haul them out and put them on display.

Dudgeon did have the appearance of a curmudgeon—75 at his death, he had a shuffle from the effects of a heart attack and a fall down an escalator in recent years, a pallid complexion from too many hours in windowless watering holes, and a voice that could pass for Deep Throat.

He even had the curmudgeon's ring of white hair around the dome and the opinions that experienced people should run things and we, by God, ought to heed history's lessons.

But curmudgeons just sit around and carp about the world going to hell in a handcart. Thomas H. Dudgeon hungered daily for fresh Statehouse action, watching it, commenting on it like a one-man Greek chorus, and more than occasionally influencing it.

"He was a camper," said House Speaker Pro Tempore William G. Batchelder, R-Medina. "He was one of the old-fashioned lobbyists who knew they had to be around or they'd miss the play."

Like the good ex-military officer he was, Dudgeon conducted covert operations. Few ever knew what he was up to. He was not a typical lobbyist who testified at hearings and took legislators out to dinner.

Instead, Dudgeon mingled after hours with the players and legislative groupies, replaying each turn of events, exchanging scraps of information and continually playing the "if" and "what-next" games.

Information. That's the staple of the Statehouse diet for the government officials who make the news and the staffers who help them, the lobbyists who profit from what happens and the reporters who write about it.

And Dudgeon was an expert at trafficking in information. Whether he was promoting the agenda of Gov. James A. Rhodes, the Ohio Petroleum Marketers Association, highway contractors or House Speaker Vern Riffe, Dudgeon kept everybody off balance. He had a gleam in his eye that said, "I know something and you don't."

Dudgeon knew more than most because he had studied the system for a long time. He would use that edge, depending on his motive, by leaking a morsel, steering you toward treasure or just giving you an angle to contemplate. Sometimes he'd direct you to a blind alley, and his record of election predictions was almost laughable, perhaps on purpose.

"I don't think the facts were as important as planting the seeds of whatever idea he thought ought to be germinating out there," said Jim Henry, veteran lobbyist for the retail merchants.

Dudgeon was in his heyday when he was publishing the Ohio News Service, a weekly political tip sheet for insiders.

He knew the Ohio Constitution and was one of the few who thought a convention should be called to modernize it. He was fond of pointing out (notwithstanding Rhodes' wild borrowing schemes) how far in debt Ohio is while masquerading as fiscally conservative.

Dudgeon drove the administration of Democratic Gov. Richard F. Celeste wild, talking about its "government grubbies" and "Mickey Mouse accounting system."

In Ohio News Service, he debunked political adversaries and know-nothings thusly: "Horsefeathers!" And he often referred to the predictable legislative push-and-pull as "the dance of the stomping buzzards."

Truth or fiction, like it or not, Dudgeon's "news" got repeated immediately and often, having the desired effect.

The tip sheet was a marquee for his vocabulary. He called a lawmaker's speech so much "borborygmus"—the rumbling sound of gas moving in the intestine, and dubbed one enemy a "foul retromingent"—an animal that urinates backward, such as a skunk.

Following the heated 1986 Republican primary for governor, won by Rhodes, Dudgeon launched this thesaurical missile at Rhodes' chief tormenter, then-state Sen. Paul Pfeifer:

"As far as we could tell, Pfeifer with his hatful of indiscriminate dings, wimpling cries of ingravescence and adamantive carps found the road to sardonicism unoccupied and took it throughout the primary, spreading splenetic rhetoric at every stop along the way. The unctuously rectitudinous hair shirt worn and smarmy grin affected did nothing to alter the rabulistic image which emerged."

Ouch! You can look 'em up.

"When he gave you advice," recalled Tim Doran of the Ohio Automobile Dealers Association, "he always gave it to you in riddles. For him, it was more fun to see if you had brains enough to decipher what he wasn't saying. He'd make it so you'd have to ask the question, 'Do you mean . . . ?' Then he'd just smile, stick the cigar back in his mouth and walk away.

"The challenge for him was the game, keeping the riddles going."

As the new legislative session begins, a major voice interpreting the intrigue is missing.

Few knew this, but Tom Dudgeon's ashes were scattered among the plantings at the northwest corner of the Statehouse—his favorite haunt—below the Senate wing and outside the governor's office. For several months, you could see them if you knew where to look. They disappeared when the gardeners applied fresh mulch in springtime.

■ ■

Colorful Tony Calabrese Brought Flair and Laughter to Statehouse

The Columbus Dispatch, July 15, 1991

He was one of the last true characters in the General Assembly—a throwback to the free and easy days when legislating was a good-old-boy network of back-scratching and palm-greasing.

Anthony O. Calabrese, a refugee from the old country, worked his way up to state senator after selling newspapers and candy on railroad cars and working as an enforcer in seedy Cleveland bars. He died last week at 83.

Born Orlando A. Calabrese, Tony went into politics and rearranged his name after Cleveland Mayor Anthony J. Celebrezze made it a winner. He rode the name to Columbus, and in the 1970s became Ohio Senate Democratic leader.

Tony Calabrese always was splendidly dressed—hand-tailored suits, silk ties and matching handkerchiefs, and Italian shoes—with not a hair out of place. In winter he favored stylish overcoats and sometimes wore a fedora.

Despite his poor upbringing, Calabrese had what one legislator called "Continental charm." His manners were impeccable, yet he was comfortable in the rough-and-tumble world of politics.

Someone asked him how he planned to vote on a bill. "I don't know yet," he replied, eyes twinkling. "I haven't heard the cash register ring."

And when asked if he was switching sides on an issue: "Once I'm bought, I stay bought."

Calabrese's office walls were lined with photos of himself with friends, legislators, presidents, popes, movie stars and show-business personalities.

"Tony always went first class," said one colleague, recalling a visit to Caesar's Palace during a legislative convention in Las Vegas. Calabrese ordered champagne for his ringside table, then slipped Vic Damone his business card while Damone was singing.

The floor show was still in progress when Damone, obeying what Calabrese had written on the back of the card, said: "Let's all toast Sen. Tony Calabrese from Ohio." Calabrese leaped to his feet, hoisted his champagne glass high in the air and acknowledged the cheers of the crowd.

At the Democratic National Convention, Calabrese would always hover over the shoulder of the delegation chairman announcing Ohio's vote so his family and friends would see him on national television.

Tony loved the glitter and glamour, and he loved the idea that a poor Italian boy had risen to the station of senator.

Calabrese had a reserved suite near the pool on the fourth floor of the old Downtown Sheraton Hotel. "He was not only dean of the Senate," recalled a colleague. "He was dean of the pool."

Calabrese was the social chairman, arranging dinners with airline stewardesses and theater stars visiting the Sheraton with the Kenley Players, many of whom were attractive young women.

The senator had a huge wardrobe locked in a closet, and Sen. Harry Meshel, D-Youngstown, recalls once asking Tony if he could wear some of those fine Italian suits while Calabrese was not in town.

"No senator should wear second-hand clothes," sneered Calabrese.

But most of the time, Calabrese would give a friend the shirt off his back. "Tony knew who his friends were," recalls Sen. Neal F. Zimmers Jr., D-Dayton. "He had a streak of loyalty, and if he liked you, he'd do anything for you."

Calabrese often would use other people's money to do things for his friends. He'd invite colleagues to dinner, then stick a lobbyist with the check.

Tony took a shine to a young lobbyist of Italian lineage, and asked for his business card. Several weeks later, the lobbyist received a bill from a local restaurant with the card attached and an order to "take care of this."

Calabrese was derided by good-government types as a buffoon who disgraced the General Assembly. He and Gov. John J. Gilligan were fellow Democrats in name only, and Gilligan wanted to get rid of Tony in the worst way. He had him reapportioned into a Republican senator's district.

One day Gilligan had the Senate Democratic caucus in his office. The governor was fiddling with a Knights of Columbus sword.

Calabrese picked up the sword and began waving it around, to the chagrin of Highway Patrol plainclothesmen. "Don't worry, governor," said Calabrese. "I no stab you in the back. I stab you in the front." Everyone laughed.

Calabrese was known and loved for his malaprops. Campaigning in Cleveland in 1974 for the Democratic nomination for lieutenant governor against Richard F. Celeste, Calabrese told an ethnic audience: "He ain't Italian. He's a Methodist."

And when senators were trying to keep the railroads from abandoning passenger lines in Ohio, Calabrese told his colleagues about flying into Cleveland Hopkins Airport and circling for two hours in the fog. "If that had been a train, we could've landed right away," he said.

Calabrese once slipped on ice in the Senate parking lot and hurt his ankle. He filed a claim for workers' compensation. Someone noticed that the senator was favoring the wrong ankle and challenged him: "Which ankle's the bad one?"

"Both of 'em," Calabrese shot back.

Later, crusty Senate Clerk Thomas Bateman was called to verify the workers' comp claim of Calabrese, who said Bateman was a witness.

"Oh, hell," an unsympathetic Bateman told the examiner. "These senators will say almost anything."

Chapter 7
Government Dynamics

This lengthy chapter of the book displays the dynamics, some of them peculiar to Ohio, that are at work, primarily in the legislature. The first section shows the terror that the small word "tax" can strike into the hearts of Ohio politicians. But the last column in the section demonstrates that when it comes to a showdown between the taxpayers and the spenders, the Capitol Square lobbyists usually win.

Budgeting, Taxes and the Caveman Caucus

Marathon Year Pitted Conservatives Against Moderates on Income Tax

United Press International, November 19, 1971

COLUMBUS (UPI)—As the weeks roll by and the swing of the legislative pendulum on taxes grows shorter and shorter, it is becoming unmistakably skewed toward Ohio's first graduated personal income tax.

Enactment of such a tax could produce some unsettling results in the game of "Heroes and Goats" that has been unfolding in the General Assembly since last March 15.

For Democrats, the object of the game has been to make Gov. John J. Gilligan a hero by getting Ohio off its traditional heavy emphasis on local property taxation and injecting new doses of state money into government programs through taxation based on "ability to pay."

Republican controlling the General Assembly have been pictured as standing in the way of tax reform.

For the GOP, the object has been to either hold the line on spending and taxation until at least after another election, or make Gilligan a "goat" by passing an income tax and branding it with his name.

Floor votes on four different tax bills during the year have shown there is a split in the Republican Party which could widen with disastrous consequences if an income tax is enacted.

Significant portions of the Senate and House Republicans, publicly but passively backed by Republican state headquarters, have favored making the GOP into heroes through fiscal conservatism which they say appeals to their constituents.

The more liberal Republicans have decided to try to install an income tax base and hope for the best.

During the long, drawn-out fiscal battle, the conservatives, firm in their belief nobody really wants an income tax, have:

- Clashed head-on several times with House Speaker Charles F. Kurfess, R-Bowling Green, accusing him of short-changing them and going so far as to wear symbols in their coat lapels in defiance of the GOP leadership.
- Accused Sen. William W. Taft, R-Cleveland, of being "the John Lindsay of the Senate" for collaborating with Democrats in writing personal income tax legislation.
- Denounced Sen. Theodore M. Gray, the Republican floor leader, for declining to take a more aggressive part in pushing their viewpoint.
- Expressed bitterness toward Republican State Chairman John S. Andrews for the same reason. Andrews has said "the general public does not want an income tax," but added it's a legislative matter and "there's room under the party umbrella for all Republicans."

There may not be enough room for the conservatives if an income tax is enacted, just as there was not enough room for awhile last year for certain figures involved in a fiscal brouhaha of another stripe.

The House conservatives already are talking about replacing Kurfess and Andrews, if they have enough muscle. While it is believed they do not have this kind of strength, they have sufficient noise-making powers and could widen the rift beyond immediate repair.

Alienating the conservatives, contributing to the long delay in passing the budget and then returning to a reasonable facsimile of Gilligan's original tax plan could severely reduce the value of the "hero and goat" trump cards Republican leaders hope to deal at the end of the long struggle.

There is a growing feeling the long legislative year, fraught with politics in its rawest form, may taint the name of any incumbent lawmaker of the ballot for re-election next year.

Simple arithmetic shows there are more Republicans than Democrats to be felled at the polls, and if the governor is to be made a "goat," he may take everybody else with him.

The reference to "the John Lindsay of the Senate": John Lindsay at one time was a New York congressman and mayor of New York. He was a Republican, but his views were so progressive that many in the GOP disowned him. So it was with Sen. William Taft.

The battle over the income tax was not over until Dec. 10, and then much of 1972 was spent in debate over an attempt, unsuccessful, to repeal the tax. Republican James A. Rhodes defeated Gilligan in 1974 in part by blaming him for the hated tax. But once in the governor's office, Rhodes made no attempt to repeal it. Instead, he used the revenues for government programs. Not until 2007 was repeal talked about in the legislature.

■ ■

With Income Tax, Ohio Joins the Big-Spending States for Good

United Press International, January 19, 1973

COLUMBUS (UPI)—Through careless error or deliberate design, the administration of Gov. John J. Gilligan has placed Ohio on an irreversible course of big government spending.

A laggard among the major industrial states for many years, Ohio is now chasing New York, Pennsylvania, California and Illinois in spending outlay.

It is catching up not only in services, but in concomitant waste.

The gasps were loud enough when Gilligan proposed a $2.1 billion spending increase two years ago. Last week, he proposed a $1.6 billion increase in a "hold-the-line" budget requiring no new taxes.

The money had to come from somewhere, and aside from federal funds, $700 million is derived from growth in the personal income and sales taxes between now and 1975.

It might appear to be poor planning that the new tax structure, enacted late in 1971 with Republican help in the legislature, furnished so much money that it can be plowed into extra government programs.

After all, the Gilligan administration was $115 million off on its estimates of sales tax collections for the current biennium, and appears to be low on its projections of the income tax yield, despite the governor's contention that the figures have been "right on the button."

The state Finance Department now reveals there will be $180 million left in the till next June 30 to spend right away, and another $155 million surplus June 30, 1974.

More likely, it was by careful calculation that the administration proposed an income tax rate high enough so that, even cut in half by the legislature, it is expanding fast enough to put Ohio on the track toward her sister industrial states.

Gilligan's philosophy that government must provide services overshadows any fear he might have that Ohio will become another New York, with legions of needless state employees doing useless and overlapping work in a maze of bureaucracies trying to solve insurmountable problems in welfare, drugs, crime, labor relations and other areas.

"Ohio state government has been weak, disoriented and inactive for a very long time," Gilligan said in a recent interview. "Local governments have had problems thrust upon them because of dereliction on the part of the state.

"I don't think we'll run into the New York or Pennsylvania or Illinois or Michigan situations because we have eight major urban communities in Ohio," the governor continued. "No one city dominates, like New York, or Philadelphia or Pittsburgh, or Chicago, or Detroit.

"We can look at our problems before they reach the dimensions of those in the big cities," he said. "We can still do it in Ohio, and we can do it with our own resources.

"We have in the past let some of these problems get away from us. And it cost us, into the billions of dollars. A classical example is the pollution of Lake Erie, which we are beginning to clean up."

As Gilligan addressed the legislature last week, he pointed with pride to advances in education and promised to improve checks on the welfare system. He called for legislation which cost practically no money, and he positively glowed when calling attention to the "no new tax" line.

It will be difficult, even for Republican legislators, to shave the governor's budget when it requires no new tax enactments.

By approving the high-powered tax package of 1971, the lawmakers closed the door on Ohio's traditional thrift in state government, and the voters sealed it with ratification of the tax in November.

■ ■

Repealing Income Tax Hike is an Uphill Battle

United Press International, August 26, 1983

COLUMBUS (UPI)—Ever since the state income tax was hiked last March, a new taxpayers' revolt has been organizing and preparing to bomb the state tax structure back to 1981 levels.

But there are growing signs that mission may not succeed.

How come, when passions against the hated tax increase and its author, Gov. Richard F. Celeste, initially rivaled those displayed at the Boston Tea Party?

Several reasons.

- Some of the passions have subsided, as Ohioans have either gotten used to the increased withholding or discovered it didn't hurt as badly as they were led to believe.
- It is one thing to holler about a miscarriage of justice, but another to get up and go do something about it.
- Groups benefitting from the tax, or those which could stand to lose from an alternative, will be putting on a vigorous media campaign this fall to torpedo the repealer.

Rep. Robert E. Netzley, R-Laura, a conservative normally on the stump against higher taxes, is not one to be deceived. He does not give the repealer a very good chance of passing.

"The people are going to blackmailed by a slick Madison Avenue public relations campaign," warns Netzley, predicting that the repeal supporters will be outspent "two or three to one." Netzley says the tax spenders, such as educators, welfare advocates and those responsible for mental health programs will air clever television advertisements, financed by Celeste's and the Democrats' funds, threatening dire consequences if the repeal goes through.

"You can make people believe just about anything with a slick public relations campaign," said Netzley in a visit to the Statehouse last week. "They will have people believing this building will fall in a hole and the state of Ohio after it if we don't keep the taxes."

Netzley ought to know. He was in the forefront of the original repeal movement in 1972 when conservatives attempted to wipe the year-old state income tax off the books.

That effort fell, by more than 2-1, to the very media barrage Netzley envisions for this year.

"It'll be closer this time," Netzley predicted. "They (the repeal supporters) have got some union people and the young people that can't afford to buy a house are getting sick and tired of taxes."

But Netzley notes that "We are starting out 600,000 votes behind, and that's awfully hard to make up."

His rationale is that 100,000 public school teachers, 50,000 university employees and 50,000 other state workers will all vote for the taxes, and each has two others (a spouse and a close friend) who will do likewise.

The most recent lesson on the effectiveness of a mass media campaign came last fall, when opponents of direct election of the Public Utilities Commission reversed an early 80 percent approval rating and knocked down the proposal by more than 2-1.

"It's the utility issue all over again," lamented Netzley, pointing out that passions against high utility bills were either doused or redirected by clever TV ads.

Netzley was right. The repealer failed. Republicans got revenge, however. They recaptured the Senate in the 1984 elections and cut the income tax by 15 percent.

■ ■

House Republicans, Newly Relevant, Feel Responsibility

The Columbus Dispatch, November 30, 1992

One time in the late 1970s, state Rep. Robert E. Netzley, a Miami County Republican to the political right of Tarzan, stuffed a handkerchief in his mouth and rose to speak on the House floor.

When recognized, Netzley opened his mouth and exhaled violently, and the white cloth sailed into the air and over the back rail. Netzley then loudly complained that he and other Republicans had been gagged by the House Speaker, Vernal G. Riffe Jr., D-Wheelersburg.

Similarly, Rep. William G. Batchelder, R-Medina, once appeared on the House floor wearing a muzzle designed for a Doberman.

Such antics are symptomatic of life in the Ohio House for the last 18 years, since Riffe has been speaker.

Half the Republicans have wanted to do more theatrics, to show their defiance of the speaker and their disagreement with the way the House is run and the governmental policies that are enacted.

The other half have preferred to recognize that Republicans are a minority in the House. They would be quiet and take whatever handouts they could get, courtesy of the easy relationship with Riffe enjoyed by House Minority Leader Corwin M. Nixon, R-Lebanon.

The Republican delegation, which in January will be the largest in 20 years, is still split down the middle between the easygoing progressives and the bomb-throwing "Caveman Caucus" of Netzley and Batchelder.

Although Rep. Jo Ann Davidson, R-Reynoldsburg, was chosen unanimously last week to replace the retiring Nixon as the GOP leader, two of the other three new leaders won with bare majorities.

One of those was Batchelder, who narrowly won the assistant leader's post and thus will represent the cave dwellers on the leadership team.

Both the Davidson and Batchelder forces tried mightily to install their own followers in the leadership slots.

But a middle-ground group of a dozen Republicans, many of whom will not be sworn in until January, recognized that a compromise was necessary for the GOP to be a force in the House.

Now, there is an uneasy truce, at least for the present, under the Davidson-Batchelder combination.

"There are some ruffled feathers, obviously," said Rep. Dale N. Van Vyven, R-Sharonville, a conservative who lost a bid for the Republican whip's position. "But I think Jo Ann is attempting to pull everybody together."

"Finally, we have a (philosophical) conservative that's part of leadership," exulted Rep. James Buchy, R-Greenville, who narrowly lost a bid for the fourth leadership post.

"With Bill Batchelder on there, we will keep the bombs in the boxes, at least for a while," said Buchy.

This was the aim of Rep. Michael A. Fox, R-Hamilton, a longtime ally of Nixon's who recognized it was necessary to keep the conservatives happy if the Republican caucus is to be at all effective during the next two years.

"The concept of governing has not crossed the minds of many of our caucus members," said Fox, who worked toward a coalition leadership. "They are too interested in throwing grenades."

Fox pointed out that with 46 members and only 50 votes needed to pass legislation, the Republicans will become "relevant" next year. "With relevance comes responsibility," he said, "and our responsibility to govern comes first."

During his 18 years in the House, Fox has worked mainly behind the scenes with Nixon and Riffe, many times infuriating the conservatives.

So it was odd to see him seconding Batchelder's nomination for the assistant leader's position, and nominating Van Vyven for job No. 3.

"This caucus has been destroyed by ambition, passions, egos, paybacks and retribution," Fox told his colleagues. "The time has come to move forward. Whatever has divided us in the past is not nearly as important as the future."

Davidson plans to have frequent caucus meetings to air things out and let the conservatives have their say. "We will have some direction, and people will be heard," predicted Batchelder, adding he expects "vigorous discussion" before caucus positions are taken.

One of the main gripes of the conservatives has been that Nixon made book with Riffe without consulting the caucus, and especially without consulting them.

"Lack of communication has caused a lot of the strife in our caucus," said Van Vyven, "and it looks like that may be over."

Fox foresees a "good-guy, bad-guy" routine in which Batchelder takes on the Democrats with his intellectual wit and speechmaking pyrotechnics, unmatched in the House, while Davidson takes the lead in working with Riffe.

Gov. George V. Voinovich should like his new Republican leadership team in the House. Batchelder, another penny-pincher, served with Voinovich in the legislature years ago. And the governor wanted Davidson to be his budget director, but she chose to stay in the House.

■ ■

Ohio Republicans Mask Their Tax Foibles by Pointing To the Democrats

The Columbus Dispatch, November 4, 2002

The favorite Halloween costume for adults this year may have been Martha Stewart in prison stripes, but for Republicans in Ohio it was Mr. Tax.

But instead of wearing the scary getup, as they should, they draped it on the Democrats.

The Republicans, after a respectful period of positive campaign advertising, have tagged their Democratic opponents with the tax label with reckless abandon in the past couple of weeks.

Everyone from "Taxin' Tim Hagan," the Democratic nominee for governor, down to the lowliest candidate for the Ohio House has been branded a taxer.

Why? Because it scares up votes.

Democrats earned the tax-and-spend I.D. during the final four decades of the last century, and Republicans are trying to prolong that view, whether it's true or not.

That's why the Republicans are running a commercial pointing out that Democratic Sen. Michael C. Shoemaker of Ross County voted to raise 34 different taxes, including the "record" 90 percent tax increase of 1983.

Spending bills sometimes include taxes, so Shoemaker's perceived indiscretions occurred over the years when he supported the multibillion-dollar budgets containing the state's educational, health care, social and other programs.

On some of those occasions, the budgets were written by Democrats, and certainly Shoemaker had a choice to vote no on the Republican ones if he wanted. But if he supported the programs, he should have been bound to support the taxes to fund them. Only an intellectually dishonest lawmaker would vote to spend money and oppose the taxes to raise it.

The Republicans have covered all bases by running ads castigating Democrats who voted against their budget last year, claiming they abandoned senior citizens, school children, the poor and the infirm.

Parenthetically, the Democrats would do the same thing if they controlled the government and had the money to run TV ads.

In fact, the Democrats have an ad accusing Republicans, including Rep. Linda Reidelbach of Columbus, of voting for $1 billion worth of taxes. That's about the figure you arrive at if you count the taxes in the current budget and the two subsequent bills required to balance it.

But back to Shoemaker and the "record" 90 percent income tax increase. Republicans recaptured the Senate in 1984 by panning that all-Democrat tax increase and displaying a padlocked wallet to show how they'd treat Ohioans.

For reasons too numerous to mention, that tax increase turned out to be only 27 percent, and in the next session, Republicans engineered a 15 percent income-tax reduction.

In 1992, the legislature passed a $1 billion tax increase—almost twice as large as the one nine years earlier. So, how can the GOP get away with continuing to give "record" status to the earlier one? Oh, that's easy, they say. It grows each year and so it just keeps getting bigger.

By that logic, the original enactment of the personal-income tax in 1971 was the biggest tax increase in Ohio history because it's grown the most. Who was in charge of the legislature that year? Republicans, in the House and Senate.

A mailer sent out by the Ohio Republican Party shows the old billfold again, some dollar bills sticking out. "What's in your wallet?" it asks, ominously, parroting a credit-card commercial.

It warns of Liberal So-and-So's "risky tax scheme" to "take even more money out of your pocket."

Sort of amusing, considering the fact that the Republican-controlled legislature had to raise close to $1 billion in taxes to balance the budget. GOP leaders and Gov. Bob Taft are not ruling out a tax increase to balance the next budget, either.

Republicans can have their fun. They can masquerade, play trick or treat, and even bob for apples with their mouths full.

But after they've painted all the Democrats as robbers who want to take your money and squander it on frills; after they've bombed them back to the Stone Age with their campaign ads, they may wish they'd followed the advice of the master: James A. Rhodes.

When someone suggested they get rid of all the Democrats, then-Gov. Rhodes smiled.

"You don't want to do that," he said. "You've got to keep somebody around to raise the taxes."

That way you can blame them for the next 20 years.

■ ■

With Experience of Past Budget Crises, State Can Weather This One, Too

The Columbus Dispatch, February 10, 2003

State government seems to have a budget crisis about every 10 years, and the current one reminds longtime Statehouse denizens of each of the past three.

The most recent was in 1992, when there was a recession, and spending outstripped revenues. Republican Gov. George V. Voinovich had to work with a Democratic House and a Republican Senate, and they reached a true compromise.

They waited until after the 1992 elections and then sprang a package of taxes that raised $1 billion over two years—at the time the largest in Ohio history but less than a third the size of today's package, discounting inflation. Voters later repealed a penny tax on soft drinks, much to Voinovich's chagrin, and, as far as is known, no legislator lost re-election in 1994 because of a vote on taxes. Voinovich was re-elected by a landslide.

The worst predicament, the current one included, was in 1980-83, when Republican Gov. James A. Rhodes had to break his pledge not to raise taxes.

The budget got out of balance in 1980 and the state fought through a series of interim budgets until, in 1983, incoming Democratic Gov. Richard F. Celeste took advantage of the Democrats' complete control of the government to increase the income tax and make permanent Rhodes' "temporary" extra penny on the sales tax. Senate Democrats paid for these moves in the '84 election, losing the majority and never regaining it. But Democrats continued to rule the House and Celeste easily was re-elected in 1986.

Republicans pushed a modest reduction in income-tax rates through a divided legislature in 1985, having persuaded even the governor that the Democrats had overreached.

There are similarities now to the theatrics of the early 1980s, although inflation, unemployment and interest rates are much lower than they were then. State lawmakers are on the verge of abandoning the two-year budget and going to short-term budgeting because they can't count on reliable revenue projections, as in 1981 and '82.

Just as Celeste and the Democrats rammed through the income-tax increase in 1983, Gov. Bob Taft's short-term budget-balancer, House Bill 40, is preceding the two-year budget bill. It contains tax increases on cigarettes, beer, wine and liquor, all of which may be dropped before the bill passes.

One big difference: Republicans controlling the government will insist on a thorough search for further spending cuts to slow, but not stop or reverse, the growth of the government.

In 1971 there was an 11-month battle over the enactment of the state income tax, sought by Democratic Gov. John J. Gilligan as a way of funding schools.

There was no economic crisis and the tax was not needed to balance the budget, but Gilligan had to convince a hostile Republican legislature that schools would be well-served. He added the sweetener of the 10 percent property-tax rollback that was later expanded to 12.5 percent for owner-occupied homes.

To lay the foundation for the income tax, Gilligan appointed a "blue-ribbon" task force of business, labor and other interest groups. That helped him win approval of the tax in the legislature and later to defeat an attempted repeal.

Taft followed the recommendations of a tax-study committee in proposing his "tax reform" package, including an extension of the sales tax to a variety of services. Taft also has named a blue-ribbon panel to lay the foundation for a new school-funding formula for 2005 and another one to recommend efficiencies in higher education.

Like Gilligan, Taft faces a legislature hostile to his two-year budget and tax package, but it is his own party causing the difficulty.

In 1971, relations grew so strained among the Republicans in the legislature, particularly the House, that some members wouldn't speak to each other because of their votes on the dreaded income tax.

The issues of cut or tax are just as passionate this time, but House Speaker Larry Householder, R-Glenford, seems to have mastered the knack of keeping communications open and the natives content. Unless things change, the conservative and moderate factions in the caucus may keep things pleasant and refrain from knifing one another in the back over taxes.

But it's a long year. Anything can happen.

Taft and the legislature weathered the 2003 budget problem and even managed to reduce taxes later. See the next column for how it was done. Five years later, Democratic Gov. Ted Strickland and the legislature got caught in a budget tsunami that was worse than any of the prior three—a projected $7.3 billion shortfall out of a $54 billion budget.

■ ■

When Push Came To Cut, Spenders Won the State Budget Battle

The Columbus Dispatch, June 2, 2003

The state budget debate was billed as a battle of the taxpayers against the tax spenders. It was to determine the direction of government for years to come, conservatives said.

Well, a lot of heat will be generated over the next month, but the verdict is already in and the winners are the spenders.

The Republican-controlled Senate and House will hiss and scratch at each other in what is expected to be a turbulent conference-committee forum in June, but the big picture is clear: There will be more spending and more taxes than ever.

The conservatives who rolled up their sleeves and drew their paring knives, intent on impeding the growth of government, had their way—for awhile.

But they were overthrown in their attempt to confine government to its basic mission and eliminate the bells and whistles.

During the past year, Gov. Bob Taft had trimmed the current two-year budget back to $44.3 billion as revenues dwindled. He proposed a $49.1 billion budget for the next two years. Conservatives had cut that back to about $47.2 billion and were going for less.

But once the idea of increasing the sales tax surfaced, the momentum was lost. If the money was going to be there, why not spend it? This became like eating peanuts. They couldn't stop. So the House passed a $48.7 billion budget.

Senate President Doug White of Manchester said the senators listened to advocates, citizens and their duly-elected representatives in coming up with the latest rewrite: a $49.2 billion spending plan that exceeds the governor's.

"Collectively, we seem to have difficulty saying no to spending," said a frustrated Sen. Lynn R. Wachtmann, R-Napoleon, who predicted the Senate's level of spending will require yet another tax increase before two years go by.

The senators might have listened to everyone, including the citizens who resent the growth of government and live miles away, but they heeded the advocates and professional lobbyists who patrol the halls of the Statehouse with regularity.

In fairness, it must be said that most of the huge increase in the budget, whether it is Taft's, the House's or the Senate's, can be traced to more state aid to schools, makeup funding for colleges, which have gone backward in the past few years, and feeding the monster known as Medicaid, which is the state-federal health-insurance program for the poor, blind and disabled. All of them are worthwhile endeavors.

Nevertheless, almost without exception, wherever the House conservatives found places to economize, the rest of the representatives and later the senators decided the effort wasn't worthwhile.

The governor said any major tax increase would have to receive public approval in advance.

But legislators were genuinely intimidated by the 4-1 public defeat of a proposed penny on-the-dollar increase in the sales tax in 1998.

Any time taxes were suggested after that, Republican legislative leaders would blanch. "The people would never stand for a tax increase," was their common refrain.

Something changed in the meantime. Taft started the ball rolling in February by proposing to balance the budget with more taxes on cigarettes and alcoholic beverages, and extending the sales tax to a variety of services.

The House proposed a temporary extra penny per dollar on the sales tax, which was to be repealed if voters approved video-slot machines at horse racetracks.

When they discovered that the sales-tax suggestion did not blow the roof off the Statehouse, senators decided to go for the new sales tax for two full years, whether or not the slot-machine proposal is approved by voters.

It was like the lawmakers stuck their toes into icy water, gradually became used to it and then called to their friends: "Come on in. The water's fine!"

Sen. Jim Jordan, R-Urbana, who bills himself as the friend of working moms and dads, is one of the few standing on the shore. "This is the largest tax increase in the history of the state," he said. By the time the new sales tax is figured on cars, appliances and satellite television, he said, "we're talking hundreds of dollars that a family is going to pay."

Some important details of the budget will have to be ironed out in the next few weeks, but one thing's for sure: The spending won't be reversed.

Slot machines at racetracks were scuttled and half the extra penny on the sales tax was later repealed. But lawmakers later voted to reduce the income tax by 20 percent over five years, and by 2008 they found themselves facing huge budget reductions just to stay even. While the budget enacted shortly after this column was written totaled $49 billion and some change, state spending had risen to just $52 billion by 2009, a remarkably low 6 percent over six years.

■ ■

Three Cavemen

Change on Board Is Taxpayers' Loss

The Columbus Dispatch, January 25, 1993

Well, they led the guard dog away from the door to the state treasury last week, and you could almost hear the sighs of relief reverberating across Capitol Square.

Rep. Robert E. Netzley, a conservative Republican from Laura, in western Ohio, was removed from the state Controlling Board because some people thought he barked too loud and acted too mean in speaking up for the taxpayers.

The result was predictable. At the first post-Netzley board meeting, Netzley's replacement singled out only two of 121 items for questioning instead of Netzley's normal 40 or 50. Time of meeting: 1 hour and 12 minutes—not the usual 3 hours.

One positive result was that the 100-or-so bureaucrats who fill the room every two weeks had time to do an extra two hours' work. Normally, they would waste those hours sitting while Netzley fished for hints of inefficiency in various agencies.

But you have to wonder whether the public was served by Netzley's removal. And you have to wonder why Gov. George V. Voinovich, who wants to get into the bowels of government and root out waste, would encourage the action.

Nothing is closer to the bowels of the government than the state Controlling Board. Every two weeks, bureaucrats come before the panel of six state legislators and one representative of the governor and expose the gory inner workings. Agency budgets are revisited and money transfers are made. Programs are re-examined to see if they are operating as designed. Unbid contracts are eyeballed to see if the state picked the best vendor. Taxpayers' funds are lent to private business.

Witnesses seldom volunteer touchy information. Until now, it was dragged out of them, bit by bit, in a buttocks-numbing, often sleep-inducing piece of theater directed by Netzley. He spent six or eight hours of his own time the previous weekend studying agencies' requests and setting traps for their hapless representatives. Other senators and representatives ask questions, too, but Netzley was by far the most tenacious. "Why can't you do this cheaper?" he'd complain. Or, "How many people does it take to do this job?"

He was especially hard on company officials seeking loans for job-producing expansions. If the companies were unprofitable, they'd get the cold shoulder from Netzley as poor risks for taxpayers' dollars.

Bob Netzley seldom won. Most requests were approved over his objection, and bureaucrats and lobbyists left the room rolling their eyes and mumbling about his obtuse attacks. But Netzley was an intimidator. His relentless questioning altered agency requests, turned the spotlight on them and sometimes embarrassed government officials. "I'm going to sort of miss the challenge," one (bureaucrat) confessed.

The opportunity to get rid of Netzley came when Rep. Jo Ann Davidson, R-Reynoldsburg, was made House Republican leader for 1993-94. Netzley had served on the Controlling Board for 14 years under House Republican Leader Corwin Nixon, but Nixon has retired. Netzley opposed Davidson's candidacy for leader, giving her the perfect excuse to oust him. But she was not alone. Though he said nothing publicly, Voinovich sent the message that Netzley should be replaced.

"The governor had been disappointed with some 'no' votes on projects that he thought were important to the state," his press secretary, Michael Dawson, said.

The clincher may have come right before Christmas when Netzley, playing his usual role of the Grinch, stepped on the feelings of Development Director Donald E. Jakeway by insinuating there might be some collusion regarding a $900,000 state loan for an office building in Canton. Jakeway was reported to be livid over Netzley's allegation that the project "smelled fishy."

"He went too far," said one insider. "He was entirely too quick to jump to conclusions."

House Speaker Vernal G. Riffe Jr., D-Wheelersburg, said Voinovich never personally asked him to remove Netzley from the Controlling Board. "If you say, 'Did I get a message?' that might be different," said the speaker.

Normally, Riffe follows the recommendations of House Republican leaders in making appointments to GOP slots. This time, however, he ignored Davidson's choice and selected Rep. David W. Johnson, R-North Canton, to be the House Republican on the Controlling Board.

As always, there was method to Riffe's intervention. Netzley's departure from the board already had made fellow conservatives boil. "We're hidin' and waitin' (for retribution)," one confided last week.

Riffe chose Johnson to enlarge any crack developing in the Republican caucus. Johnson, who had been in the Republican leadership for a number of years, was unceremoniously pushed aside for this session.

By selecting him for Controlling Board, Riffe gave Johnson something the Republicans wouldn't give him, and Johnson now owes him. Riffe may want to collect when he needs a vote on a bill sometime down the road.

Netzley played no favorites. He was equally hard on Republican and Democratic administrations. He was the longest-serving state representative in Ohio history, completing 40 years when he retired at the end of 2000.

■ ■

Thomas A. Van Meter was classified with the "Caveman Caucus" in the Ohio Senate, but he was not the prototypical arch-conservative. He actually tried to find workable solutions to problems, and he would co-operate with his political adversaries to get a solution. But he wasn't wishy-washy, either. He held to Republican principles. "You've got to stand for something," he would say.

Van Meter Reincarnated as George Bush Supporter

United Press International, December 14, 1986

COLUMBUS (UPI)—Resilient Tom Van Meter, who's been kicked more times than an alley cat and has returned the kicks with relish, is back again—this time as an early Ohio booster of Vice President George Bush for president in 1988.

Van Meter, a conservative state legislator from Ashland, is not afraid to wear his ideas or his candidates on his sleeve.

And while his fellow Republicans are hunkering down, trying to analyze the fallout from the Iran-Contra arms debacle before choosing sides in the 1988 Presidential sweepstakes, Van Meter has marched front and center carrying the Bush flag.

How do we know? Because twice now, Van Meter has furnished Statehouse reporters with copies of articles in the Washington press and the national media about Bush's impressive record as a combat pilot and his stance on the Iran-Contra issue.

Van Meter tries to downplay his involvement, saying he wants Ohio reporters to be properly backgrounded when the 1988 follies reach the Buckeye State. "It is not done from the standpoint of trying to generate any publicity on it," said the former state senator and soon-to-be former state representative, who leaves office in two weeks.

Van Meter said he has been in contact with Bush's political people, but other potential Republican presidential candidates also have made overtures to him for exploratory work in Ohio. Has he agreed to help the others? "No," was Van Meter's response.

And that response is telling. For among the 1988 hopefuls are Rep. Jack Kemp, R-N.Y., like Van Meter the quintessential conservative, and Gen. Alexander Haig, a right-hand man to former President Nixon. Van Meter is a former military officer and a strong admirer of Nixon.

"I've always liked the guy personally," said Van Meter of Bush. "The guy is tough, especially in foreign affairs. The real guts of a president to me is his ability in foreign affairs. I don't think there's a person in either party that can hold a candle to George Bush when it comes to foreign affairs. From my position, he's rock solid."

Van Meter, who supported former Texas Gov. John Connally for president in 1980 before skipping over Bush to Reagan, believes Bush's record in Congress actually was more conservative than the way he is perceived.

Why is it important who Van Meter supports? He has lost a Republican primary for Governor (1982), been rebuffed by Republican state senators in his bid to return to the Senate (1985), been rejected by Republicans in his old Senate district (1986), and backed a loser in the governor's race, James A. Rhodes (1986).

Van Meter is well-known in GOP circles. He is well-grounded in the knowledge of Ohio politics and running statewide campaigns, and has access to an impressive money-raising list of names. Van Meter would be an asset to any presidential candidate he chooses to support.

It's also important to know that Van Meter isn't finished politically despite four rough years. If George Bush carries Ohio and gets nominated, possibly elected, he's going to remember Tom Van Meter, who stuck his neck out, and not some faint-hearted folks in three-piece suits who sat on their hands when things looked bad.

Van Meter has established credit with Rhodes, and now Bush. He will be back.

Tom Van Meter did not come back. He died early in 1992, too soon to see his prediction come true that Republicans would overthrow a 20-year Democratic reign in the Ohio House. Actually it took two years longer than he predicted.

■ ■

Like Tom Van Meter, Buz Lukens was fun to write about because he was colorful and always on the move. He was a flitter and a glamour boy. He had a beautiful Japanese wife and the gift of gab. He was a classic conservative, and he stayed around long enough to play a role in the legislation cleaning up after the Home State banking scandal of 1985.

"Buz" Lukens Does Exciting Things But Annoys Some Colleagues

United Press International, April 24, 1971

COLUMBUS (UPI)—State Sen. Donald E. Lukens, R-Middletown, who has already served in Congress and run for governor, has proven himself an interesting specimen for "Senate-watchers" during his brief tenure in Columbus.

To say the least, the young senator has lived up to his nickname—"Buz."

Ever since Lukens traded seats with Republican Congressman Walter E. Powell last January, he has been on the go. He already has made visits to China, Korea and Latin America, and there is no indication he is slowing down.

Watching Lukens operate in the Senate chamber is like watching a tennis match. While most freshmen are content to stay in their seats during floor sessions, Lukens darts hither and yon, engaging in private conversations with Republicans and Democrats alike.

"I think he just makes small talk," said one senator. "He is aware of the tension under which he came in here and I think he's trying to settle any qualms some of the members have."

Lukens beat out former state Rep. Barry Levey, also of Middletown, in a private Republican squabble over Powell's seat, and some of the wounds may not yet have healed.

"He's a flitter, just like he always was," said one Republican colleague. "I don't have much use for All-American boys, and that's what he is. He reminds me of somebody out of 'The Rover Boys.' That's a book that was popular when I was a kid. Sam had an airplane and somebody else had a race car and they were always doing exciting things."

Lukens does exciting things. Earlier this month, he made a 10-day jaunt to Costa Rica as one of President Nixon's appointees to the U.S. delegation to the first regular session of the General Assembly of the Organization of American States.

Hardly typical of the freshman state senator. But then Lukens is not typical. The first week he was here, he was holding news conferences in the office of Senate President Pro Tempore Theodore M. Gray.

He also is the only senator who has dared to cut in on Gray's practice of answering "Aye" to roll calls instead of the customary "Yes."

And instead of sending the announcement of his Costa Rica trip and a statement on My Lai to the Statehouse press room, he sent them to wire service offices to insure statewide and possibly nationwide publicity.

Despite his quick pace during floor sessions, Lukens answered 81 of 83 roll calls through March 25. His absence during the Costa Rica trip cost him in that regard, and he has voted at a poor 30 percent clip since then.

Lukens has authored but one bill—calling for a prayer room in the Statehouse. His committee participation, while sporadic, is stimulating because his questioning of witnesses often points up his experience in Washington and his consciousness of the federal government's role in legislation.

Senate Republican leaders have looked on Lukens' activities in semi-amusement. Since they don't always know where he is, they are unable to depend on him as part of the team. But they haven't publicly knocked him.

One Democratic colleague, Sen. Ronald M. Mottl of Parma, has high praise for Lukens.

"So far, he's been just a great guy," said Mottl. "I would rate him 'A'."

Lukens and Mottl had a common point of reference before Lukens became a senator. Both used to date Kathy Lynn Baumann, the gorgeous girl from Bowling Green who was Miss Ohio and came within an eyelash of being Miss America last year.

One disgruntled Democrat, however, has no use for Lukens and the way he eased into the Senate after battling Roger Cloud for the GOP gubernatorial nomination in 1970.

"He doesn't belong in here, a man who went against his own party," said the old-line politician. "They shouldn't reward him. I'm glad he's not in my party. If he was, I'd be the first one to knife him. God may forgive him, and Christ may forgive him, but not me."

Reporters followed Lukens' movements because he had already been in Congress and there was always the possibility that he was going to run for higher office. He had put a scare into the Republican hierarchy in 1970 when he finished second in the primary for governor. One of the author's clear memories is of Lukens in a yellow baseball cap, scurrying around the 1976 Republican National Convention in Kansas City as one of the regional floor managers for Ronald Reagan. He wasn't successful and when Reagan's time came in 1980, Lukens was not a factor on Team Reagan.

■ ■

Rural vs. Urban and State vs. Local

Legislators from rural and urban areas just view things differently. The term "cornstalk brigade" was used to describe rural lawmakers, who dominated the Ohio legislature before districts were apportioned according to population.

Rural, City Lawmakers See Tow Trucks Differently

United Press International, February 29, 1980

COLUMBUS (UPI)—Leap year day this past week gave state legislators an extra day to favor the people of Ohio with some more laws. Fortunately, they were home and didn't take advantage of the opportunity.

Earlier in the week, senators demonstrated what mischief they can make while waiting to grapple with one of the important issues of the day. They passed a bill creating a special licensing category for tow trucks.

The reason? Too many unmarked tow trucks are cruising around the cities of Ohio, hauling away parked cars and collecting money for the parts and scrap metal. They strike like thieves in the night. Nobody knows who they are, and they vanish before they can be identified.

The solution? Make all private tow truck owners get a special license from the state Bureau of Motor Vehicles; display their name, address and permit number on their truck; and have "authenticated authorization" every time they move a car.

Debate on the bill boiled down to a classic confrontation between the big-city Democrats trying to solve a problem by passing a new law, and the last of the cornstalk brigade—Republicans who saw the proposal as another unnecessary intrusion by government creating another pile of paperwork.

Sen. Thomas E. Carney, D-Girard, the chief sponsor, was joined by Democratic Sens. William F. Bowen, D-Cincinnati, and Michael Schwarzwalder, D-Columbus, in pleading for passage of the measure.

They said unmarked tow trucks are a plague in their districts.

Republicans made a strong case against the bill, pointing out that if someone is going to use a tow truck as a front for car theft, how are they going to be stopped by a little identification requirement?

Some paint and a stencil, and "Joe's Towing Service" is born, with a cover of respectability. Who's to find out? If nobody pays attention to unmarked tow trucks, a marked one will arouse even less suspicion.

Sen. Thomas A. Van Meter, R-Ashland, a rabid foe of bureaucracy, pointed out that tow trucks already have identification. They're called license plates, and they're probably more reliable than any decals.

Finally, Sen. M. Ben Gaeth, R-Defiance, told the tale of driving his car into a snow bank in rural Ohio and being pulled out by a "good Samaritan" who had a tow truck which he used for helping people in trouble, not to make money.

"This is another classic example of a problem that cannot be solved by legislation," complained Gaeth. He warned that the fellow who has a tow truck as a "sideline" is not going to keep it if he has to fork over an extra $25 a year and go through the hassle required by Carney's bill.

"Tell him to go play with a wagon and a hay rake," grumbled Carney, who happened to have just enough votes to pass his bill.

It's easy to understand the frustration of discovering that your car has disappeared on the business end of a tow truck while you're shopping. But it's hard to understand how another layer of paperwork in Columbus is going to help.

■ ■

Lawmakers Wrestle in School-Ruling Mud

The Columbus Dispatch, April 15, 1997

The Ohio Supreme Court's landmark school-funding decision has touched off a display in the legislature about who can do what to whom, and it's not pretty.

The high court told the legislature to fix the schools, something the legislators thought was their exclusive turf. Like a small boy beaten up by the neighborhood bully, lawmakers have been looking around for somebody to take it out on. And last week, some of them found punching bags.

In the House, the target was the hated "E-check" program of testing motor-vehicle exhaust systems for ozone emissions. This is the state's response to the federal government's clean-air standards that require a reduction in ozone in 14 Ohio counties. It applies mainly to northeast Ohio and the southwestern Ohio air basin, but it could be coming to Franklin and surrounding counties under "new" and "improved" stricter federal standards. To reregister their vehicles, motorists have to take them to a central testing station and get a certificate that the exhaust system is clean. For that privilege, they pay about $20.

State legislators have long regarded such programs as "federal blackmail," since receipt of federal highway funds is dependent on states' compliance. Some legislators would like to tell the feds to stick their regulations where the grass doesn't grow. However, the more moderate legislators have tried to cooperate and write a bill that would comply with the federal regulations in a way that's the least burdensome to taxpayers.

So what started out last year as a move to kill E-check came to the floor in the form of carefully worded House Bill 172, which replaces E-check with a simpler tailpipe test, possibly for a lower price. The bill also sets up local clean-air councils to decide how to stay in compliance with the air standards.

Parenthetically, the latter provision also gets the monkey off the legislature's back. Local control, local control, that's the catch-phrase around here, especially with respect to schools. But what the legislators want is for county commissioners and mayors to get the irate phone calls about lawn-mowing and backyard barbecue bans.

During the House debate, conservatives and legislators from E-check districts tried to tilt the bill in their direction. One succeeded. Rep. Diane Grendell, a Republican from Geauga County, got the House to go along with an income tax credit for the cost of the emissions check.

Other attempts were beaten back by the moderates, including Grendell's proposal to thumb Ohio's nose at Washington and scrap the entire testing program.

It was amusing to watch, as Republican leaders had more difficulty wrestling with members of their own caucus than they did with Democrats, with whom they had a mutual admiration party only three weeks ago.

House Speaker Pro Tempore William G. Batchelder, R-Medina, a conservative leader, had to put philosophy in his back pocket for the moment and argue vehemently against a broadside at the federal government.

"I yield to no one in their contempt for the federal government," said Batchelder, a curious statement from someone whose wife is a federal judge. "We're entitled to a good temper tantrum, but we're past the point where we can ignore the federal government because we've made book with them. We don't have the will to give up the gas tax money. The best we can do for our people is to pass this bill." And the House did.

Rep. Bryan C. Williams, R-Akron, wanted to rename the program "Fed-Check" so people would know whom to blame. But Rep. Lynn R. Wachtmann, R-Napoleon, perhaps even more conservative than Batchelder, had a sudden attack of practical politics. He remembered that Republicans control Congress, and they might get blamed.

"While it would be fun to kick Congress . . . we have a lot of new congressmen," he said, blaming "our weakling President Bush" for signing the Clean Air Act that started the whole mess.

In the Senate, the issue was Senate Bill 15, prohibiting local governments from requiring their employees to live within city, county or township limits. Sen. Gary C. Suhadolnik, R-Strongsville, clearly was aiming the measure at the city of Cleveland.

Suhadolnik also had to compromise, so as the bill came to the floor, it allowed cities to restrict employees' residences to any surrounding county. A more restrictive requirement could be negotiated with the employee union.

"Who's supposed to run the local communities, the local communities or the state of Ohio?" barked Republican Sen. M. Ben Gaeth, a former mayor of Defiance who started out supporting the bill but was now opposed. "I thought we had changed our minds about sending mandates back to local governments, but apparently we have not."

"This is about local control," agreed Sen. Scott R. Nein, R-Middletown. "I found out there are no such things as local school systems because somebody across the street (the Supreme Court) told us that."

Suhadolnik's bill was defeated and local control was saved except, apparently, for schools.

Nein's quote at the end of "no such things as local school systems" referred to the Ohio Supreme Court's recent ruling that the state was responsible for a "thorough and efficient" system of funding Ohio public schools. To some, that meant the end of true local control of schools because if the state provided a preponderance of the money, it could tell the locals how to run their schools.

■ ■

This column deals not only with the tension between state and local governments, but differences between elected and appointed public officials.

Smoke Screen: The Debate on Local Control of Tobacco Rules

The Columbus Dispatch, April 3, 2000

Last week's debate in the Ohio House about city councils ratifying tobacco-related rules was all about power to the people, wasn't it? Or was it?

On the surface, the proposal seemed reasonable. Rep. Robert L. Schuler sponsored House Bill 298, requiring that local legislative authorities approve any smoking-related rule or order of a board of health before it takes effect.

The Cincinnati Republican said boards of health are appointed, and that any smoking-related order (read that as *no-smoking rules*) should be ratified by elected officials, such as city council members.

Schuler said the bill is a lifeline for small businesses, including restaurants, bars and bowling alleys. They could be put out of business by heavy-handed no-smoking rules.

"We talk about taxation without representation," said Rep. John A. Carey Jr., R-Wellston. "Regulation without representation is tyranny."

Carey said defeat of Schuler's bill would be a step toward Big Brother. But there's another view: Should public policy always be made by elected officials? Or are there times when appointees answering to elected officials are better?

"The best way to kill the efficacy of a board of health is to subject it to political whims and lobbying," said House Minority Leader Jack Ford, D-Toledo.

Of course, you could say that appointed boards are just as vulnerable to politicking and lobbying as elected officials are. The elected vs. appointed debate carries into a variety of areas.

There's a difference of opinion over whether judges ought to be elected or appointed. U.S. Supreme Court justices are appointed for life. In some instances, they've become tyrants. In others, they've shaped our society for the better *because* they've been independent of politics.

Ohio elects its state attorney general. Some states appoint theirs, reasoning that the attorney general is the governor's lawyer.

At one time in Ohio, some forces attempted to make the post of public utility commissioner an elective office. The regulators of public utilities are appointed by the governor. As a hedge against politicizing the commission, no more than three of the five commissioners may be from one political party.

More recently, former Gov. George V. Voinovich wanted to appoint the members of the state Board of Education; historically they had been elected. He reasoned that if he was responsible for education, he should control the board. The legislature saw fit to let the governor name eight of the 19 members. The rest are elected.

Rep. Priscilla D. Mead, R-Upper Arlington, said House Bill 298 is unconstitutional because it overrides charter cities that have independent boards of health. Mead ought to know. She's been both a councilwoman and mayor of Upper Arlington and has been president of that city's health board.

Mead said cities that have their own charter, ratified by the voters, should be able to set up independent boards of health whose decisions are not subject to approval by a city council.

She said Columbus suburbs treat health oversight differently. Upper Arlington and Grandview Heights contract with the Franklin County Board of Health for services. Worthington has no board of health but contracts with the city of Columbus, she said. Bexley has a health commissioner and a staffed department.

Mead said Schuler's bill would disrupt local control on smoking-related matters. Next, it might be zoning rules that have to go to a council, she warned.

Mead tried to exempt charter cities from Schuler's bill but she was voted down. She'll try pushing state senators to take it up again in their chamber.

Despite the sponsor's professed goal of allowing folks to have their say on smoking-related rules, another agenda might have been at play.

Why, after lawmakers struggled for months to distribute $1.2 billion in tobacco-settlement money for anti-smoking programs, would they want to hamstring local boards of health by subjecting their rules to a council's votes? Perhaps the tobacco companies were involved. Rep. Jerry W. Krupinski, D-Steubenville, thought so.

Cigarette company lobbyists on Capitol Square denied involvement, but the lobbying could have been done from afar.

It didn't seem to bother House members to pass House Bill 298, then visit an Atrium luncheon for them sponsored by the Ohio chapter of the American Cancer Society. Society representatives were philosophical: They expected Schuler's bill to pass but hope to win the Senate round.

The skirmish over local tobacco rules became moot. A statewide ban on smoking in public places, and some private ones, was enacted.

■ ■

It was the early 1970s when funding Ohio's schools began to be a problem. Thirty-four years later, despite an order from the Ohio Supreme Court to reduce reliance on the property tax for school money, the problem persisted. This might be the best summary written about the dilemma.

Don't Look for Solution to Ohio's School-Funding Mess Soon—If Ever
The Columbus Dispatch, November 29, 2004

If the Governor's Blue-Ribbon Task Force on Financing Student Success has taught one lesson, it's that Ohio's school-funding problem will never be solved.

Not that it was going to be solved anyway. The Ohio Supreme Court found the system wanting and made broad recommendations, but the court refused to enforce its order when the legislative remedy fell short.

And not everyone wants the funding problem to be solved. Ohioans like the idea of having veto power over school levies and bond issues. It's their means of control over the schools. Never mind that folks in other states give you that open-mouthed stare when you tell them you actually get to vote on how much to give the schools. In those states, it's not an option. The schools write their budgets, and you pay up.

No, the school-funding system will remain for three basic reasons:

- Ohioans won't give up their constitutional right to vote on school taxes.
- Property taxes provide a stable source of revenue.
- The Buckeye State is too diverse for a one-size-fits-all method of distributing the money.

Under a new system, funds would be shifted from one district to another unless the overall pot grows. There would be winners and losers, and backing a loser is not an option in the political realm.

State Sen. Joy Padgett of Coshocton suggested during her recent campaign that maybe there should be three school-funding formulas—one for the urban areas, one for rural areas and one for the suburbs. Not a bad idea.

But even that wouldn't work out. There are too many divergent interests clawing for a share of the pie, and each thinks it's the most important. You say: The children; do what's best for the children. They all think they're doing the best for the children.

You have the teachers and the parent groups and the taxpayers and the school administrators and the elected school-board members and the school employees and the government and business and organized labor and the ivory-tower educators. Each sees funding from a different perspective.

They sure did when the governor's task force recently got together to discuss a draft report after months of study. These folks are men and women of good intention, each representing a piece of the primary and secondary education puzzle. They weren't trying to reinvent the wheel. They were just trying to come up with something doable. And when push came to shove, somebody found fault with almost every suggested change.

The panel could not even reach unanimity on a plan to correct a flaw that cheats some school districts out of state aid by basing their grants on an artificial local tax figure. One influential senator said he'd work against a proposed correction because it would cost the state too much money.

A survey commissioned by the task force showed that Ohioans want to see the funding fixed but they want to ensure that the new system is going to improve education and help students.

Voter concern, according to the survey, is not so much about eliminating local school levies as it is about providing a stable source of revenue that will allow schools to focus more on teaching than on money.

The most stable source of revenue is the property tax. But the court has called for the state to move away from the property tax. It's unfair to those on fixed incomes and to low-wealth districts.

Voters want schools to be accountable and efficient, just like businesses. They want schools to live within their means. Then the "means" should be a tax based on income. When income is up, school expenses can be up. When it's down, that's the time for schools to cut back. But nobody's looking down that politically treacherous road.

The court could have mandated a solution. The governor's task force, with all the players in the room, could throw out caution and recommend a plan. Term-limited legislators with no political future could put something together. But they didn't, and they won't. And even if they did, it wouldn't work because any workable plan has to have the confidence and blessing of the people.

Ohioans don't understand the current system because it's too complex. It is complex because Ohio is so diverse. The legislature won't start over because that's too much of a risk, and the people want a guarantee that any change will bring success.

Best chance for a solution? Ask Santa.

When he took office in 2007, Democratic Gov. Ted Strickland foolishly promised to solve the school-funding mess. He held public forums to seek ideas for a solution. All the ideas had surfaced already. It was a matter of getting the interest groups in a room, finding out what they had to have and forging a compromise.

The only hope for a solution is for the governor and the legislators to muster the political will to do it. Some interest groups will be hurt. Others will be helped. But there isn't a "no-lose" solution, which is what is always sought at the Statehouse. Strickland lost any chance of a meaningful solution when the American economy collapsed in the fall of 2008 and Ohio's budget was shrunk by about 25 percent.

■ ■

Labor vs. Business

Business and Labor Each Want the Edge in Campaign Funding

United Press International, October 27, 1973

COLUMBUS (UPI)—As the special legislative session on campaign financing proceeds, it is clear that the single major issue standing in the way of complete reform is the question of how to treat political contributions by labor unions, corporations and other heavyweight pressure groups.

There seems to be no common ground for agreement between Democrats and Republicans. Their philosophies are directly opposed and their future strengths in Ohio are at stake in the matter.

Democrats are calling for unlimited contributions of $10 or less to labor unions and trade associations for political purposes. They claim this would encourage more average working people to participate in the political process through small donations.

Republicans want "equal treatment" for labor unions and business interests. Under the terms of a bill on the way to the Senate floor, members of unions and trade associations would be able to make voluntary contributions and earmark them for the candidate or party of their choice.

Moreover, employers—that is, leaders of business and industry—would be allowed to set up political action groups like the labor unions have to receive voluntary political contributions.

Most of the debate in the legislative corridors and committee rooms has centered on the provision for unlimited $10 contributions, which the administration of Gov. John J. Gilligan believes vital to any equitable campaign financing law.

The arguments on both sides are vehement and rational. Republicans claim contributions to labor unions ought to be voluntary, and that the money should go to the candidate or party of the member's choice.

House Democrats, the United Auto Workers, the Ohio Education Association and the Ohio Democratic Party reply almost in unison.

Their basic argument is that union members are not coerced into supporting political action groups and that they have a choice in who gets the money by attending democratically-operated union meetings. The recipient is the selection of the majority.

"Since when is it un-American to organize?" asked one House Democrat last week in attempting to make the point that the political punch would be taken from unions and trade associations if contributions were earmarked for various candidates and parties.

The answer seems to be that it isn't un-American to organize for political clout. Such organizations are called political parties, not unions or trade associations, and anyone is free to contribute at any time.

Labor unions and trade associations already have legitimate clout around the bargaining table in the private sector. Their interests in government-related activities might not match all their members' concerns.

Although labor unions and trade associations are democratically-operated, they share one trait that seems out of line with modern democracy. They follow the "winner-take-all" concept, which breeds power, not the idea of proportional representation fostered by reform Democrats.

Thus, in campaign financing, the winner of union or association support takes all the money. In some cases, this is fair but probably not in all.

Finally, when the governor called the special session on campaign financing, one of the main goals seemed to be to eliminate the influence of money on elections, that is, the "buying" of elections.

The lawmakers have established their intentions to set spending limits to equalize candidates, and to dull the effects of wealthy individuals and business tycoons by limiting contributions to $3,000.

It would seem logical, then, that the last vestige of "organized money" be removed from election campaigns by writing into law a provision for voluntary, earmarked union and association gifts.

Lawmakers and other elected officials struggled mightily for the next 35 years to come up with an equitable campaign finance law. They made some improvements. Corporations were allowed to have political action committees. Individual donations to candidates were limited to $2,500 per election. But contributions to political parties and caucuses were unlimited. And the courts ruled against spending limits. The tension between organized labor and business remained.

■ ■

Tax incentives for industry are a continual thorn in the side of organized labor. The business community, on the other hand, thinks it's taxed too much in Ohio.

Dems Cave in to Rhodes on Tax Breaks for Industry

United Press International, December 17, 1977

COLUMBUS (UPI)—Gov. James A. Rhodes is winning another hand of "Jackson County Poker" with his archrivals—the Democratic leaders of the Ohio General Assembly.

For the uninitiated, Jackson County poker in this instance is the helter-skelter way Rhodes runs the affairs of state, charging off in all directions and changing the rules in mid-game.

The governor has dragged his adversaries kicking and screaming into the world of tax incentives for industry, and he may never let them up.

Rhodes is so elated over the acquisition of a Ford Motor Co. transmission plant in Clermont County he could probably fly to Florida for his Christmas vacation without a plane.

Last week, he heaped praise on the legislative leaders for their part in attracting the Ford Plant, claiming the passage of House Bill 828 tipped the balance between Ohio and Michigan by offering substantial tax reductions on Ford's new investments.

The governor shared the credit despite the fact he has been hammering the legislature for the tax breaks without success for three years.

Democrats immodestly accepted the applause and said the tax package "gives Ohio the finest climate in the country for attracting industry."

That's a hedge against any future overtures for more tax abatement. The Democrats had trouble enough squaring themselves with organized labor to vote for the package and betray the time-honored tenet that individuals' taxes must be lowered before corporate taxes are cut.

As for Rhodes' profuse praise, that will be forgotten in six months and he will once again be claiming his rightful credit for attracting Ford and Honda plants, and flaying the legislators for their snail-like reactions.

Meanwhile, the governor has tossed another time-bomb to the lawmakers. Rhodes, who often complains too many things are studied to death, said he favors a "blue ribbon" legislative committee to study Ohio's school financing problems.

Shunning a role of leadership, the governor said he will not assemble any formal recommendations for solving the school crisis, but will merely offer input to the legislative committee.

"I've already talked to some of them," he said. "They know how I stand."

Thus, Rhodes will not run the risk of having to propose any drastic changes in taxation or school finance during an election year, and if the situation becomes worse, you-know-who will receive the blame.

■ ■

Prevailing Mood in Statehouse Was Nasty During Wage Debate

The Columbus Dispatch, May 12, 1997

The dynamite was in place and the plunger was about to be pushed. If it hadn't been for a cooling-off period, the cupola might have come off the Statehouse last week.

Angry and restless over a threat to their pay, trade union workers filled the rotunda, lined the stairways and crammed into the Ohio Senate chamber.

At issue was Senate Bill 102, offering state aid for school-building construction and repairs. What motivated the workers was a section eliminating the prevailing union wage on such school-building projects.

The atmosphere resembled a sporting event and the workers didn't need scorecards to identify the players. As senators approached their desks, they were greeted as if emerging from the tunnel onto the field. Heroes were cheered; foes were booed.

Union members called out: "Let's cut *your* pay!" and, "We have to make a living, too!"

Leaning on the brass rail around the chamber were laborers in cut-off sleeves that bared tattooed arms. Some looked like they could bench-press Utah.

Senate President Richard H. Finan, a Republican responsible for the anti-wage clause in the bill, attempted to establish order, warning the unionists they would be ejected if they didn't observe decorum.

When comments and catcalls continued, the Cincinnatian loudly lectured the offenders, warning that they would be banished to the rotunda if they kept it up. "It's your choice," he bellowed.

When a presentation to a high-school all-American soccer player was interrupted, the red-haired Irishman lost it. Slamming his gavel repeatedly until chips flew from it, he unleashed a tirade unparalleled on either the House or Senate dais in more than 28 years.

"At least you ought to have enough common sense to shut up!" he screamed, trembling and red-faced.

A recess was called for Republican and Democratic caucuses, and Senate Minority Leader Ben Espy, D-Columbus, asked Finan if he could help defuse the situation.

Finan accepted and Espy urged union leaders to get their members to cool it. When the session resumed, Espy spoke to the crowd. "This is a very sensitive issue," he said. "We understand your emotions." He told them they'd get more out of the session if they listened to the debate instead of interrupting.

The union members restrained themselves and Finan never reached another flash point. In fact, he permitted applause from the sidelines, not normally allowed.

"Cool heads prevailed on both sides," Finan said later. He and Espy agreed that the situation came close to the point of no return. To the union members, Finan represented a red flag. "Him trying to quiet them was like me trying to quiet a roomful of bankers," said Espy.

Had Finan thrown out the workers, there's no telling what might have happened when they rejoined several hundred brothers and sisters outside. A good guess is a loud and possibly dangerous confrontation with security officers.

What caused this demonstration in the first place, and why did tempers flare?

A showdown on prevailing wage—the union scale paid on public projects—has been coming for a long time. Conservative Republicans want to get rid of it, and now that the GOP controls the legislature and the governor's office, they might have a chance.

Senate Bill 102 is designed to move up to $300 million in state aid to poorer school districts before summer. The Republicans decided to use school construction as a test for canceling the prevailing wage. They said it would save 15 percent to 20 percent in costs, and who could argue against stretching school construction dollars to the max?

Sen. Leigh E. Herington, D-Aurora, said his calculations showed the maneuver would save 2 percent to 5 percent, and that would be more than offset by nonunion workers taking longer and doing inferior work.

School-building renovation and repair is only a small part of the construction picture, but the real fear for the unions is that Senate Bill 102 would set a precedent for wages on other public projects, especially if it is shown the schools can save money.

As for Finan, he's new at presiding over the Senate, and he's a stickler for decorum. He honchoed the three-year restoration of the Statehouse and wants to see the institution respected.

It probably was an unnecessary political gimmick to include the nonprevailing-wage section in the bill, but the Republicans wanted to try it. They passed the bill and escaped a nasty situation.

The stage is set for another round in the House, where the bill will be voted on in the next couple of weeks. Speaker Jo Ann Davidson of Reynoldsburg, also a Republican, may want to strap on a helmet and take a tranquilizer.

The "cupola" referred to in the first paragraph above is what passes for a dome on the Ohio Statehouse.

The Republicans had their way on Senate Bill 102 in the House, although the labor demonstration in the Senate was unmatched on the other side of the Statehouse. A subsequent study showed little savings by eliminating the prevailing wage on school construction projects.

■ ■

The Irony of Issue 2 Isn't Lost on Ohio's Republicans

The Columbus Dispatch, November 10, 1997

The irony was delicious: Conservative lawmakers who have zealously protected the people's right to referendum over the years saw it rear up and bite the General Assembly last week—on behalf of organized labor.

"It's like an appendix," Rep. William G. Batchelder said of the referendum process. "You don't know what it's about, but once it starts to hurt, it hurts."

Batchelder, a conservative Republican from Medina, has taught a generation of House members to uphold the right of referendum by opposing emergency clauses on bills. An emergency clause makes the bill effective immediately when the governor signs it, eliminating the people's right to petition for a referendum and try to keep it off the lawbooks.

Of course, that's what happened last week for the first time in more than a half-century in Ohio: Opponents of Senate Bill 45, changing a variety of workers' compensation procedures, got Issue 2 on the ballot and nullified the law.

The irony is that Batchelder is a strong supporter of the business community that pushed the workers' compensation changes. He's also a constitutional scholar and a firm believer in the institution of the legislature, yet he grudgingly admired the folks who so skillfully used the referendum to allow the people to override the legislature.

"This is important," Batchelder said of the results of Issue 2, "because it is a brake on legislative action."

It's not easy to use the referendum in this manner. It took a massive effort to gather 414,924 signatures within 90 days of the bill's passage to put the issue on the ballot.

Although various repealers and initiated laws have been tried by citizen groups in the past, it's been 58 years since a law was subjected to referendum in Ohio, and not since 1920, when the people rejected a state law on the prohibition of liquor sales, has a referendum succeeded.

In the last 25 years, Ohio has had mainly a bipartisan government, with each party exerting at least some control. Legislation, especially bills affecting business and labor, had to be compromise efforts. It became common for legislative leaders to demand "agreed" bills between warring factions before the bills were even introduced.

One exception was in 1983, when Democrats took over the governor's office and both legislative chambers. They rammed through a hefty increase in the state income tax without consulting minority Republicans.

Some observers have compared the Republicans' efforts on workers' compensation to the 1983 escapade. The GOP took over the Statehouse in 1995 and then, apparently, tried to overreach by slanting the workers' compensation law in favor of the business community. The result was Issue 2.

House Minority Leader Ross Boggs Jr., D-Andover, said business was just waiting for the Republicans to retake the Statehouse. "It was payback time," he said of the workers' comp bill.

Organized labor started getting ready for the referendum before the bill even passed. Robert E. Kopp, state coordinator for the United Auto Workers, said newsletters constantly updated the membership on the progress of Senate Bill 45. Paycheck envelopes were stuffed with literature, mailers were sent out and calls were made.

"They were like the cat at the mouse's hole," said Batchelder.

Kent Darr of the Ohio AFL-CIO said organized labor joined with health-care workers, farmers, ministers, attorneys and the NAACP, among others, to mount a grass roots campaign. "For the first time in a long, long time we actually put together a broad-based coalition," he said.

Thomas R. Winters, a Columbus attorney and a member of the Ohio Ballot Board, said the referendum was not used frequently by lobby groups for fear of alienating the legislature. "You're basically saying the powers-that-be are wrong," he said. "Now, with term limits coming up, they don't care."

Will Ohio see more of the public referendum? Secretary of State Bob Taft thinks so.

"To some extent, the representative government process is eroding," said Taft. "Voters feel they are more informed than ever. I think the voters want to have a direct say on issues."

Perhaps talk radio and the Internet have given folks confidence to express their opinions.

"There's a disassociation of people with their government," said Columbus political consultant Greg Haas, a Democrat. "There's a basic distrust." Haas also believes employees are less trusting of their employers, a feeling that contributed to the defeat of Issue 2. He said workers have not shared in the rewards of the robust economy, while business profits have soared.

Herb Asher, a professor emeritus of political science at Ohio State University, said there'll be more referenda but doesn't think "it's going to become commonplace."

■ ■

Ralph Nader Meets His Match in Vern Riffe

United Press International, February 1, 1987

COLUMBUS (UPI)—Consumer advocate Ralph Nader breezed into town last week to take on the giant insurance industry and the corporate world over a civil justice and insurance reform package now in the legislature.

He wound up taking on Ohio House Speaker Vernal Riffe, D-New Boston, who makes the wheels turn in the Statehouse, and may have overplayed his hand.

Nader's message to the House Insurance Committee was simple: Forget about changing the system of handling lawsuits; that would only hurt the little people. Instead, crack down on the insurance companies. Their ineptitude is why liability insurance isn't available at affordable rates.

Nader told reporters Ohio's bill, except for those states which put a ceiling on damage awards, "is the worst bill in the country."

This is the same bill over which lawmakers agonized for nine months last year, and which Riffe is protecting as a model of compromise.

Nader didn't stop there. He publicly flogged Riffe, saying he has maintained iron-fisted control over the House, discouraging diversity of opinion by "reprimand and removal," and staying on top for a record 12 years by "an ingenious deployment of political power."

"If he's going to run for governor in this state of Ohio, he's going to pay a penalty for straight-arming the workers and consumers," warned Nader. "This issue is going to track him from New Boston to Cleveland."

Nader said Riffe will be described as "soft on crime" for keeping consumers from recovering adequate compensation for wrongful acts.

What made Nader's attack even more interesting was that he had spent the previous evening at the Governor's Mansion as the guest of Gov. Richard F. Celeste.

Celeste only recently had a meeting of the minds with Riffe over civil justice and insurance reform. Alone in the governor's office, they agreed to work together on a solution. Celeste, who had vetoed last year's version at the request of Nader and others, said he would negotiate language on defective product lawsuits.

Yet here came Nader, after having slept at the governor's house, saying Celeste was not convinced that product liability had to be part of the settlement.

"Ralph Nader doesn't speak for the governor," said Brian Usher, Celeste's press secretary, who also denied the governor was going to allow Nader to drive a wedge between himself and Riffe.

"The governor still thinks Vern is his friend, his mentor," said Usher. "He listened to Ralph Nader. That doesn't mean he agrees with him."

But why beard Riffe by having Ralph Nader stay overnight?

"He's a prominent figure in the ranks of consumer advocates," said Usher. "He's a nationally known figure, the kind of a guy the governor would like to have a little chat with. He (Celeste) is not going to disassociate himself from people who have differences with Vern Riffe."

As for Riffe, he coolly endured Nader's barbs, knowing he still holds the high cards in the game that's about to unfold.

And Riffe laughed heartily when one House Republican told him, "That's the best thing that could have happened for you, Ralph Nader coming here."

Tort reform is a perennial bone of contention between labor and business at the Statehouse. Mainly it manifests itself in campaigns for Ohio Supreme Court justice because that's where the ultimate battle is always fought. Consumer groups and organized labor want an unfettered right to sue. But business and insurance groups seek predictability for the bottom line. They want limitations on lawsuits.

■ ■

Energy vs. Environment

This battle rages on today. Most of the conflict in Ohio involves the mining and burning of high-sulfur coal, and clean air standards. But the first two columns here point out that Americans were aware of their dependence on foreign oil, and of the need to preserve the environment, thirty years ago. The natural gas exploration proposal in 1977 was occasioned by a severe coal shortage the previous winter.

To Drill or Not to Drill under Lake Erie

United Press International, June 4, 1977

COLUMBUS (UPI)—There was "man-bites-dog" news in the Ohio General Assembly last week.

The Senate acted, more than a year ahead of time, on a bill dealing with the ban on drilling for minerals under Lake Erie.

Normally, the legislature does not act much ahead of time on anything, except maybe pay raise bills or other mischief. Legislation by crisis is a habit.

One time, the ban on drilling under Lake Erie expired for three months because the legislature forgot to re-enact it.

But the Senate gets the "Gold Star" award for passing last week the bill making a permanent ban on oil drilling under Lake Erie and authorizing a pilot program for a limited search for gas in the eastern portion of the lake.

The last ban on all mineral production, enacted in 1974, expires July 1, 1978. Far-sighted lawmakers, concerned with fuel supplies, figure something ought to be done before then to determine if the mineral resources of the lake can be used without polluting it.

So they have prepared a carefully-drafted bill authorizing the state to drill three test gas wells to check fuel reserves and environmental impact on the lake.

Senate debate last week was spirited and thoughtful. Sen. J. Timothy McCormack, D-Euclid, author of the four-year ban, was dead set against removing any part of it.

McCormack recalled how many allies he had for keeping the lake clean in 1974. "The mood has changed, but the conditions have not," he said, adding that "with tons of waste being poured into the lake every day, it ages 10,000 years in a very short period of time."

The senator said three state agencies cooperating in the pilot gas-drilling project represented "an ominous choir of voices" which would put the camel's nose under the tent and result in wholesale drilling in a few years.

"Where will the voice of caution come from?" asked McCormack.

It seems the voice of caution has already spoken in the form of the bill, which eventually received 21-10 Senate approval and went over to the House.

After the pilot drilling projects conducted by the Ohio Energy and Resource Development Agency in cooperation with the Ohio Environmental Protection Agency and state Department of Natural Resources, a report would be written and submitted to the legislature.

The General Assembly would decide if it wanted to permit commercial gas drilling. If so, it would write a law to govern the drilling. Further safeguards would be incorporated in rules adopted by the Division of Oil and Gas in the Department of Natural Resources.

There would be no drilling for oil anywhere under the lake, and no drilling for gas in the western basin. Production of oil or wet gas containing liquid hydrocarbons would be prohibited. Offshore wells capable of producing oil would have to be plugged. Drillers would have to carry adequate liability insurance.

How much more caution can reasonably be expected?

Freshman Sen. Michael Schwarzwalder, D-Columbus, probably best summarized the rationale of supporters of the test program and the change in attitude since the fuel shortage.

"We've got to find out, in fact, what we have in Lake Erie in the way of a gas supply," said Schwarzwalder. "There are varying estimates, and I think the time has come that we know what is available in Ohio. Our dependence on the southwest for gas is almost absolute."

Schwarzwalder joined with one of the Senate's more conservative members, Thomas A. Van Meter, R-Ashland, in pointing out it will take three or four years to get commercial production of gas in the lake, if it is authorized.

By then Ohio's fuel supply, as well as the impact of drilling in the lake, will be more in focus.

For once, a bouquet to the Senate for being a step ahead of the game. Perhaps the House will maintain the pace.

■ ■

Rhodes Pushes for Independence from Arab Oil

United Press International, January 18, 1980

COLUMBUS (UPI)—Every once in awhile, you will pass a car with a picture of Uncle Sam or Mickey Mouse in the rear window, making a rude gesture at Iran, the Ayatollah or another public enemy of the day.

If cartoon warfare is an example of this country's best line of defense; if people actually believe that a show of scorching humor will put down all foes, then America's in a heap of trouble.

One person who doesn't buy this approach, though he's not above laughing at a good joke, is Gov. James A. Rhodes.

Rhodes was out selling again last week, peddling his latest plan to free the country from dependence on foreigners.

The governor has what he views as a constructive alternative to shelling out billions of dollars to the oil-producing nations—increase production here at home and use our own oil.

"Inflation, unemployment, weakened national defense, a weak dollar, higher interest rates and a lower standard of living are all the direct results of our ill-founded energy policies," said Rhodes.

"We must find the national determination to end our addiction to OPEC oil, and develop our own reserves."

Simplified, as are all Rhodes' plans, this one calls for improved recovery techniques to get more oil out of existing wells, drilling on western land made off-limits by the federal government, and an end to federal bureaucracy which has blocked offshore drilling.

Rhodes was selling his plan to Republicans in Washington by week's end. Maybe it will work and maybe it won't. But it's considerably more productive than driving around with a sign in your back window.

One can only be thankful that mentality wasn't afoot 40 years ago. Hitler dartboards would have been a great defense against buzz-bombs.

Jim Rhodes may have acted like a buffoon at times, but he read the Wall Street Journal every day. Note the similarity of concern here about foreign oil and some thirty years later—nothing changes.

■ ■

This was the start of the strip mine wars that lasted several years in the 1970s. Environmentalists prevailed with a strong reclamation bill that basically held up into the next century, although some concessions later were made to the mine operators.

It was a tough issue because coal was a big part of the economy in eastern Ohio. Local utilities wanted to burn it because it was nearby and cheap. Reclamation of the scarred land added to the cost.

Later in the 1970s, the battle turned toward Washington over clean-air standards. Ohio coal has a high sulfur content and there was no easy way to clean it, as subsequent columns will point out.

Pennsylvania Strip Mine Owner Praises Strong Reclamation Standards

United Press International, March 18, 1971

COLUMBUS (UPI)—Those who say there's nothing worse than a reformed drinker might have had second thoughts last week if they had attended the first (Ohio) House committee hearing on tough strip mine legislation—especially if they were a coal mine operator.

The House Environment Committee was treated, if that is the word, to a fist-thumping, ear-splitting plea for strong regulations from, of all people, the owner of a strip mine company in Pennsylvania.

"You must pass this bill," thundered Russell Haller of Kittanning, Pa., operator of the West Freedom Mining Co. Part of the audience, presumably coal operators or miners, stared in disbelief. Some waved their hands in contempt.

Haller appeared before the committee on behalf of the strip mine reform bill with two of his former arch-enemies from Pennsylvania.

One was William E. Guckert, director of conservation and reclamation who personally supervises backfilling and replanting of strip pits in western Pennsylvania.

The other was Pennsylvania State Rep. John F. Laudadio, a spokesman for conservation and a strong ally of the sportsmen's lobby in the Keystone State.

"Eight or nine years ago, I said the new Pennsylvania law would put me out of business," Haller told the committee. "It passed in January, 1964, and I said 'There I go, down the drain.'"

But he explained that after he was required to plan and engineer his projects to meet the requirements to reclaim the land as he mined, he became a better businessman and was still able to make a profit.

"I used to go down to a fraternal organization or someplace and people would ask me, 'What do you do?'" he related. "I'd tell them I was a strip mine operator, and they'd say, 'What a hell of a thing to do.' Now, they say, 'Aren't you the guy that did that beautiful thing up there on the hill?'" Haller said, referring to a landscaping job he had done on his coal pit.

Haller's reclamation reputation is such that he can lease land from farmers to mine because they know he will leave it in as good or better condition than he found it.

Guckert showed the committee color slides of huge strip pits, some gouged 100 feet into the earth. Then he showed the areas after compulsory reclamation, turned into lush hay and buckwheat fields or beautifully landscaped lakes.

"They can do it, gentlemen," he said repeatedly. "They tell you they can't, but they can."

At one point there was laughter from the audience.

"Don't let them laugh at you, gentlemen," retorted Guckert, whose predecessor had been fired in Pennsylvania because he was not treating all coal mine operators alike. "They can do it if you make them."

Guckert said he makes them, and "we get along just fine. I'm not afraid to tell them when they do a good job, and they're doing a good job."

Debate on the Ohio strip mine bill is likely to be long and controversial, but it probably will produce no greater irony than Haller standing side-by side with Guckert and Laudadio, with whom he once fought bitterly.

And the committee may not soon forget the color slides documenting the sharp transformation of wasted land through proper conservation techniques.

"They can do it if you make them" is a point that state legislators need to hear whenever they are confronted with a decision that might be unpopular but is in the public interest. Too many times, lawmakers take the easy way out. So do elected officials in the executive branch.

The author was personally acquainted with John Laudadio and Bill Guckert, having covered them in Harrisburg in the mid-1960s.

■ ■

Gov. Rhodes and President Carter Spar, Showbiz-Style, Over Coal Emissions

United Press International, February 8, 1980

COLUMBUS (UPI)—Politics and show business went head-to-head with science last week when it came time to decide how Ohio's air should be cleaned up.

Science lost.

The occasion was the announcement by the federal government—anticipated for six months—on whether Ohio's plan was acceptable for reducing sulfur dioxide emissions to the atmosphere after utilities and industries burn high-sulfur Ohio coal.

The U.S. Environmental Protection Agency, through its Midwest regional office in Chicago, spent months weighing the plan submitted by the administration of Gov. James A. Rhodes—the last such plan in the country to be approved.

The Carter administration, to which the EPA supposedly answers, agonized through those same months over whether to make Ohio conform to the rest of the nation or secure crucial votes in the coal region by taking a relaxed stance.

When the decision came, it was pure Barnum & Bailey.

Coordinated by the state Democratic Party and president Carter's re-election operatives, the U.S. EPA sent its personnel to Columbus to make the announcement, plugging in Democratic state legislators from the coal region for maximum mileage.

As luck would have it, Gov. Rhodes—Ohio's top "fed"-baiter—was taking an entourage to Washington that very morning to continue his attack on the EPA before a U.S. Senate Republican policy committee.

The Rhodes group and the EPA passed each other at Port Columbus International Airport, one on the way in and the other on the way out, like a pair of professional wrestlers running past each other to bounce off the ring ropes.

Then came the EPA's carefully-orchestrated announcement: Most of the Ohio plan for reducing sulfur emissions was acceptable. As for the part that was not—using a 30-day average to calculate emissions instead of measuring heavier spot discharges—The EPA would ease up on enforcement and honor that method for 12 months.

There were huzzahs from the Democrats. Except for one.

State Rep. Wayne Hays, who enjoys being the ant at the picnic, grumbled that maybe, just maybe, the moratorium would last long enough for Carter to rake in the coal region votes this fall and then the crackdown would come. What would happen to the coal companies and miners in his district then? Hays wondered.

He was told by John McGuire, the regional EPA director, to hold his own press conference and stop throwing a wet blanket on the love feast.

Meanwhile Rhodes was in Washington. Cut off from the entire issue which he had been fighting for months, what could he do? Certainly not hail it as victory. He had been pre-empted there by Carter and the Democrats.

But he couldn't denounce the decision either, for after all, it gave Ohio's coal region a year's breathing space, in a manner of speaking.

So what did Rhodes do? Just what he always does, being the politician without peer. He did a fast shuffle and changed the subject without missing a step, attacking the environmentalists on another front. He wasn't about to call timeout on his war with the EPA.

Bright and early the next morning, Mrs. Charlie Smith, a regional coordinator with the U.S. EPA, was testifying before an Ohio House Committee on acid rain. She is an attorney but not a politician, and she had been invited there to open a dialogue between the state and the federal government, hopefully to foster mutual understanding.

After some calm and thoughtful discussion by Mrs. Smith and the committee, James F. McAvoy, director of the Ohio EPA, began blustering through a press release from Rhodes saying Ohio was the "target of a scurrilous attack by no-growth environmental extremists using scare tactics."

That was the end of the uneasy truce, but certainly not the end of the politicking and showbiz that will accompany the issue of Ohio's clean air through this presidential election year.

■ ■

How to Make Good Politics Out of a Blizzard

United Press International, March 2, 1984

COLUMBUS (UPI)—Gov. Richard F. Celeste took his first test in snowstorm politics last week. He passed.

This was important for Celeste's future in government. Having raised taxes last year and taken the accompanying brickbats, he didn't need the hassle of blowing a blizzard.

The handbook for Blizzard Politics 101 was written in 1978 when former Gov. James A Rhodes forged a re-election campaign out of behavior during a heavy winter storm.

Rhodes set up a command post in his office, slept there, and declared that "A killer blizzard is stalking Ohio, looking for victims."

He barked orders to the Ohio National Guard, the Ohio Department of Transportation, the Highway Patrol and everyone else at his command. They responded.

Rhodes' troops rescued hundreds of stranded travelers and residents, set up temporary shelters, provided food and medical care, coordinated efforts with local governments and private groups, and opened drifted highways.

The indefatigable Rhodes staged press conferences in his Cabinet room, complete with colored highway maps and briefings from the military hierarchy during the four-day blizzard cleanup, which lasted through the weekend.

One evening, Rhodes called for the fourth media event of the day and was advised by an aide to forget it and let the reporters go home.

"You don't understand," admonished the governor. "People want to hear from us. They're scared." Taking command during the blizzard was an issue made to order for Rhodes, who had performed listlessly in the late '70s and was in danger of losing his bid for a fourth term.

His Democratic opponent, Celeste, made the mistake of promising a solution to the school-funding problem. Fearful of calling for new taxes, he changed his mind and said he would appoint a committee to study the situation.

That was all Rhodes needed.

"We didn't need a committee to solve the blizzard," he snorted at his campaign kickoff. Two months later, he was re-elected.

When last week's snowstorm of near blizzard proportions hit, Celeste was in Washington at a meeting of the National Association of Governors. He lost no time in following Rhodes' playbook.

Cancelling a series of meetings late Monday, the governor flew back to Columbus and showed up at the National Guard armory where the state's command post was located.

Celeste appeared on TV, but he avoided a carnival public relations atmosphere and let the 900 national guardsmen and 2,000 Ohio Department of Transportation employees do their work in the field.

Wednesday, the governor made the obligatory flight to Port Clinton and Cleveland to survey the situation. Then he put in for federal assistance.

Almost everything went smoothly because the battle plan was in place. Equipment had been inspected and a dry run conducted.

Fighting snowstorms is a matter of personnel, equipment and communications. All seemed in order. "We've been through this before," said one ODOT employee.

Celeste didn't match Rhodes' Academy Award for acting, but he passed the test because he was prepared.

■ ■

This is a balanced column—it gives both sides. But it makes the unmistakable point that when push came to shove, Gov. George Voinovich, as did most Ohio governors, would side with business and industry on environmental questions. They called the tune because they represented jobs. "Green" had not yet come into fashion.

Voinovich's Environmentalist Claims Open to Question

The Columbus Dispatch, September 6, 1993

The sun was hot, and the sky was perfectly blue, lined with a handful of wispy clouds. A hawk circled lazily overhead, and a monarch butterfly fluttered high.

Below, on Earth, at Horwath's Landing by the Upper Cuyahoga River in Geauga County last week, Gov. George V. Voinovich was telling reporters and others how good his administration has been for Ohio's environment.

A subsequent 7-mile canoe trip down the sparkling river helped create the impression that Voinovich, as advertised in his 1990 election campaign, has become the "environmental governor."

But if they had been allowed, some dark thoughts might have crept into that sunny day:

If Voinovich is the environmental governor, where were the environmentalists? How come they were battling the governor instead of embracing him?

Why do protesters continue to hound the administration, calling for closure of the new hazardous-waste incinerator near East Liverpool?

Why would the Voinovich administration permit a southern Ohio coal company to dump millions of gallons of an acid substance resembling thick tomato soup into 75 miles of creeks and streams?

Possible answers will appear below, but first a word about the governor's environmental accomplishments.

Voinovich said he has been fighting for a way to curtail out-of-state trash shipments. He said he has increased funding for the Ohio Environmental Protection Agency by 60 percent, chiefly by charging fees to the waste-generating companies that use the EPA services.

The governor said the fees will fund Ohio's solid-waste disposal program, double the state's ability to monitor rivers and streams and allow the first regular oversight of small drinking-water systems.

He took credit for a law requiring the recycling of scrap tires—actually proposed by a couple of Akron-area lawmakers—but he didn't mention the bottle-and-can recycling bill. That was central to the environmental plank in his campaign platform, but it flopped in the legislature.

Voinovich highlighted his efforts to get manufacturers generating tons of toxic chemicals to reduce emissions by 50 percent by 1995. He released the names of the top 100 offending companies and said he will personally write company officials urging their compliance. But when asked if he would underscore his commitment by rejecting campaign contributions from anyone affiliated with the offending companies, he replied, "Absolutely not!"

"I don't think accepting campaign funds from companies that emit toxic substances as a byproduct disqualifies them from participating in good government," he added.

When Voinovich tries to disassociate campaign contributions from results on Capitol Square, he draws horselaughs from cynics who believe "participating in good government" is a euphemism for having your way with those who receive your gifts—the government leaders.

Voinovich came into office in 1991 saying he was going to alter the way business is done at the Statehouse—no more insider favoritism, no more influence peddling through campaign donations.

His refusal to forswear contributions from polluters and his preference for the jawbone over the whip merely reinforces the perception that the governor has fallen, unwillingly perhaps, into the get-along, go-along game he abhorred.

Voinovich, through his press secretary, Michael Dawson, said environmentalists were represented on the canoe trip by Frances S. Buchholzer, the natural resources director, and EPA Director Donald R. Schregardus.

Dawson said the governor has banned future hazardous-waste incinerators, but inherited the East Liverpool burner from the previous administration. He said Voinovich is doing all he can to ensure safety.

Regarding the pumping of the Southern Ohio Coal Co. mine in Meigs County, Dawson said the decision to reopen the mine was shared by federal and local-area representatives from both political parties.

"Without pumping, you would destroy the lives of 800 families who have no prospects for other jobs," said Dawson. "A choice had to be made, and we made the right one."

Dawson scoffed at the notion that Voinovich is in bed with industries. He said they vigorously fought the fees he proposed.

When it comes down to the environment and industry, Voinovich's outlook is remarkably similar to that of former Republican Gov. James A. Rhodes, under whom he served as lieutenant governor.

At the end of the canoe trip, Voinovich cautioned a group of conservation-minded students from Chardon High School, "We've got to achieve a balance between environmental concerns and our economic concerns."

"We'd like to ask him, when is he going to start putting the environment into the balance?" said Richard Sahli, executive director of the Ohio Environmental Council, representing 162 local environmental groups.

Voinovich's annual canoe trips with the press corps were fun, even if your canoe swamped or you felt the governor got the better of you with his rhetoric.

CHAPTER 8
FROM THE COLUMNIST'S PERSPECTIVE

The next series of columns involve the media, some precursors of things that would happen later, some personal commentary and some humor, often inspired by the absurd happenings at the Statehouse.

Media

Paul Leonard was not related to the author, although they called each other "cuz" (for cousin). This column is included because it's rare for a politician to speak plainly to the news media.

Lt. Gov. Paul Leonard Speaks Frankly With Editors

United Press International, May 17, 1987

COLUMBUS (UPI)—Ever since he returned to the Statehouse this year, a lot of observers have been wondering about the makeup of Lt. Gov. Paul R. Leonard. Inquiring minds want to know.

When he was in the legislature in the 1970s, Leonard had the reputation of a free spirit. Obviously, his strong suit is in communications. He's a graduate of Ohio University's journalism school, a rock band singer and a part-time actor in community theater. He has the gift of gab.

Just the ticket for lieutenant governor, right? Don't have to do anything but travel around and talk it up, spread it on thick.

A week ago, Leonard showed the editors of the state's newspapers he may be made of a little more than marshmallow fluff, hairspray and a toothsome grin. One day after Gary Hart quit the presidential race, Leonard stood before the annual meeting of the *United Press International* Ohio Editors' Association and said flatly that "stakeout journalism" has no place in assembling a story on a politician's personal character.

He also said the appearance of sexual indiscretion should never have become an issue in the presidential campaign, and that the media had best be careful how far it carries the First Amendment. "You are a professional limited only by your own code of conduct," he said.

The lieutenant governor said he felt Hart behaved wrong, and that the media should not be blamed for being the messenger. He said politicians have to learn that it's a "People Magazine" society where the public is interested in the private lives of public figures.

Nonetheless, it took a certain amount of courage on the part of Leonard, who will be in the thick of the governor's contest in 1990—and thus in need of newspaper support—to say what he did to the editors, and without checking the wind of public opinion first. It was sort of refreshing.

Leonard's balanced standup presentation showed he is capable of cutting to the core of important issues on little notice, and can do more than Watusi in yellow suspenders and a pair of pink heart-shaped shades.

Political life is fragile and sometimes fleeting. Paul Leonard was not in the thick of the governor's contest in 1990, or even in the "thin" of it. He left state government and became development director, first in Athens, then in Lima. Later he returned to Dayton, where his political career started, to practice law in relative obscurity.

■ ■

The Statehouse Press Corps Will Miss Its Cal Ripken

The Columbus Dispatch, April 24, 2000

When Len Unger, a retired Pennsylvania state-government reporter for the *Associated Press,* died in the mid-1960s, the Harrisburg press corps went to the funeral and then returned to the Capitol newsroom. They cracked open a bottle of Jack Daniel's, lit their Camels, rippled the deck and irreverently launched the "Len Unger Memorial Hearts Game," which continued for the rest of the afternoon.

Earlier this month, another retired state-government reporter for the *Associated Press* passed away, this one in Ohio.

Although Bob Miller, a mainstay in the Statehouse for 35 years, cut his teeth in the Len Unger era, he was a different kind of newsman.

Miller worked in the days when Statehouse reporters smoked, drank and caroused with sources, government officials and lobbyists. He was still working when consorting with lobbyists was frowned on and spin doctors set the political agenda. And through it all, Miller was the nice-guy reporter who helped his colleagues and cared for those he wrote about.

"He was the rock," said Mike Cull, a former reporter for the *Akron Beacon Journal*. "He was the go-to guy. He was your Cal Ripken."

Miller, a former schoolteacher, joined the *Associated Press* in West Virginia, his home state, and migrated to Columbus to cover Ohio government.

And that's what he did. He didn't try to influence the government or take potshots at politicians or prepare for a possible run for office.

His crisp, spare reports were dispatched to the big-city papers and to dozens of medium-size and small newspapers around Ohio. Because of Miller, thousands of Ohioans in such places as Wapakoneta, Alliance, Fremont, Portsmouth and Steubenville were informed daily about their state government.

"He was a true observer of the process who didn't get caught up in the process," said Bob Schmitz, a veteran Statehouse lobbyist. "I never saw him get excited. He was just steady. He reported the news. He didn't try to make it."

Miller's stories were neither interpretive nor slanted. He gave readers what they say they want: fair and balanced reporting so they can form their own opinions. Miller told both sides of the story.

"I cannot honestly tell you whether he was a Republican or a Democrat," said Tom Diemer, who worked side by side with Miller in the *AP*'s Statehouse cubicle for close to eight years.

"People say we (reporters) can't be objective," Diemer said. "Anybody who believes that never worked with Bob Miller."

"One thing about Bob," recalled former Statehouse reporter Jim Underwood. "He never lost view of his readers. Every once in awhile he would take a step back and see how it was playing outside the beltway."

Miller did that with *AP* features known as "perspectives," which give readers context for daily news stories. His hallmark was accuracy.

After interviewing then-Gov. James A. Rhodes one day, Miller called Robert F. Howarth, the governor's executive assistant, five times that night to make sure he got the story straight on Rhodes, who talked in a language all his own.

In 1990, Bill Chavanne, a former colleague of Miller's, was helping then-Attorney General Anthony J. Celebrezze Jr. campaign for governor. Speculation was hot over Celebrezze's running mate.

Miller cornered Chavanne and tried to worm it out of him, but Chavanne walked away, shaking his head, refusing to talk about it.

"Would I be wrong if I wrote that it's Gene Branstool?" Miller asked. Chavanne continued to shake his head, which Miller interpreted to mean, "No."

Miller broke the story that Branstool was going to be Celebrezze's running mate, and he was right.

Celebrezze's people were furious and accused Chavanne of leaking it to Miller. Chavanne had no defense.

"Bob was too reliable a reporter to write something somebody didn't say," he said. "No way they were gonna believe me. He had too many years, too many hundreds of stories. I couldn't get out of it."

Miller did make mistakes. When he did, Diemer says, he'd confess. "He'd say, 'Tore my britches on that one.'"

Competing against Bob Miller, as I did for 20 years with rival *United Press International*, was like facing a pitching machine.

You could write five stories on a given day and have a first-rate exclusive, but you could not relax.

Because you knew that Miller would be right back the next day, relentlessly serving up another portion of the Statehouse diet for people all over Ohio to consume.

Schmitz recalls: "Every time I saw him, I'd ask him if he had the scoop. He'd just laugh and say, 'I'm still lookin' for it.'"

Right now, Bob Miller is probably getting his daily scoop without even looking for it.

■ ■

Bob Hughes was a dominant force in Republican politics in the Buckeye State, chiefly because he was closely allied with James A. Rhodes, a proven winner. Hughes was co-chairman, then chairman, of the Cuyahoga County Republican Party. He could win races in the heavily-Democratic county, and he could hold down the natural Democratic edge there to help GOP candidates statewide. He was a favorite of news reporters, as you can see from the following:

Bob Hughes to GOP Leaders: Befriend Reporters, Don't Fear Them

The Columbus Dispatch, Nov. 25, 1991

In the summer of 1983, Bob Hughes, chairman of the Cuyahoga County Republican organization, invited state and county Republican leaders from across the nation to Cleveland for a two-day seminar.

Republicans came from San Francisco and Texas and Minnesota to learn how Hughes beat the Democrats in a county they dominated 5-to-1. The men came in their pin-stripe suits and wingtips, and the women came in colorful dresses and high heels. The odor of country club was in the air.

Hughes put a quick end to that. He had invited the best black politicians he could find, and they were good ones—Carl B. Stokes, the first black mayor of a major American city; George Forbes, the Cleveland City Council president; and Virgil E. Brown, now the state lottery director.

Hughes also had invited Ohio's political reporters, who enjoyed cramming into booths in smoke-filled taverns, loosening their ties, sitting on their topcoats and rapping, just as he did.

The state and local party officials were forced by Hughes to rub elbows with all these unsavory characters at a reception. Then the fun began.

Stokes and the glowering Forbes, both Democrats, sat before the GOP leaders and told them in blunt English why Republicans never won many elections below president.

Next came the panel of reporters, whom Hughes assigned to tell the assembly why scribes never liked Republicans. "Don't be afraid of these guys (the reporters)," Hughes admonished. "They're not going to bite you."

Then Hughes took over. He broke every rule in the book, trying to get the Republican leaders to see that they could no longer ignore the black vote, that they ought to be recruiting women candidates and that they ought to make friends with reporters and not treat them like lepers.

Hughes told his well-bred audience what reporters loved to hear. "Rhodes is nuts!" Hughes shouted about the 16-year former Republican Gov. James A. Rhodes. "But he wins!"

There were gasps at such irreverence, and you could almost hear the starched shirts crackling as neck veins bulged. It was vintage Hughes, and by the end of the conference the Republican leaders, with some reservations, agreed to try his recipe at home.

This is why Ohio's political reporters were especially saddened last week when they learned of Hughes' death at age 63 in the Cleveland suburb of Lyndhurst.

Robert E. Hughes was one of them—a former sportswriter in Warren, a graduate of The Ohio State University's Journalism School and a former employee of three different Columbus daily newspapers.

Hughes rarely sugarcoated anything; he told reporters the unvarnished truth, and it served him well. He was always in motion, sucking on cigarettes in short, violent puffs, and slurping coffee equally vigorously as he championed the large urban counties at state Republican meetings.

Hughes said you had to be in the mainstream to win, that conservatives lost every time they were handed the ball. He preferred the pragmatic style of politics practiced by Rhodes.

"People say smoke-filled rooms and back-room dealing are bad," Hughes said in 1979. "But there's one thing about those people (professional politicians). They want to win, and they put their best candidates forward, not some Horatio Alger (sic) at the bridge."

Hughes backed Rhodes through his disastrous defeat in 1986, and Robert T. Bennett, the No. 2 man in the Cuyahoga County party, went on to be the state party chairman.

Although Bennett was the architect of last year's big Republican win, some of the early spadework was done by Hughes, one of the last old-style political leaders in Ohio.

Bennett, who played second fiddle to Hughes until he came to Columbus, certainly got his chance to shine and took advantage of it. In Hughes' heyday, no Capitol reporters would have predicted Bennett's sterling accomplishments.

Hughes' time-tested formula for a Republican carrying Ohio (lose Cuyahoga County by less than 100,000 votes) misfired when Jimmy Carter beat President Gerald Ford in 1976 by over-performing for a Democrat in rural southern counties. And Hughes obviously backed the wrong horse when Rhodes led the GOP ticket to defeat in 1986.

Ohio politics changed, and Bennett kept up with it. He recruited female candidates—whom he said provided a built-in 5 percent edge—and courted the female vote. Conservatives moved to the fore and helped George W. Bush win and retain the presidency despite Hughes' disdain for them. The GOP's relationship with news reporters deteriorated after Hughes' demise.

Republicans got their black candidate for governor in 2006, and J. Kenneth Blackwell was creamed, setting back the movement for years to come. Ray Bliss disapproved of the Hughes-Rhodes tandem, but surely he had to respect Hughes' work in Cleveland. The thought of Rhodes' longevity always drew a wheezy cackle from Hughes. His eyes twinkled when he'd fuel reporters' speculation about the next election: "If he's breathin', he's runnin'!" That, too, came to an end.

■ ■

End of an Era: Government Goes Into Hiding

United Press International, Jan. 15, 1989

COLUMBUS (UPI)—Whether you know it or not, your state government is gradually slipping away from you. From now on, you will have less control; it will have more. You won't be able to watch it; it will be watching you.

It's scary.

The process didn't start yesterday, but its significance was underscored by the completion of the new state office tower in downtown Columbus.

Members of the Ohio House of Representatives, led by Speaker Vernal Riffe Jr., D-Wheelersburg, have already moved out of the Statehouse and over to the new tower. That was planned.

But more alarming, Gov. Richard Celeste and his staff of 65 will vacate the Statehouse at the end of this month in favor of the entire 30th floor of the tower. That was never part of the scheme for the building.

The tower was built, officials said, to consolidate agencies with leased office space all over the Columbus metropolitan area. And it's true that 32 agencies have moved in under the new 503-foot tent.

But the Ohio Environmental Protection Agency, for example, got its own building in the northwest section of town, leaving room enough for Celeste to travel across the street and take up the penthouse.

Debra Phillips, press secretary to the governor, defends the move on grounds it will make the governor's office function more efficiently. "His office and staff are basically working on top of each other and this place (the Statehouse) is not wired for computers," she said.

"It's not very functional."

To reporters based in the Statehouse and covering government operations on a day-to-day basis, the move is a pain in the neck. House members, their staffers and governor's office personnel—until now no further away than a good nine-iron shot—will be reached only by telephone or by a hike amounting to a city block.

Tough, you say. Nobody cares about the inconveniences of a reporter's job. Just do it.

And you're right. But there's something more sinister about these moves; something beyond the control of reporters.

Riffe and his members have moved out of sight. Included on their four floors in the new tower are two committee rooms where they can, if they choose, consider legislation out of view of the public.

The governor also is moving out of sight. He'll be able to leave his car under the new tower and go by private elevator to his hideaway on the 30th floor without anyone knowing.

State government reportage involves the senses—touch, feel, glimpses, sniffs—watching who's talking to whom.

It has meant intercepting the governor when he arrived at or left the Statehouse, asking him questions on important issues of the day, and generally observing the comings and goings of other government officials, lobbyists and groups and individuals.

By seeing the interaction, two and two could be put together about what was going on. Questions could be asked, news stories obtained to inform the public.

No more. The speaker and the governor, hidden in the tower, can do business as they please, without prying eyes. When they get their stories straight, they can feed them to the media. Their interaction with the high-powered lobbyists about whom we've read so much in the last two years—the ones that receive five figures a pop to get things done—will be invisible.

These are the same lobbyists who will sell the government the sophisticated electronic equipment that can be programmed to know everything about your life.

So while the government watches you, your eyes and ears are slowly being obstructed. It's unnecessary, and a shame.

Gov. Ted Strickland moved back into the Statehouse when he took over in 2007, although he still could retreat to the 30th floor of the Riffe Center if he wanted to stay out of sight.

The House speaker and House members remained in the office tower, where security and privacy were valued more than they had been at the Statehouse. Reporters became accustomed to the situation and learned to "stake out" certain offices in the Riffe Center, but much of the forgoing came to pass.

■ ■

Opinions

Warning: Repeal of Fair Trade Laws Will Hurt Community Retailers

United Press International, July 12, 1975

COLUMBUS (UPI)—Most Ohio House members last week rushed to embrace yet another idea "whose time has come"—repeal of the state's 39-year old fair trade laws.

It wasn't all that easy at first persuading the Democratic-dominated House to do away with a law that upholds "fair trade."

But as Rep. William G. Batchelder, R-Medina, said, "words sometimes get twisted around," and the law couched in "Mom and the flag terms" is really nothing more than price-fixing. It allows manufacturers to set minimum prices for their goods sold at the retail level.

Chief sponsor of the repealer bill, Rep. Michael P. Stinziano, D-Columbus, had done his homework well, and by the time he finished his explanation, he had convinced 75 of the 99 House members to abandon "fair trade."

Stinziano's main lure was cheaper prices for Ohio consumers, "Your constituents," he told his colleagues.

The Columbus lawmaker spewed forth tantalizing figures to support his claim:

A collective $80 million savings per year for Ohio consumers.

Retail price reductions of 18 to 27 percent on most items in a free trade situation and, in less frequent cases, savings of 44 to 60 percent.

Markdowns of $61 on a $510 color television set, $84 on a $220 set of golf clubs and $445 on a $1,360 stereo.

The excess money, he explained, now goes to retailers and manufacturers because of artificially-inflated prices. The items could just as well be sold far cheaper by discount houses in a free market, Stinziano claimed.

There were 13 House members who remained unconvinced but only one, Charles R. Saxbe, R-Mechanicsburg, was prepared to stand up and challenge Stinziano. Saxbe stood alone, like his father, William B. Saxbe, does on many issues.

Young Saxbe made some strong arguments for retaining fair trade restrictions.

He raised the spectre of discount chains slashing prices to drive the local corner stores out of business, then raising prices beyond fair trade levels.

Saxbe said the discount houses could use certain items as loss-leaders to draw customers, charging higher prices on the rest of their stock.

"You may be paying less for one item, but you can guarantee that the other items are marked up so the store isn't losing any money," he said, claiming profit margins for the discount stores are as high as 33 percent.

Saxbe predicted the demise of the "mom and pop" neighborhood stores, and said mug shots for check cashing, electronic frisking at the storefront and bulldozers at the edge of town would become a permanent way of life.

It seemed a trifle odd to see House liberals lining up on the side of large corporate stores, and many Republicans abandoning their traditional leanings toward local business.

Stinziano's and Saxbe's conflicting versions of the effect of fair trade repeal will get another airing in the Senate, where the bill goes next.

Can you say "Wal-Mart"? Saxbe pretty much had it pegged in that third paragraph from the end, didn't he?

■ ■

If the following scenario wasn't a harbinger of the housing and credit crash of 2008, nothing was.

Often-Deaf Legislators Lent Ear to Advice On Predatory Lending

The Columbus Dispatch, February 4, 2002

Sometimes the little kid gets Superman's attention by tugging on his cape. And sometimes state legislators get out of their rut and listen to the small voice of the average citizen.

But not often. That's why it was noteworthy last week when the Senate Finance Committee called time out on a bill dealing with predatory-lending practices as the measure sped toward Gov. Bob Taft's desk.

A modified version of the bill no doubt will resume the sprint toward the governor's office this week, but only after some input, however limited, from the consumers who have been victimized by lending gimmicks that should have been outlawed long ago.

The legislative radar went up on predatory lending last year, and a bill was passed in June regulating mortgage brokers and loan officers. But that wasn't enough to suit consumer groups. Reputable banks and finance companies have plenty of safeguards to avoid bilking consumers. One of those safeguards is refusing to make the loan. That doesn't do the prospective borrower much good.

Easy credit is tempting these days, and companies are not shy about exploiting the craving. Consumers are flooded with e-mail, direct mail and telemarketing pitches on how they can fulfill their dreams on credit. No payments until 2004. Turn the equity on your home into cash.

Senior citizens and unsophisticated individuals may bite on these offers and later regret it.

Like companies that offer insurance to high-risk drivers, some loan companies are only too eager to provide money to people who are poor credit risks: They can extract a high price for such services.

House Bill 386, aimed at solving parts of the problem not solved by last year's bill, zipped through the House in three weeks.

When consumer groups complained it didn't go far enough, top Senate Republican leaders thought they merely would incorporate federal oversight rules into state law, give the Ohio Department of Commerce more power to investigate and appoint a study committee to tie up the loose ends.

The bill was on track for quick passage last week when opponents set up a line of defense in the Finance Committee. Much of the opposition came from local-government officials, who said the bill would preclude their cities' stronger lending requirements. Individual consumers offered first-person stories of loans gone bad.

Most times, such testimony goes into the ozone, as lawmakers wander in and out of the committee room, talk to their aides and stare into space. But during a grueling six-hour hearing, some of the 17 witnesses scored enough points that a vote was postponed.

"I was pretty depressed going in," said Bill Faith, executive director of the Coalition on Homelessness and Housing in Ohio. "But as I testified, I could see the expressions on the senators' faces."

They were especially impressed with Faith and with Jacqueline King of the Federal Reserve Bank of Cleveland, who addressed the global nature of the problem and told what's being done in other states.

"I thought we had put a lot in the bill that people cared about," said Sen. James E. Carnes, R-St. Clairsville, chairman of the committee. "But these people (borrowers) need help. That came through loud and clear."

Sen. Robert A. Gardner, R-Madison, who buys and sells homes as a sideline, said he has a trusted title company look over the fine print on his loan documents. Most folks can't afford that kind of help.

"These (questionable) loans are 100 percent legal," Gardner said. "The question is, how do we make them ethical as well as legal?"

Sen. Robert F. Spada, an accountant and business owner from Parma Heights, said Faith was "very compelling." He also was touched by a story about an individual whose refinanced home resulted in $10,000 in payments above the original loan because of "some high-pressure, savvy salesman."

It's easy to chalk up the prior legislative inattention to the campaign contributions made by bankers, mortgage brokers and finance-company brass.

"It's not entirely about the money and politics," Faith said. "It's about the people they (legislators) see all the time . . . the industry. That's who they're getting their information from."

So, for one evening, anyway, the lawmakers pushed themselves away from the whirlwind round of cocktail parties and assorted feeds that make Columbus their home away from home for much of the year.

"We listened," Carnes said. "We're going to come up with something to help them. It isn't going to be the end-all, though."

Faith, who has represented the downtrodden at the Statehouse for 14 years, is suspicious of study committees.

"At least we'll be at the table," he said. "I hope they come around and really do something to help the consumer."

■ ■

This column was written during the dog days of the endless summer of 1971 in Columbus when Gov. John J. Gilligan and the Republican-controlled legislature toiled daily through a stalemate over whether to enact the state's first personal income tax. Nixon, normally a free-market advocate, called for a voluntary wage-price freeze to help stabilize the economy.

Odd Bedfellows, Nixon and Gilligan Bravely Try Austerity Measures

United Press International, August 20, 1971

COLUMBUS (UPI)—Last week, both the American economy and Ohio's budget became strained to the point where the chief executives of the nation and state coincidentally gave a yank on the reins.

"Belt-tightening" and "austerity" were the watchwords of President Nixon and Gov. John J. Gilligan, who respectively instituted a wage-price freeze and threatened a cutback in state government services. Both actions were taken to restore fiscal balance. Both required forethought and courage. Both necessarily would result in a certain amount of indiscriminate hardship. And both (actions) were taken by men whose political views are widely divergent.

It is interesting to note that these twin calls to sacrifice were most poorly taken by the same people who are responsible for a major share of the bickering over Ohio's budget and tax problems—lobbyists and special interest groups. Not all the special interest groups protested loudly. Some were silent. Some pledged grudgingly to go along with the president. Many understood the position of the governor.

Two particular Ohio lobby groups tied firmly to the budget-tax problem flashed their colors when the call came to put "self" second.

Frank King, president of the Ohio AFL-CIO, wondered for quotation whether President Nixon had ever heard of "involuntary servitude."

The labor organization's weekly publication, "News and Views," sarcastically lamented that Nixon had pre-empted "Bonanza" and the "Sunday Night Movie" to tell the American people that "someone was going to be forced to make a sacrifice until this nasty inflationary spiral becomes unwound."

"Guess who?" the publication inquired. "Yep. You . . . the working people of America, have once again been selected to make the supreme sacrifice.

"Mr. Nixon's Sunday special boils down to this: the working people of America must forget about any upcoming pay raise so Tricky Dicky can get re-elected next November," the publication reported.

John H. Hall, chief lobbyist for the Ohio Education Association, was more polite in sending 275 school teachers into the Statehouse to "bug" their state senators for more money for education.

But he scorned the idea that it would be patriotic for the teachers to back off in view of the president's message. "They (the senators) are going to tell you that you are unpatriotic if you don't follow the president's order," Hall said. "They'll say 'we've got to go along with the president and tighten our belts.' Well, anyone who backs away from getting the funds that are needed is educationally irresponsible."

It was slightly ironic that both the AFL-CIO and the OEA were complaining when Nixon took action to curb the rocketing prices they had long protested. But it took the governor, for whom both groups no doubt have more respect, to crystallize the situation. Without naming names, the governor condemned the "King Midas" attitude of the lobby groups and blamed it for the current budget impasse.

"Nine months ago," Gilligan told a Cleveland audience, "I called together representatives of every facet of Ohio's society. Every special interest group, every lobby, every citizens' organization was given a voice in our Task Force on Tax Reform.

"These people worked in the glare of public attention—and in that glare all of them agreed that we could solve our problems, if we were willing to sacrifice and to compromise and to work together.

"But now, these people have gone back into the dark corridors of the Statehouse, out of the glare of public attention, and they have abandoned that spirit of cooperation, that spirit of optimism for our state.

"We have permitted our selfish motives, our concern for ourselves first and society second, to creep over us again, and we see the awful sight of our system of government paralyzed by self-doubt." The "glare" popped up again last week and cast an unfavorable light on the special interest groups.

> How similar the reaction of the United Auto Workers in 2008 toward opponents of a bailout of the Big Three auto manufacturers! And would President George W. Bush ever have considered a wage-price freeze to stabilize the economy?

■ ■

Lesson of Challenger Ignored in Workers' Comp Legislation

United Press International, February 2, 1986

COLUMBUS (UPI)—Eight hours after the space shuttle Challenger burst apart off the coast of Florida last week, the Ohio House Commerce and Labor

Committee observed a moment of silence in memory of the seven astronauts aboard.

It was a nice touch by the chairman, Rep. Clifton Skeen, D-Akron, representing the hometown of Judith Resnik, one of the fallen astronauts.

But then Skeen and the majority Democrats ignored the lesson of the day as they trotted out a workers' compensation bill retaining most of the broad provisions (that) hamstring industries by subjecting them to expensive lawsuits in addition to their contributions to the state insurance pool.

The lesson of the day from Challenger was that nothing important gets done without risk. The National Aeronautics and Space Administration risks its reputation and support of the space program with every launch. And certainly seven brave people risked their lives last Tuesday, and lost.

In Ohio businesses and industries, large and small, are taking risks every day in expanding operations and opening new ventures (that) provide jobs for people. Gov. Richard F. Celeste is staking his political career in part on his ability to entice them to do it.

It seems, then, that the people who are receiving the jobs ought to be willing to take a little risk. They ought not try to write a law giving them loopholes to file million-dollar damage claims for every conceivable injury or illness when they are on lunch break, on their way home from work, suffering from stress or working long hours.

Such loopholes would be great if companies had bottomless pockets, but they don't. So workers need to share a little bit of the inherent risk of doing business and a little of the care that goes along with it.

The space shuttle calamity probably will provoke a lucrative lawsuit but the lesson remains, nothing worthwhile gets done without risk.

In Ohio, workers' compensation is what one attorney referred to as a "lawyer's banquet," and will continue to be so until the concept of shared risk is put into play.

■ ■

Maintaining Infrastructure Lacks Taxpayer Appeal, but Neglect Is Costly

The Columbus Dispatch, September 1, 2003

Not long ago, a letter to the editor indicated that the recent sales-tax increase, courtesy of Gov. Bob Taft, allowed the Ohio Department of Transportation to embark on a huge 10-year highway construction program, and that the public was "duped again."

Not to nitpick, but this letter was misleading. The beloved sales-tax increase was the brainchild of the Republican-controlled General Assembly, not the governor, although he certainly went along with it. And the highway program is being funded in part by a 6-cent increase in the gasoline tax, not the sales tax.

The sales tax was increased and applied to a variety of services to balance the general state budget. There is a misconception that the gasoline tax could be used to balance the budget; under the Ohio Constitution, that tax can be used only for highway purposes.

If these kinds of misconceptions are common, then it's no wonder people react with skepticism, even to the sensible solutions put forth by government.

The 10-year highway-construction program is portrayed as a boondoggle gobbling up tax money, when it is an attempt to upgrade the road system to present-day needs and standards, with safety and easing congestion the top considerations. Who in their right mind would not protect this investment?

In the late 1980s, the state established a bonding program to help local governments repair and replace aging infrastructure by awarding state grants based on a demonstration of need on a regional basis. The program has worked very well, enabling local governments to upgrade roads, bridges and water and sewer systems.

The state established a multibillion-dollar bonding program for repairing and replacing school buildings. Some local officials loudly cried that the state was trying to "blackmail" their school districts by dangling the state money out there and demanding a local match.

While the school-facilities program has traveled a somewhat rocky road, schools have been built, renovated and modernized in a wide variety of districts.

The Taft administration is involved in multistate negotiations to protect the Great Lakes from those who want to raid the waters for their own purposes. Not that this will cost a great deal of money, but Ohio has an interest in Lake Erie and in the other lakes.

Now comes the Great Blackout of 2003, and everyone wants to know who is responsible and how it could happen.

The electrical system is not unlike the highway system that ODOT is trying to upgrade, except that switches aren't thrown to allow cars access to the road or to push them off.

But just as the highways have developed cracks or become clogged with traffic, so has the electricity transmission grid on which Ohio and other states depend.

Maybe the flaw that caused the blackout was in Ohio, on FirstEnergy turf; maybe it was somewhere else. But the government officials crying the loudest two weeks ago were responding to people's outrage that this could happen to them: the lights went out, they couldn't turn on the water, their televisions and air conditioners didn't work and, in some cases, they couldn't use their cell phones.

Yet any suggestion to upgrade the electrical infrastructure before the Aug. 14 blackout would have come to naught, because there was no perceived urgency to it. Expanding the grid would cost billions in capital expenditures, thus increasing the cost of electricity for everyone.

And nobody likes to pay more, whether it's for lighting their homes, watching their cable TV, talking on their cell phones, sending other people's kids to school, having safe drinking water, fixing the curbs in their neighborhood or driving on smooth, wide roads.

As a society, we have become so preoccupied with the next generation of technology that we have neglected to maintain the building blocks. We are willing to spend top dollar on clothing, entertainment and the latest electronic gadgets, but putting money into infrastructure has no sex appeal.

Protecting our networks of roads, water, education, electricity and telecommunications is expensive.

Yes, the state should investigate and find out whether an electric utility skimped on maintenance to fatten its purse. But we should also remember the adage, "You can pay me now or pay me later."

■ ■

Humor

This is a testament to lawmakers' outsized egos and a spoof of entrenched legislators, specifically the legendary House Speaker Vern Riffe. The oddities, artifacts and great moments described in the following piece are all real except for the senator's stinky shirt. And the credit card was requested by carousing legislators, but never sent by the lobbyist.

A Pols' Hall Of Fame? No, How About Blame?

The Columbus Dispatch, April 25, 1994

Well, term limits have finally made them daffy. They've proposed a Hall of Fame for members of the General Assembly who've been there 20 years or more. They ought to call it the Hall of Blame.

Rep. Casey Jones, D-Toledo, introduced a bill last week establishing the hall for veterans of 20 years or more. Needless to say, Jones qualifies. He's retiring in December after 26 years in the House.

In the interest of speculating what it would be like should the idea ever catch on and pass, we take you now to the General Assembly Hall of Fame located, not in Cooperstown but, ah, Wheelersburg, Ohio. Yeah, that's a good location.

We approach the building, shaped like a miniature Statehouse. The docent greets us warmly and ushers us into the foyer. He identifies himself as Vernal G. Riffe Jr., a former member of the House and, it just so happens, a famous resident of Wheelersburg.

Riffe has just recently retired from the House, where he spent 36 years, 20 of them as speaker, so naturally he is a charter member of the Hall of Fame. He took the job as a guide to combat boredom in his retirement.

Riffe takes us into a room exhibiting "How a Bill Becomes Law." For the pre-1994 era, it shows giant photos of himself, Senate President Stanley J. Aronoff, R-Cincinnati, and the governor shaking hands. The photo of the governor changes periodically from Gov. George V. Voinovich to former Gov. Richard F. Celeste to former Gov. James A. Rhodes.

In the post-1994 era, the bill-becoming-law display is different. It is a photo of a demolition derby, featuring various legislators and lobbyists bearing down on each other in total chaos.

The sounds are excruciating, and Riffe beckons us toward a more serene spot for quiet contemplation. This is the infamous "smoke-filled room," where laws were made in a bygone day. There's a lifelike representation of Rep. Patrick A. Sweeney, D-Cleveland, another Hall-of-Famer, showing how to put a tax on private detectives in the budget without their detecting it. Nearby is the modern equivalent, the "smokeless room," where laws are made in secret but the participants have to go outside to smoke.

We now walk to the "Ripley's Believe it or Not" room, commemorating such oddities as:

- Rep. John Galbraith, R-Maumee, who once introduced a bill to outlaw February as a way to solve Ohio's fuel shortage in the 1970s.

- Rep. Gene Damschroder, R-Fremont, who once called on President Carter to round up all Iranians in the United States and send them to liberate American hostages in their homeland. It would be easy for them, he reasoned, because they would blend in with other Iranians.
- Sen. Ferald L. Ritchie, R-Wapakoneta, who served the shortest Senate term on record: 17 days, in 1979.

Another room commemorates great moments in the annals of the General Assembly, with filmed highlights of the 11-month battle to enact the state income tax in 1971, the Six-Day War of 1975 and the three-month effort to bail out depositors of the Home State Savings Bank in 1985.

Still another room contains artifacts of legislative history, much as Cooperstown displays uniforms, baseballs and bats:

- The shirt once worn by a senator to 117 consecutive sessions until colleagues, holding their noses, passed his bill.
- The credit card once sent by cab to legislators in a bar by a lobbyist who declined to join them because he was ready for bed.
- The high-backed chair once pilfered from the Ohio Supreme Court by a House member for his own office.

Finally, we arrive in the Hall of Stars, where the 20-year members are enshrined with bronze plaques. This is what visitors have waited for, a chance to see the giants who played the game: Sen. Theodore M. Gray, R-Columbus, 43 years; Riffe; Aronoff; Sweeney; Jones; and Rep. Ronald M. Mottl, D-North Royalton, who liked the legislature so well he came back after a few terms in Congress.

The hall is small, but then it won't be expanding very much, because there won't be any more 20-year legislators to honor. Terms in the House and Senate are limited to eight years.

As we exit the hall by the back door, we view the dumpster commemorating the guy who put legislative term limits on the ballot and got it passed.

In the real world, a "pay-to-play" scandal, detailed elsewhere in this book, ended the cozy relationship among the governor and the two top legislative leaders, known as "The Big Three." Lawmakers learned how to survive term limits, chiefly by running for the other chamber when their time was up. Some even went back and forth. Of course, Jones' bill for a Hall of Fame was consigned to the aforementioned dumpster by the back door.

■ ■

Memo to Driver: If You've Got Ohio-1, Don't Speed

United Press International, Aug. 28, 1969

COLUMBUS (UPI)—Terry Shannon's prize-winning safety slogan may not be driving him to death but it's driving him and his family to distraction, and taking the governor's office and Highway Safety Department along as passengers.

Back in April, Terry submitted the best safety slogan in a statewide contest. His entry was: "Are you driving yourself to death?" His prize was a 1969 Mustang and Ohio license plate No.1.

Four months later, Aug. 6 to be exact, one S. W. Anderson of Syracuse, N.Y., was driving along Interstate 71 between Columbus and Cincinnati when an auto flashed past at an estimated 85 miles an hour. Anderson swears the license was Ohio-1. He wrote the governor's office a stern letter on speeding by chief executives. The letter was shunted over to Warren C. Nelson, state director of highway safety, who quietly relayed it to Shannon for his edification.

That apparently would have been the end of it, no questions asked, except Shannon, a Bowling Green State University sophomore from Bellevue, panicked.

Perhaps he was afraid Nelson would take away his Mustang on grounds he was driving himself to death. Anyway, he fired back a letter to Nelson thanking him for the reminder about the responsibility which goes with the highway safety title and the No. 1 license plate.

He allowed as how drivers must use good judgment, and such judgment might have been lacking in the person behind the wheel of his prize car that fateful day of Aug. 6—his sister Candy.

It was poor Candy's 16th birthday that day and she had just gotten her driver's permit. Perhaps, conceded Shannon, she just might have exceeded the speed limit when her passengers egged her on to pass some slow-moving cars.

Well, the story leaked out, as such stories have a habit of doing. There were headlines all over the place—the No. 1 car was seen traveling 15 miles an hour over the speed limit and Shannon had confessed.

This sent Mrs. Victor E. Shannon, the mother of Terry and Candy, into a tizzy. She got on the telephone to John McElroy, assistant to the governor, and accused the governor's office of leaking the story. She would be in touch with her attorney, she said.

Furthermore, said Mrs. Shannon, her son had not been driving the Mustang in early August—she herself had. Also, the auto had never been on

Interstate 71 and in fact on the day in question, Candy was driving on the Jackie Mayer Highway toward Sandusky, far from where Mr. Anderson was.

Her family, Mrs. Shannon continued, has been subjected to embarrassment by kids who titter and point their fingers at the "safety-minded" people who go 85 M.P.H. Not only that, she said, but she works for an insurance firm that boasts: "We insure Ohio's No. 1 safe driver." That would be none other than Terry Shannon.

All this was played back to Anderson by the Highway Safety Department. Perhaps he had mistaken another license for Ohio's.

"There's nothing the matter with my eyesight," was Anderson's reply.

But the department notes that Anderson was not correct on the color of the car and claimed it was larger than a Mustang. Shannon has been cleared in the eyes of the state. Now if the homefolks would only get off his back, maybe the governor's office could breathe a little easier.

■ ■

This is a device used when column material is scarce—take an offbeat news item and apply it to the Statehouse. Fiction can approach reality.

Two Years Sealed in Biosphere Solitude Might Benefit Ohio's Leaders

The Columbus Dispatch, September 30, 1991

You may have heard that eight scientists and agricultural experts have gone into isolation near Oracle, Ariz., to learn more about the Earth in a controlled climate. These brave (some think daffy) individuals will live and interact in Biosphere II, a glass-and-steel geodesic dome the size of three football fields, conducting experiments with 3,800 species of plants and animals.

The "biospherians" are locked in, unable to leave for two years except for an extreme medical emergency. They have their own doctor.

Their capsule, sealed by steel airlocks, includes simulated ocean, rain forest, savanna, marshes and a farm. There is also habitat for humans, including apartments, laboratories, workshops, observatories and a library.

The dome is built to last 100 years, but the eight biospherians will be out in two years. What to do with it for the other 98?

In the interest of conservation—doing more with less, and all that—it has been suggested that the next inhabitants of Biosphere II be Ohio's government.

After all, our politicians have been haggling year after year over the problems of the environment, health care and education. Maybe those problems could be solved in a carefully controlled atmosphere with no worldly distractions. Here's the way we see it:

A select group of Ohio House and Senate members, along with staff members from the governor's office and a few lobbyists, enter Biosphere II for two years.

They are not allowed to leave unless they have an extreme medical emergency—or they run short of re-election campaign funds.

Otherwise, this encapsulated mini-government operates as it normally does, holding "think" sessions, caucuses and hearings to thrash out the great issues of the day.

To assist, the public is allowed to demonstrate outside the dome, chanting and carrying signs, pressing their faces up against the glass. Unfortunately, the capsule is soundproofed, so their voices can't be heard. Nothing much new there.

The Biosphere II landscape will be reconfigured to fit the new process. Instead of oceans, deserts and savannas, there will be:

- The Smoke-Filled Room, where leadership will practice cutting deals. This room also will be used as a test area for the long-term effects of air quality on the human body.
- The Log-Rolling Rain Forest, where political favors are repaid. It's near the Pork Barrel River, adjacent to the Public Trough.
- The Windsock Observatory, where the new biospherians can test the political winds on various issues.
- The Duck Pond, a wooded area to which they can escape to avoid voting, usually after visiting the Windsock Observatory.
- The Watering Hole, where an ample supply of food and drink will lubricate the participants, aiding the negotiations.
- The Lobby (close to the Watering Hole). This is self-explanatory.
- The Filibuster Arena, an empty room where they can make speeches and no one will be bothered.
- The Bureaucrats' Haven, a windowless room with lots of file cabinets and drawers, and stacks of paper piled around.

Come to think of it, the Statehouse is being remodeled right now. There's a glass-enclosed atrium going up between the Statehouse and the Annex. Many of the aforementioned features are already in place.

Maybe we don't need to send them to Arizona after all. Pass the keys.

■ ■

Rip Van Twinkle, patterned after the character Slats Grobnik invented by *Chicago Tribune* columnist Mike Royko, was awakened every few months to comment on the absurd happenings at the Statehouse.

Waking Up To the Doings at the Statehouse Can Shock a Guy

The Columbus Dispatch, April 5, 1999

He was easy to spot among the horde of youngsters rolling colorfully dyed eggs and scavenging for candy on the Statehouse lawn.

This "kid" was 6 feet tall and had a long, scraggly white beard. He was wearing an OSU sweatshirt and a khaki cap that said "Final Four." It was my old friend, Rip Van Twinkle.

"Hey, Rip!" I yelled across the grassy expanse. "Where you been?"

Van Twinkle stiff-armed a 10-year old, tripped a 6-year old and whacked an 8-year-old with his cane as he homed in on a chocolate bunny nestled in the grass. "I been up on campus," he said, gesturing northward. "They woke me up the other day with the most godawful noise. This silver-haired guy with a New York accent—I think his name was O'Flaherty or somethin'—was thanking people, and they were cheering the Buckeye basketball team.

"They said the Buckeyes won something, but that couldn't be possible. I was awake last year and they stunk. I think I was still dreaming."

"No, Rip," I replied. "That was real. The Buckeyes made a remarkable turnaround and were among the top teams in the country."

"You don't say!" said Van Twinkle, biting the ears off his bunny. "Now I hear Taft is governor. Which one is it, the tubby guy who was president or Mr. Republican, the senator?"

"Neither," I answered. "This is Bob, great-grandson of the president and grandson of the senator."

"Wow!" said Van Twinkle, rummaging through his Easter basket for another treat. "I must have been asleep a long time. But he is a Republican, right?"

"Well," I said. "Some of the conservatives think he's acting like a Democrat because he's not necessarily a chip off the old block. For example, he wants to give any surplus tax money to the schools and not back to the taxpayers. And he collaborated with the American Civil Liberties Union to help a guy visit a prison to be with his wife while their child was delivered."

"Far out!" said Van Twinkle, chewing a marshmallow chick with gusto. "At least he probably hates those unions just like his grandfather did. I remember Sen. Taft wrote that anti-union Taft-Hartley law years ago."

Again, I had to tell Rip the shocking truth. "Gov. Bob Taft went before the Ohio AFL-CIO and told them the union movement was welcome during his administration. They gave him a standing ovation."

"I gotta get outta the sun," said Van Twinkle, his face flushed and his eyes bugging out. "I'm gettin' dizzy. I can't believe what you're telling me."

We went into the cool Statehouse basement and I showed Van Twinkle where George V. Voinovich had posed for his official portrait as Ohio's 66th governor.

It was in front of a bronze sculpture called The Modern Classroom, showing children taking a history lesson. In the background were Ohio icons: the Wright Brothers' plane, John Glenn, Neil Armstrong.

Voinovich chose to pose in front of this sculpture because of his keen interest in children, I explained.

"Hmmph!" muttered Van Twinkle, popping a handful of jelly beans into his mouth. "For all he's done for children's education, he should have posed in front of that sculpture," he said, motioning toward a bronze representation of a one-room school called The Historic Classroom. "That's how a lot of kids go to school in Ohio. Hey! The last time I woke up, the court told 'em to come into the 20th century. How's that goin'?"

I had to explain that a judge threw a shutout at the General Assembly by nixing everything lawmakers had done in the name of improving schools and sending the issue back before the Ohio Supreme Court.

"What we need is more lawyers involved," Van Twinkle said sarcastically. "I don't think I can sleep long enough for this thing to get solved."

I wasn't sure how much more my whiskered friend could take, but I felt obligated to bring him up to date. So I told him that Voinovich and Mike DeWine, Ohio's other Republican U.S. senator, had combined their Columbus offices to save money.

"Awww!" cooed Van Twinkle, running a bony finger through his marshmallow-coated beard. "Ain't that sweet? Those two never wanted to be apart, ever since one was governor and the other lieutenant governor."

I had to tell Rip that the linkage was only for staff purposes, to eliminate duplication on constituent requests and to save the taxpayers money.

The sugar had a grip on Rip. He turned surly. "I'll give 'em a constituent request," he said. "Tell 'em to close their offices and they'll save us a lotta money."

With that, the old boy headed for what's known at the Statehouse as the crypt, and another nap.

This was the last of about eight years' worth of the Rip Van Twinkle columns. Statehouse doings had turned so bizarre, the humor looked tame by comparison and the effect was lost. You couldn't make up anything zanier than what was going on. And there couldn't be a better way to end this collection of columns about the Ohio Statehouse.

Index